To the Vast and Beautiful Land

NUMBER FORTY-SEVEN

Elma Dill Russell Spencer Series in the West and Southwest
Andrés Tijerina, General Editor

To the Vast and Beautiful Land

Anglo Migration into Spanish Louisiana and Texas, 1760s–1820s

Light Townsend Cummins

TEXAS A&M UNIVERSITY PRESS
COLLEGE STATION

First edition

This paper meets the requirements of ANSI/NISO Z39.48–1992
(Permanence of Paper).
Binding materials have been chosen for durability.
Manufactured in the United States of America

Library of Congress Cataloging-in-Publication Data

Names: Cummins, Light Townsend, author.
Title: To the vast and beautiful land : Anglo migration into Spanish Louisiana and Texas, 1760s–1820s / Light Townsend Cummins.
Other titles: Elma Dill Russell Spencer series in the West and Southwest.
Description: First edition. | College Station : Texas A&M University Press, [2019] | Series: Elma Dill Russell Spencer series in the West and Southwest | Includes bibliographical references and index.
Identifiers: LCCN 2018046041 | ISBN 9781623497415 (book/hardcover (printed case) : alk. paper) | ISBN 9781623497422 (e-book)
Subjects: LCSH: Southwest, Old—Colonization—History. | British Americans—Southwest, Old—History. | Southwest, Old—Relations—Spain. | Spain—Relations—Southwest, Old. | Louisiana—History—To 1803. | Texas—History—To 1846. | Louisiana—Emigration and immigration—History. | Texas—Emigration and immigration—History.
Classification: LCC F396 .C94 2019 | DDC 976—dc23 LC record available at https://lccn.loc.gov/2018046041

A list of titles in this series is available at the end of the book.

Contents

Preface

THIS BOOK contains eleven essays I wrote between 1988 and 2015. They appeared in various academic journals and one book. All of them deal in one way or another with the migration of English speakers into Spanish Louisiana and Texas from the 1760s until the 1820s. They are presented here without revision because each in its original form remains relevant to understanding this topic. The volume closes with a new bibliographic essay of recent scholarship that updates and supplements the sources cited in the essays. Every chapter begins with an introduction written by me that places it within the larger focus of this volume. Each introduction concludes with mention of one recently published historical monograph by a historian who has written on that particular subject, building on it in some fashion to expand the essay's analysis and topical coverage into the current historical literature.

The premise of this book is my assertion that commerce and land acquisition by Anglo-Americans went hand in hand as dual motivations for the migration of English speakers into Louisiana and Texas. Mercantile trade dominated by Anglo-Americans increasingly tied the Mississippi valley and western Gulf coast to the English-speaking ports of the Atlantic world during the decades covered in this book, shifting it away from earlier French and Spanish commercial patterns. As a result, Anglo-Americans moved to the region as residents and secured land from Spanish authorities, who often welcomed them with favorable settlement policies. These settlers came first to the lower Mississippi valley as early as the 1760s, with the last stages of this demographic movement arriving in Texas during the 1820s. New Orleans evolved to be the linchpin of this process, becoming the central entrepôt and commercial center that energized this migration throughout the region. The movement of English speakers into Louisiana and Texas represents one historical continuum across two generations of Anglo-American settlers, from their first arrival along the lower Mississippi before the American Revolution to the appearance of Moses Austin in Texas. The Louisiana Purchase of 1803 and the Texas Revolution of 1836 as political events legitimized the domination of a stable Anglo-American hegemony already existing in those areas.

In 1893 historian Frederick Jackson Turner presented one of the most important scholarly papers ever delivered before the American Historical Association. Entitled "The Significance of the Frontier in American History," he postulated that the frontier constituted the preeminent historical process that influenced the development of the United States, observing, "the most significant thing about the American frontier is that it lies at the hither edge of free land." Turner traced the history of the movement westward in broad outline, from the colonial Atlantic coast, over the Appalachians, into the Mississippi valley, and beyond to the Far West. This evolving frontier, he noted, was located at any given time at the area of transition between civilization and savagery. Turner's frontier pushed westward as vacant land welcomed successive waves of new settlers, with these migrants eventually arriving on the Pacific coast. The motivation for this grand demographic expansion, according to Turner, came from the settlers themselves. Frontier folk made their treks to the west because of their individual desire to possess free land. Over the years, of course, several generations of historians have questioned and refined Turner's frontier thesis, pointing out a number of problems based on his generalities. It is my contention that Turner completely ignored the fact that much of this movement in its early stages entered lands belonging to Spain, both in Louisiana and Texas, not "unsettled" areas between savagery and civilization. English-speaking settlers, coming first from British colonies and later the United States, existed side by side with other Europeans already established in fully functioning colonial provinces. Moreover, the motivation for this migration did not come only from the settlers' expansive and restless nature. Instead, Spain specifically invited them into its Mississippi valley and Gulf coast possessions, the colonial governments of Louisiana and Texas actively courting them as potential new residents. These English-speaking settlers were therefore answering a call to settle there and put into operation by Spanish policy.

By the time of the American Revolution, outbound migrations from Pennsylvania and Virginia had brought English speakers into the Shenandoah Valley and the eastern foothills of the Appalachian Mountains. Just beyond lay the vast Ohio River, a natural highway into the midcontinent and gateway to the Mississippi valley and Spanish Louisiana. The intrepid frontiersman Daniel Boone, who became the first iconic figure of a grand demographic event lasting almost two centuries, helped accelerate this process when he blazed the Wilderness Road in 1775 and led the first group of Anglo-Americans into what would become Kentucky. Others followed, even during the course of the American War of Independence. George Rogers Clark brought settlers into the Ohio River valley during the 1770s. After the revolution, other undertakings brought new settlers into the lower Mississippi valley and the western Gulf coast as a result of policies administered by Spanish authorities at New Orleans, who encouraged Anglo-Americans to migrate. Anglo-American merchants had already successfully integrated these areas into trade networks linked to the coastal United States, thereby creating profitable avenues of capital exchange along with lucrative commercial markets for these newly arriving settlers.

The essays in this volume do not seek to be inclusive regarding all aspects of the Anglo-American, English-speaking advance into Spanish Louisiana and Texas. For example, the institution of slavery played a significant role, touching on almost every aspect of this migration. Slavery per se is not my historical concern in the chapters that follow. I have not analyzed it as an institution, commented on the lives of slaves, or assessed how human bondage drove this migration; other historians have undertaken accomplished analyses of such topics. My interests have instead rested on aspects of the slave trade as a commercial venture and the importance it had on underpinning land acquisition by planters. In addition, the ongoing and significant role played by Native Americans in their relationships with all of the Europeans living in the region falls outside my scholarly work. Like historical studies of slavery, the history of Native Americans and their effects on the developments in Spanish Louisiana and Texas are not reflected in the essays collected here. The bibliographic essay, however, does note the important academic studies that explicitly address the relationships of slavery and Native Americans to English-speaking migrations into Louisiana and Texas.

The essays in this book as well provide no cognizance of the interpretive frameworks of Atlantic World history, a topic more fully addressed in the bibliographic essay. History written from this historiographical approach is based on analytical assumptions that view the colonial experience as part of an extended, interlocking, and integrated Atlantic basin constituting one historical entity—namely, a unitary system of economic, cultural, and imperial enlacements, with each component part playing a symbiotic role in the larger whole. As historian Allison Games notes in a 2006 essay in the *American Historical Review,* considering the entire Atlantic basin and its imperial relationships as one single unit of historical analysis "is a way of looking at global *and* regional processes within a contained unit" of historical analysis. In the last decade or so, Atlantic World history has increasingly informed studies about Louisiana during the eighteenth century and early nineteenth centuries, although this approach has not yet influenced scholars of Spanish colonial Texas very much. Cécile Vidal offers a firm opinion regarding these historiographical developments in her 2014 book *Louisiana: Crossroads of the Atlantic World,* a collection of essays by various historians writing from this viewpoint. "One cannot write Louisiana history," Vidal notes, "without adopting an Atlantic perspective or study Atlantic history without including Louisiana."

All of the essays in this book were researched and written before the rise of Atlantic World history. For that reason, they do represent, as Vidal has aptly characterized my historical writing, "an earlier historiography that belongs to a more traditional kind of colonial history but constitutes an indispensable pedestal on which one can build a more innovative social and cultural history" rooted in an Atlantic World history.

In that regard, my essays embrace topics that to some extent provide foundations for the ex-post-facto imposition of such an approach over them. Several of them might be called "cisatlantic world" history at best, although I pay little attention to matters that do not relate to Spain, Great Britain, or the United States. Heavily influenced by the "imperial school" in my own graduate training decades ago, my approaches seem institutional by today's historiographical standards, especially for Atlantic World historians. That is the case because the essays in this book almost exclusively deal with commercial and landholding activities that motivated English speakers to move into the lower Mississippi valley and Gulf coast regions up until the 1820s. They address patterns of English-speaking demographic movement, lifestyles related to these populations, and the blending of Hispanic and Anglo cultural patterns without any emphasis on black, Native American, or nonimperial considerations of a social or cultural nature.

Within that explicit context, however, this volume challenges two assumptions that have been stipulated in much of the historical literature dealing with the expanding English-speaking frontier into the Mississippi valley and Gulf coast. First, there was no "westward movement" during the late eighteenth or early nineteenth centuries bringing a steady stream of English speakers into the colonies of the Spanish Borderlands. Turner's implicit conceptualization of a western frontier moving in contiguous stages across territories from the Atlantic coast to the Mississippi valley is not accurate. Instead, it was maritime in nature, explicitly tied to trade patterns that evolved between the Gulf coast and the Atlantic Seaboard. Many settlers came in boats instead of wagons, floating down the inland waterways directly to Louisiana without stopping or coming by ship across the Gulf of Mexico to the lower Mississippi. This migration was disparate, occurred in fits and starts, and most often took place along the routes of trade and commerce. Much of this expansion fanned out either in a northward direction from New Orleans or from the Mississippi down toward the Crescent City, with Kentucky waystations on the Ohio, bypassing all of the interior South from the Appalachians to the great river.

Second, the trading networks that brought English-speaking merchants to the lower Mississippi and Gulf coast followed established lines of capital migration and commerce that tied these regions to the major port cities of the Atlantic coast, especially Philadelphia. English-speaking settlement in these areas took place because of commercial and mercantile activities of the first Anglo-Americans to arrive in Spanish Louisiana. It was a process that began in the decade before the American Revolution and accelerated for the rest of the eighteenth century. Retail trade and investments in land as a commercial enterprise proved more popular than agriculture in the early stages of this migration. Merchants from the Atlantic Seaboard who settled in areas such as New Orleans thus provided significant stability to the success of Anglo-American settlers coming to the region.

The title of this volume of essays references a book that I read in 1974 while pursuing my doctoral studies in history at Tulane University, Marshall Sprague's *So Vast, So Beautiful a Land: Louisiana and the Purchase*. That volume came into my hands soon after I decided to specialize in studying the Spanish Borderlands, with a research concentration on Louisiana as a colony of Spain. This focus proved consistent with my interests, having grown up in south Texas and along the Gulf coast, which provided me with both a facility in Spanish and a historical appreciation for the role Spain had played in the history of the region. As an undergraduate I had taken a course in Texas history from the noted historian William C. Pool, who gave me a useful context for understanding the larger parameters of the Spanish Borderlands as they related to Texas.

Having never taken a course in the history of Louisiana prior to my graduate studies at Tulane, I lacked a detailed background for putting that Spanish colony into a comprehensive frame of reference. The faculty in the history department did not offer a general Louisiana history course, so I sought one in the offerings of Tulane's University College. That division of the university offered classes to nontraditional students seeking a bachelor's degree as well as noncredit courses for continuing education. Many instructors who taught in University College did so as adjuncts unaffiliated with Tulane's regular academic departments.

Such proved the case with the teacher of the course in Louisiana history, Charles "Pie" Dufour, who permitted me to audit his course on a non-credit basis.

Pie Dufour was a fixture of the Louisiana literary community who knew just about everyone involved in the state's arts and letters, many of whom I eventually had the pleasure of meeting over the years through his auspices. When I first met him, Dufour had almost a half century's experience as a journalist for various New Orleans newspapers besides being a widely read author of almost two dozen popular books dealing with Louisiana history and heritage. He was the person who recommended that I read Sprague's newly published *So Vast, So Beautiful a Land*. Like Dufour, Sprague was not an academic historian, having a background in journalism and writing historical nonfiction for the general reader. His history presented a delightful look at Louisiana from the time of European settlement to the purchase of 1803. I found Sprague's volume a readable and informative introduction to the topic, steeped with high narrative adventure. The joy of reading that book has stayed with me because it helped set me on the academic path I have followed during the last four decades. I pay homage to Marshall Sprague by referencing the title of that volume in this one.

My book of essays, *To the Vast and Beautiful Land*, grew from a series of conversations I had with two respected colleagues in the study of the Spanish Borderlands: Caroline Castillo Crimm and Jesús F. de la Teja. Both enjoy stellar scholarly reputations because of their important publications. Crimm has long been interested in the era of Mexican Texas and has published important studies on the subject. She is also involved with a civic group, the Granderos de Gálvez, who promote greater historical recognition of Bernardo de Gálvez, the governor of Spanish Louisiana who commanded Spain's armies in the Gulf region during the American Revolution. De la Teja's research and writing have redefined the historical interpretation of Spanish Texas; he is an authority on Spanish colonial San Antonio. Both encouraged me to assemble the group of essays that compose this volume.

A note is in order about the terminology used to describe the various groups of people denoted in the essays that follow. We seek as historians to give all peoples in the past a distinctive voice, over time in the historical literature leading to an inconsistency in nomenclature. For many people in the past, the way they defined group identities for themselves changed according to how they perceived themselves at a particular point in time. Their ethnic orientation, language, and place of residence variously determined for them who they were. For example, a person of Irish lineage who came to the American colonies in the 1770s would not have identified as English, even though Spanish speakers in Louisiana or Texas would have considered them as such. Spanish authorities in the region had difficulty discerning any differences between British, English, Irish, and Anglo-American identities, the last being citizens of either Great Britain or the infant United States, sometimes both across time.

Labels based on citizenship are thus difficult for historians to apply regarding English speakers, a challenge compounded because various groups in the past often used inaccurate terms to describe each other. I therefore use the term "Anglo-American" to mean any person of European heritage who was not Gallic or Hispanic. I also employ "English speaker" as a term analogous to Anglo-American. Historian F. Todd Smith uses the term "Anglo Protestant" in his recent survey of the Louisiana and Texas Gulf South, but I avoid it because of the Anglo-Catholic merchants and landowners who were important to my investigations. A more precise academic term might be "Anglophone," but using it seems pretentious.

Several editorial decisions reflect the way these essays appear in this book. Other than correcting obvious typographical errors, no changes have been made to the narrative. Each essay appears as it was published in its respective journal of origin. For that reason, a certain amount of redundancy appears in both the narratives and in the citations across this entire volume. Discussions of Oliver Pollock, for example, take place in a similar fashion of first reference in several of the essays since each had an independent existence as separately published items across twenty-seven years.

It is my pleasure to thank Caroline Castillo Crimm and Jesús F. de la Teja for the roles they played in making this book possible. I would also like to acknowledge my faculty colleagues in the Austin College Writing Group, led by Randi Tanglen, a program sponsored by the Robert and Joyce Johnson Center for Faculty Development, especially Melinda Landeck for making me aware of writing techniques that facilitated my work on this project. Above all, I acknowledge the help and support of my history department colleague and wife, Victoria Hennessey Cummins, for all she has done to help bring this book into print.

To the Vast and Beautiful Land

CHAPTER 1

An Enduring Community

Anglo-American Settlers at Colonial Natchez and in the Felicianas, 1774–1810

The English-speaking settlement of the lower Mississippi valley and Gulf coast began with the peopling of the British colony of West Florida after the Seven Years' War during the early 1760s. Prior to that decade, there had occurred no coordinated or large-scale attempts by subjects of Great Britain to establish themselves in territories previously claimed by France or Spain along the northern coast of the Seno Mexicano, as the Spanish called the Gulf of Mexico. The Seven Years War, or the French and Indian War, as the British colonists styled it, marked a change in the international fortunes of the lower Mississippi. The Peace of Paris (1763), which ended that conflict, brought significant transfers in territorial sovereignties to the European colonies in North America: Canada became British, French Louisiana became a Spanish province, and Spain ceded Florida to Britain. Consequently, France ceased to be a colonial power in North America, while the British and Spanish Empires now for the first time faced each other across the Mississippi River and along the northern Gulf of Mexico.

Great Britain thereafter moved to establish two new colonies along the southern Atlantic and Gulf coasts. The former Spanish areas south of the Carolinas and Georgia became British East Florida. Britain also established the colony of West Florida, which ran along the Gulf coast westward from the Apalachicola River through Pensacola to the Mississippi, passing to the north of Lakes Pontchartrain and Borgne, with the Isle of Orleans to the south belonging to Spanish Louisiana. Along the Mississippi, Bayou Manchac separated British possessions to the north from Spanish territory and New Orleans to the south. British troops arrived in Pensacola in 1763, establishing that longstanding post as the military and civil headquarters of West Florida, with George Johnstone as its first governor. A representative assembly met there for the first time in 1764. Royal officials encouraged settlement by British subjects, issuing land grants both to absentee owners and to colonists moving into the region. Most of the latter group came to West Florida from the older colonies on the Atlantic coast, although some arrived from England. Almost all of them traveled to the new colony by means of maritime transport. While a few floated down the Mississippi River from Pennsylvania, ships from London, New York, Baltimore, and Philadelphia brought the bulk of these new settlers to the colony. This marked the beginning of English-speaking settlement in the lower Mississippi valley and along the northern reaches of the Gulf coast.

The settlement of British West Florida has historical importance because it served as the "jumping-off" place for many of the individuals who would later settle other parts of the lower Mississippi valley and Gulf coast, with some of the children and grandchildren of early West Florida setters ending up in Texas during the 1820s and 1830s. That historical reality motivated me to craft a research strategy that sought to comment on the role West Florida colonists played as an opening wedge for the English-speaking settlement of the region. How many of these people remained across the various sovereignties that controlled the areas north of New Orleans on the east side of the Mississippi from the 1760s to the 1820s? I therefore consulted the 1774 William Wilton map. Compiling names from that document, I cross-referenced these landholders with various names in notary proceedings, court cases, tax records, and similar sources down into the antebellum period. This confirmed that the settlement of British West Florida produced an enduring community of people in the area, some of the children from which later went to Texas. Andrew McMichael has subjected the English-speaking population in West Florida to detailed analysis for the time period following the American Revolution to the Rebellion of 1810, using many of the sources that underpin this essay. This research resulted in his 2008 book, *Atlantic Loyalties: Americans in Spanish West Florida, 1785–1810*.

Light Townsend Cummins, "An Enduring Community: Anglo-Americans at Colonial Natchez and in the Felicianas, 1774–1810," *Journal of Mississippi History* 55 (May 1995): 133–54.

IN JUNE 1772, His Catholic Majesty, King Charles III of Spain, convened a royal audience with his principal advisors at the Palacio del Oriente in Madrid. The purpose of this meeting was to consider a recent report from Luis de Unzaga y Amezaga, governor of Louisiana, that the British were settling along the eastern bank of the Mississippi River, north of and adjacent to Spanish Louisiana. Consequently, Charles III also invited General Alejandro O'Reilly to attend because of his familiarity with conditions in the lower Mississippi valley. The general had compiled a distinguished record of service in Cuba and Louisiana. In fact, O'Reilly was responsible for establishing Spanish authority in Louisiana during 1769.[1] Consequently, the general possessed firsthand information about the entire region, including the area to the north of New Orleans being settled by the British. By the terms of the Peace of Paris (1763), Great Britain had acquired this territory as part of West Florida. News of these British settlements worried the Spanish king and his ministers. Were these settlers a presage to possible British territorial encroachments into Spanish Louisiana?

Pressed for his views about British intentions, O'Reilly explained the motive for this expansion was probably not an official British policy of aggression. Instead it came from the personal desires of the settlers to better themselves.[2] Authorities in West Florida had made land grants to individuals who sought to push the frontier into rich and unsettled territory along the Mississippi. These settlers were eager to profit individually from rising land values and new agricultural opportunities. According to O'Reilly, British territorial expansion was a byproduct of land hunger, personal initiative, and individual desire for wealth. The arrival of new settlers along the Mississippi River, he believed, was therefore not an indication of hostile intentions directed toward Spanish Louisiana by the British government.[3]

This essay is also concerned with these very same British settlers who so worried King Charles and his ministers over two centuries ago. The purpose herein, however, is not to examine Spanish policy regarding them, which came to little because of O'Reilly's advice. It is to determine what happened to these particular Anglo-American settlers during the remainder of the eighteenth and early nineteenth centuries. Did some of them stay to live under Spanish rule after the 1779 conquests of Bernardo de Gálvez during the American Revolution? Did some later continue as United States citizens in the Mississippi Territory, while others of them remain in the Spanish district around Baton Rouge? Did some from this latter group stay into the American period, which began unofficially with the West Florida Rebellion of 1810? By popular tradition and lineage, it has long been known to genealogists and local historians of the region that several families today prominent in the area between Natchez and Baton Rouge descended from settlers in British West Florida.[4] No systematic effort, however, has been made to substantiate this assertion. No historian has attempted to determine the numerical extent to which Anglo-Americans from British West Florida might have stayed in the region.

This essay will examine the extent to which these Anglo-American settlers became an enduring community across the shifting territorial domination of Great Britain, Spain, and the United States in the Natchez District and in the Felicianas. The grantee listings enumerated on the William Wilton map of 1774 provide a potentially fruitful foundation upon which to base an analysis of this community. William Wilton's map of grants along the Mississippi River between Baton Rouge and Natchez is one of the earliest extant cartographic records of these settlers. All of the discussion which follows in this essay is, as a case study, based upon the two hundred forty-seven names noted on that particular map.[5] The documentary records regarding the lower Mississippi valley between 1774 and 1810 are indeed rich in detail about many individual Wilton map grantees, especially in matters touching upon their land-grant filings and reconfirmations; notarial transactions (or, as they are known in the British system, chancery-court proceedings) such as slave transfers, conveyances, mortgages, and powers of attorney; and ecclesiastical matters such as births, marriages, and deaths. These records trace the careers and lives of the Wilton map grantees. "With Wilton's map," as the distinguished Louisiana geographer Milton B. Newton Jr. observed in his study of this important plat, "we have the documentation of the arrival of tangible British order upon the land of the Old Natchez District."[6]

The geographical area comprehended by the Wilton map runs the entire east bank of the Mississippi between present-day Baton Rouge and Natchez (containing their hinterlands), including some of the inland settlements along the rivers and bayous flowing from the east into the great river. It covers northward to the vicinity of present-day Vicksburg, although very few grants are noted upriver from Bayou Pierre. At various times in history, this area has been known popularly by different names with a fair degree of imprecision. The British of the 1760s and 1770s generally called it the Natchez District. After the American Revolution and the advent of Spanish domination over the area, the northern part came to be known more specifically as the Natchez District while the southern part nearer to Baton Rouge came to be styled "Feliciana." The Peace of Paris (1783) failed to define a clear boundary along the lower Mississippi between the territory of the United States and Spain. Pinckney's Treaty of 1795 resolved this boundary dispute. A joint boundary-line commission later surveyed a dividing line between United States and Spanish territory. That survey line is today the southern boundary of Mississippi as it touches West and East Feliciana Parishes in Louisiana. In 1803, the United States purchased most of Louisiana, including the City of New Orleans. Feliciana, however, specifically remained a part of Spanish West Florida. The areas north of the boundary line became part of the Territory of Mississippi, while the zone to the south became the Spanish District of Feliciana, with administrative headquarters at Baton Rouge. In 1810, Anglo-American planters in the Spanish District of Feliciana rebelled against the government of Spain and formed the short-lived Republic of West Florida. Shortly thereafter, Governor W. C. C. Claiborne of the Orleans Territory accepted United States jurisdiction over the district from the Transcontinental Treaty of 1819. Today, the area south of the boundary line in Louisiana is therefore popularly known as the "Florida Parishes" or as the "Felicianas."[7]

The William Wilton map of 1774 was the first finished map of this area to make an extensive listing by specific name of the various grantees who received land in this region.[8] Wilton served as deputy surveyor general of the Province of West Florida during the early 1770s in addition to being a landowner and planter. His map is entitled *Part of the River Mississippi from Manchac to the River Yazous for Governor Chester by William Wilton.*[9] The grantees listed on it were most certainly an integral part of the British population influx that so concerned King Charles when he sought the advice of General O'Reilly in June 1772. Beyond the fact of its providing a relatively large listing of early grantees in the region, however, the Wilton map has no special cartographic significance that compels its use. Moreover, it is not comprehensive, since there were indeed other grantees in the area who did not appear on the map. The Wilton map, in point of fact, was probably not an official government document created for the use of West Florida land authorities.[10]

Nonetheless, the names on the map do provide a group of Anglo-American settlers convenient to the historian for sampling and analysis. Hence, the William Wilton map—by the nature of its listing of early landowners, its geographical focus on the area between Baton Rouge and Natchez, and its pre–American Revolutionary chronological status—constitutes for the historian a ready-made, contemporaneous set of British grantees eligible for historical tracing. In doing so, a broad-based survey in a wide variety of records from the British, Spanish, and United States periods can logically provide documentary evidence regarding the subsequent careers of these individuals. Notary records, census data, loyalty oaths, tax rosters, birth and death records, and marriage registers are valuable sources in documenting the continued residence of these settlers in the Natchez District and the Felicianas.

The search for this information must begin at the British Public Records Office, especially the Colonial Office Papers, Section Five (America and the West Indies), which are particularly useful for British land-grant information.[11] The Papeles Procedentes de Cuba in the Archivo General de Indias also provide a wealth of census data, militia muster rolls, loyalty oaths, and settler listings useful for identifying by name British settlers who remained.[12] The survey records for grants of land made by the Spanish government also provide information about British-era settlers who continued to amass holdings after 1781. These papers, which have had a complicated provenance, are today widely scattered, with the majority being found in the Pintado Papers at Louisiana State University and the Louisiana Land Survey Papers at the Historic New Orleans Collection.[13] Notarial records from the Spanish era are also important sources of information about early settlers. Especially valuable are the New Orleans acts of Estevan Quinones, which contain data about marriages and marital discord; the Spanish Archives of West Florida, which contain transactions and conveyances for the District of Feliciana; and the notarial proceedings today known as the Spanish Court Records of Adams County, Mississippi, located at the courthouse in Natchez.[14] Finally, the *American State Papers: Public Lands* contain much information touching on the reconfirmation of British West Florida land grants by the United States government in the decade after the Louisiana Purchase.[15] The basic research design for this essay consisted of the conceptually simple but time-consuming attempt to locate mention of each Wilton map grantee in the above sources, or in the secondary literature written from these documents, for the years between 1774 and 1810.

This research task was made easier by the fact that, unlike in other of the eighteenth-century British colonies, the majority of individual grantees actually resided in the province. "The remoteness of this far borderland colony from familiar sea lands and trade routes, its obscurity and lack of glamour," as Bernard Bailyn has noted of West Florida, "meant that the metropolitan entrepreneurs plunging into overseas land speculation were relatively uninterested in its possibilities and hence tied up less of its land in absentee grants."[16] This was certainly the case, in spite of the fact that an often-cited, earlier historian of Anglo-American immigration into British West Florida presented an opinion different from that of Bailyn. Unfortunately, some scholarly studies still reflect the view of W. B. Hamilton, who noted in 1937: "It is certain that a large number of grantees were absentee, and never made a gesture of settlement."[17] The information developed in this essay supports Professor Bailyn's conclusion instead of that held earlier by Hamilton. There was a minority of absentee landowners (at the very maximum no more than approximately 26 percent, at least among those noted on the Wilton map).[18] Over 74 percent of the grantees noted by William Wilton on his map were physically present in British West Florida.

Research in the documentary base used for this essay indicates that the two hundred forty-seven persons noted on the Wilton map can be divided into three demographic groups: (1) those for whom no record other than a Wilton-map listing can be found or who were explicitly identified in the documents consulted as absentee grantees, with sixty-five names falling into this category of "demographic invisibility"; (2) those persons noted on the Wilton map and for whom another document established proven residence in British West Florida, but for whom no record can be found after 1781, and hence it may be conjectured they did not remain to live under the Spanish government, with ninety names appearing in this category of "departed persons"; and (3) those Wilton-map grantees for whom a post-1781 record can be found, thus indicating they remained to live under Spanish if not American domination as "permanent residents," with a total of ninety-two names in this latter category.[19] This means that, of the two hundred forty-seven grantees appearing on the William Wilton map, 26.3 percent are at present unaccounted for in the modern documentary record surveyed and are to date "demographically invisible," while 36.4 percent left West Florida by the end of 1781 as "departed persons." Lastly, 37.2 percent remained in the province as "permanent residents." Less than 1 percent of the total were those persons definitively identified by the documentary record as absentee grantees who never came to the province.[20]

It is, of course, the 37.2 percent "permanent residents," or their immediate families, listed on the Wilton map of 1774 who are the primary interest of this study. Nonetheless, some attention should be given to Wilton-map grantees who departed West Florida before, or upon, its transfer to Spain. Many of these individuals were British loyalists. They departed the colony with the end of British sovereignty, although others in this grouping left the colony at a time previous to the Revolution for reasons unrelated to the conflict.[21] The largest number in this group was composed, understandably, of provincial officials and military officers. Forty-two persons fell into this category of Wilton-plat grantees, a classification that includes some of the best-known historical personages of British West Florida. Governors George Johnstone and Peter Chester, along with several of their relatives, were Wilton-map grantees. So too were Lieutenant Governor Monforte Browne, General Frederick Haldimand, Surveyor General Elias Durnford, Provincial Chief Justice William Clifton, Colonel Alexander Dickson, Council Member Philip Livingston Jr., Indian Commissary Charles Stuart, Attorney General Edmund Rush Wegg, Provincial Secretary Elihu Hall Bay, several dozen other council members, and various other government employees.[22]

A second group of Wilton-map grantees who left no post-1781 documentary record was the merchants, artisans, and planters who had close ties to the British mercantile system, or who had personal ties to the British government or some of its officials. Forty-one of these grantees did not remain under Spanish control after the American Revolution. Many of them lived at Mobile or Pensacola, although they held land grants noted on the Wilton map. They were involved prior to 1781 in a wide variety of economic activities that ranged from planting and agriculture to supplying British troops as commissaries, investing in real estate, engaging in slave ownership, and operating extensive export-import commerce from the province's major ports. In modern terms, they constituted British West Florida's established, port-city economic elite. Merchants including James Amoss, Thomas Bentley, John Falconer, Joseph Garriov, John Gradenigo, and Charles Strachen were among them. Others included the physician John Lorimer, Henry Fairchild, David Hodge, and Walter Hood. A significant number of persons from this grouping had regular contact with the British administration, with some of them engaging in government-supply contracts while sometimes serving on juries and panels and attending as delegates to the provincial assembly on the occasions when it met.[23] All of them departed by the end of 1781.

British ship captains and pilots were a third group of the Wilton-map grantees who did not remain after 1781. They were a small number, with only six such persons in this category. They were Arthur Clark, William Gosling, Alexander Moore, Thomas McMin, John Vaughan, and Ephraim Wolfe.[24] These persons probably held their grants only for purposes of land speculation.

The departure by late 1781 of these ninety individuals from West Florida did not necessarily indicate that they subsequently lost personal interest in their Wilton-map holdings. After the Louisiana Purchase, the government of the United States undertook a process to legitimize land grants north of the boundary line surveyed between Spanish Feliciana and the Mississippi Territory. Acts of Congress provided that persons resident in American territory could seek reconfirmation of their British and Spanish land grants by meeting certain provisions. Such persons, or their legal heirs, had to furnish the United States General Land office with documents substantiating the colonial-era land grants, along with proof of actual residency on the land. Only applicants who were then current residents on the land and who could prove they had occupied their holdings prior to Pinckney's Treaty had the right to seek such reconfirmation. In the first decade of the 1800s, however, various Wilton-map grantees (or their family members or other lawful heirs) who had departed West Florida by 1781 tried to have the United States reconfirm their British-era titles. In many cases, these grants had been superseded by ones made to other individuals during the Spanish era.[25] The general confusion associated with this quieting of land titles in the Mississippi Territory made the process complex and cumbersome. "One or more persons," as one historian has noted without much exaggeration, "claimed to be the rightful owner of every tract of land under cultivation and many that were not."[26]

The heirs of Archibald Montgomerie, the Earl of Eglington, undertook the most blatant of these spurious reconfirmation attempts. Eglington was an absentee landholder resident in London who had been awarded a mandamus of 20,000 acres in the Natchez area during 1767, primarily because he was a drinking companion of George Johnstone, the province's first governor. Wilton noted the grant on his map. In the early 1800s, Eglington's heirs in Great Britain filed a motion before the land-office commissioners seeking a United States title. The commissioners refused to confirm this title, ostensibly because Eglington never met the residency requirement. They also refused to confirm Eglington's title because "this land is entirely covered by Spanish patents, being one of the most flourishing settlements in the district."[27]

Elihu Hall Bay, the former provincial secretary prior to the American Revolution, departed West Florida shortly after the Spanish conquest of Pensacola. Later, after the Revolution, he became a United States citizen and eventually resided in Charleston, South Carolina, during the early 1800s. By 1809, he had filed over a dozen claims for reconfirmation of British titles, not only for himself but in the names of other former settlers, including William Garnier, William Grant, Dr. John Lorimer, John Smith, James Barbour, Thaddeus Lyman, and James Provost. Bay, in partnership with his associate Robert J. Turnbull, particularly attempted to claim four plantations on the Mississippi that appeared on the Wilton map. The United States commissioners, however, failed to sustain any of Bay's claims because he did not meet the legal criteria of residency established by Congress.[28] Alexander MaCullaugh, the nephew and namesake of the West Florida provost marshal, also unsuccessfully attempted to secure reconfirmations of grants as his uncle's legal heir. By 1809, most of his claims had been denied by the United States due to poor documentation.[29] Only those grantees who could prove they had actually lived on their land during the late eighteenth century successfully secured reconfirmation by United States title.

Among these, of course, were some of the ninety-two Wilton-map grantees (or members of their immediate family) who stayed in the region during the shifts of British, Spanish, French, and United States sovereignty. They constituted an enduring residential presence in the region for generations. This may be seen in the distribution by five-year period of the "last date of reference" for these ninety-two grantees or their immediate family members. The dates are 1781–85, twenty-one persons; 1786–90, fourteen persons; 1791–95, nineteen persons; 1796–1800, eight persons; 1801–5, eighteen persons; and after 1805, ten persons. A majority of the ninety-two Wilton-map grantee families who remained in the area were either planters or were general merchants. In some cases, particular persons engaged in both activities. Some of them enjoyed great prosperity, became well known in the region, and established lineages that continue in some cases to the present day.

Many of the Wilton-map grantees and their families stayed in the region because, in the ultimate analysis, the Spanish government by the mid-1780s accepted "the fact that a large number of English-speaking Protestants had sunk permanent roots in the province, and that a policy of dislocating them would be difficult to carry out and unwise."[30] In part, the Spanish government came to this realization because some of the Anglo-Americans (including Wilton-map grantees) explicitly made known their strong desires to stay. William Johnstone, a Wilton-map grantee, expressed such sentiments when he wrote to Spain's minister of the Indies, José de Gálvez, during April 1783. Johnstone asked that he be permitted to keep over three thousand acres of his landholdings. As well, he offered the Spanish minister various suggestions for improving the economy of the province, including tax exemptions, in the hopes of increasing the agricultural productivity of the region.[31] William was not the only Anglo resident to petition the Spanish government about remaining in Spanish territory after the American Revolution. Others made similar requests to the governor of Louisiana.[32]

Those who desired to stay were understandably concerned because the Peace of Paris (1783) required that all citizens of the former British province of West Florida depart the lower Mississippi valley within eighteen months after the promulgation of the treaty. Those Anglo-American settlers who chose to remain could therefore do so only with expressed permission. Spain, it turned out, had a very accommodating disposition toward them. Louisiana governor Esteban Miró soon embarked on a plan that would make possible the continued residence of Anglo-American landowners on their British-era holdings. Spain, eager to populate the territorially expanded province of Louisiana with colonists, had already experienced difficulty inducing Iberian immigrants to the lower Mississippi valley. This was due both to financial problems in underwriting a trans-Atlantic migration of Spanish subjects and the unwillingness on the part of individual Hispanic colonists to relocate in Louisiana, which many of them saw as an isolated, economically backward, and undesirable place of potential residence. Hence, Louisiana needed loyal settlers who might come from any acceptable quarter. This realization prompted a 1785 proposal from Governor Miró that would permit British-era residents to retain their holdings. They could become loyal Spanish subjects by taking an oath of allegiance to the king of Spain and adopting Roman Catholicism as their publicly professed religion. Implementation of this plan began during the spring of 1786. Miró created two parishes that covered the former British Natchez District. Each parish received a priest, a military commandant, and a detachment of troops for the protection of the parish.[33] These new parishes covered much of the area noted on the William Wilton map.

Stephen Minor soon thereafter became Spanish adjutant at the town of Natchez, the center for the northern parish. Born in Virginia in 1760, Minor had come to the Mississippi valley during the American Revolution and settled in the Natchez area. He sincerely gave his allegiance to the Spanish king, in whose employ he would serve for decades thereafter. Minor's solid leadership skills, which served him in good stead at Natchez for the remainder of the Spanish period, made an important "step toward mutual understanding and respect" between the Anglo-American residents of the region and their new Spanish masters.[34] By 1785, a process of assimilation was well underway in spite of tensions and problems remaining from the tumult of the American Revolution. In that year, Spanish official Francisco Bougligny wrote of Natchez: "The majority of the inhabitants of this town are natives of North America, others are Englishmen, with a few Frenchmen, and it is very rare that a Spaniard is encountered."[35]

Thus, by the mid-1780s, many Anglo-American residents of former British West Florida began to play significant roles as citizens of Spanish Louisiana, including some of the ninety-two who were Wilton-map grantees. William Wilton himself stayed in the region. He had received a British grant, which appeared on his own map, for two hundred acres on the east bank of the Mississippi to the north of Baton Rouge across from Point Coupee. The governmental papers of Spanish West Florida contain records of his commercial transactions, and with the transfer to the United States, his family successfully sought confirmation of his British- and Spanish-era holdings.[36]

Daniel Hickey is a good example of a Wilton-map landholder who enjoyed success during the decades of Spanish domination. A native of County Clare, Ireland, where he was born about 1740, Hickey came to West Florida in the 1760s and worked as the overseer on Monforte Browne's Dauphin Island plantation. He briefly served as Indian commissary at Pensacola. After several years in Browne's employ, he moved to British Manchac and opened a tavern. On June 10, 1768, Hickey received a grant of five hundred acres, which was noted on the Wilton map. The Spanish government confirmed this grant in 1789, and the United States government granted title reconfirmation in 1804. Hickey served as an officer in the Spanish militia for the District of Baton Rouge during the early 1800s. In this capacity, he helped maintain public order in the district when a United States gunboat took as prisoners several American fugitives from justice who had fled into Spanish territory.[37] Hickey, who died in 1808, established a family dynasty that continued in the region for generations.[38] His son Philip married the daughter of James Mather and participated in the West Florida Rebellion of 1810, where he served as a delegate to the convention held at St. John's Plain in August 1810. There the younger Hickey worked to validate British-era landholdings belonging to longtime residents. Article four of the proposed West Florida constitution of 1810 confirmed all such holdings, even in cases where no written title or document of legal grant could be produced. Once the Felicianas joined the United States, Philip Hickey Jr. served as a Louisiana state senator, saw active duty in the military during the War of 1812, and erected the first sugar mill in East Baton Rouge Parish.[39]

David Williams, also a grantee on the Wilton map, emerged during the Spanish period as another important resident, and his family was prominent in the area between Baton Rouge and Natchez after his death in 1792. Williams, along with three of his brothers, came to British West Florida from South Carolina. He received a thousand-acre grant on the Mississippi in 1769 and amassed numerous other landholdings during his business career in the area. He played an active role in the Natchez uprising of 1781, during which some former British subjects protested Spanish control in the wake of Bernardo de Gálvez's victories. Along with John Blommart, William Easton, and other rebel leaders, he was sent as a prisoner to New Orleans in 1781. He later returned to the Felicianas and rehabilitated himself in the eyes of the Spanish. He named one of his sons Gayoso in honor of the Spanish governor, Manuel Gayoso de Lemos. In the census of 1782 for Baton Rouge, he was one of the largest slaveowners of the district as well as owner of the area's most extensive timber-producing operation. He was held in high esteem by virtue of his acting as executor to his neighbors' wills in addition to serving as witness in various land disputes. An active trader, he augmented his agricultural profits by buying and selling slaves. After his death, David Williams's heirs continued to operate plantations along the Mississippi between Natchez and Baton Rouge.[40]

Francis Poussett also came to the Mississippi valley during the 1760s. After serving as speaker of the West Florida Assembly in 1766, he received grants of land along the Mississippi. Several of these holdings appeared on the Wilton map. Poussett eventually moved to Baton Rouge, where he resided until his death in 1802. He held office as the syndic for the Bayou Sarah District in the late 1790s. An Anglo-American by birth and culture, he steadfastly complained about his often being mistaken for a Frenchman because of his Gallic surname. On one occasion, he formally filed records of his birth before a Spanish notary at Baton Rouge in order to prove his Anglo-American background.[41] Along with the Poussett, Williams, and Hickey families, the descendants of Thomas Comyns established roots in the area. Thomas and Stephen Comyns were London merchants during the 1760s. They specialized in trade with British West Florida, and in the late 1760s, Stephen sent his sons Valens and Phillip to the province in order to superintend the family business. They later received various grants of land, which they farmed as income supplements to their prosperous merchant activities as specialists in the importation of rum and textiles. They and their descendants, including a grandson also named Thomas, settled in the Felicianas area during the 1780s, where they remained for several generations.[42]

The list of Wilton-map grantees and their families who stayed in the Felicianas region and Natchez District should be extended to include the Jones brothers and Hezekiah Russ. The Jones brothers may have become the wealthiest of the Anglo-Americans who stayed. They established a mercantile operation in the lower Mississippi valley that lasted well into the nineteenth century. Evan Jones was born in New England in the late 1730s and immigrated to Mobile from New York as one of the first Anglo-American merchants to arrive in that British West Florida port. He imported flour, along with the usual assortment of manufactured goods so much in demand along the Gulf coast. Evan also served as the corresponding commercial agent for Logan, Terry, and Company, while his brother John, a merchant in New York City, supplied him with goods from that major Atlantic port.[43]

In 1765, Evan moved to New Orleans and founded his own firm. There he quickly ingratiated himself with the government and was permitted to engage in mercantile pursuits. New Orleans society welcomed Evan into its fold. He married the Creole beauty Marie Verret and became a citizen of substance. Meanwhile, another brother, James, moved to West Florida, and by the early 1770s, they together managed a successful trans-provincial mercantile house based both at British Pensacola and Spanish New Orleans. James took an active role in West Florida politics and was elected to the provincial assembly. In 1772 and 1773, the Jones brothers received several relatively large British land grants that appeared on the Wilton map. Both brothers became Spanish citizens upon the territorial transfer to Spain. James moved to New Orleans, where he bought a home on present-day Bienville Street. The brothers' firm centered its operations in Spanish Louisiana. Under the regime of Miró, the Spanish government reconfirmed the title to their extensive landholdings in the Natchez District and in the Felicianas area. Evan served in the Spanish militia and operated as the vice consul of the United States at New Orleans. After 1803, the brothers willingly shifted their allegiance to the United States as Evan was elected to the New Orleans City Council and served as a director of the Louisiana branch of the Bank of the United States. In 1805, the United States land commissioners reconfirmed American titles to the Jones brothers' British land grants, including those that appeared on the Wilton map.[44]

Hezekiah Russ, although he did not live into the American period, also established a family dynasty that endured along the lower Mississippi for several generations. Russ came to West Florida in the early 1770s as a prosperous planter. A man who clearly valued family, he and his wife Rebecca had a dozen children, most of whom lived into adulthood. In 1772, the Hezekiah Russ family received a grant of one thousand acres along Thompson's Creek, which William Wilton noted. As various sons left home, they too became landowners. The Spanish census of 1782 listed his son William Russ and six grandchildren as residents of the Baton Rouge District, while it noted that Hezekiah's son Abaza also owned land in the area. By 1794, two others of the Russ children, John and Abiyah, had established themselves along False River in Point Coupee. By 1802, at least seven of the Russ grandchildren had been baptized at St. Joseph's Roman Catholic parish in Baton Rouge.[45]

The American Revolutionary merchant Oliver Pollock is perhaps the most well-known of the Wilton-map grantees to have established a permanent presence in the lower Mississippi valley during the late eighteenth century. A native of Ireland, Pollock came to Pennsylvania in 1760, where he resided at Carlisle, later moved to Philadelphia, and thereafter established a lifelong trading relationship with Hispanic America. Pollock, after living at Havana for several years, came to the lower Mississippi valley in 1769. Although he resided at New Orleans, where he was fully accepted as a merchant by the Spanish government, he also maintained his British citizenship until 1777, when he joined the rebel cause during the American Revolution. He thus took full advantage during the early 1770s of British land policy and received several valuable tracts of land, including one noted on the Wilton map near the location of the Tunica Indian village north of Baton Rouge. Pollock, once the Natchez District fell to Spanish sovereignty during the Revolution, expanded his activities in the region. Some of the Pollock family, including his nephew Hamilton, settled there permanently. Hamilton managed the Pollock lands until his health broke during the summer of 1814. By that time, the unfortunate Hamilton had become mentally deranged and died shortly thereafter. During his final illness, family members had to keep him chained to a post inside one of the plantation barns to avoid his doing injury to himself or others.[46] Oliver's daughter, Mary Pollock Robinson, and her husband thereafter took charge of the Pollock plantations. They lived at Pinckneyville, in Wilkinson County, well into the American period. It was at Mary's home that the aged Oliver Pollock died in 1824. His grandson Oliver Pollock Robinson lived in West Feliciana Parish, Louisiana, until the Civil War.[47]

Other Wilton-map settlers who remained along the lower Mississippi, however, were not as uniformly upstanding in their good citizenship as Philip Hickey, David Williams, Hezekiah Russ, and Oliver Pollock. James Lovel must certainly be excluded from this group since he became one of the district's most notorious criminals during the Spanish period. Lovel had come to the region during the British era and received a 1769 grant of one thousand acres, which appeared on various tax and landowner rolls. Along with two of his sons and several others, he became a member of a criminal gang that robbed and terrorized the area during the mid-1780s. His final crime spree occurred in August 1786, just before the gang fled to American territory, reputedly bound for rural Georgia. They robbed the home of Manuel Texada, where they took horses, bridles, and other supplies at gunpoint. Lovel and his gang moved on to other nearby homes, where they took at gunpoint various valuables from the residents before fleeing to the United States.[48]

Daniel Ward, another Wilton-map grantee, also ran afoul of Spanish authorities for different reasons. Ward, along with Luis Forneret, became a participant in the longest-running and most spectacular adultery case in the history of Spanish Louisiana. Forneret, a resident of Louisiana since the French regime, became the public interpreter at Mobile and Baton Rouge during the Spanish era. In 1767, he had married a woman named Isabel Alexandre. The two lived together for several years, but Forneret traveled to France in the 1770s for an extended stay in order to conduct family business. Upon his return, he found that his wife had allegedly become the mistress of Daniel Ward, apparently living in

Ward's household and sharing his bed and board. Isabel claimed that she was simply a domestic servant and acted as Ward's lawful wife. Almost a decade's worth of adultery suits and countersuits followed while Ward, Isabel, and Forneret engaged in an almost bewildering array of charges and countercharges. Finally, in the 1790s, the ecclesiastical court at New Orleans ordered Isabel to vacate the Ward home and to resume living with Forneret as his wife.[49]

Sarah Joiner, sister of William Joiner, who appeared on the Wilton map, also had difficulty with the ecclesiastical courts because of marital problems. Sarah filed a divorce suit against her husband, James Smith, in 1792. She contended, and her brother supported her before the Spanish courts, that Smith drove "her from him with two helpless children, and has taken every means of support from her and the children, although she had greatly contributed by her industry to acquire what little property they have." Testimony in this case determined that Mrs. Smith had sufficient reason for securing a divorce, which was granted. A comprehensive inventory of the Smith possessions revealed that they were a family of clearly modest means living near Bayou Sarah.[50]

For the most part, however, the Anglo-American residents of West Florida who remained led quiet lives of simplicity and hard work. They farmed, bought and sold slaves, and willingly met their obligations as citizens of the Felicianas and the Natchez District. This was so because agriculture was the primary activity in West Florida.[51] Although very few of the original grantees actually lived to see the Louisiana Purchase of 1803 or the West Florida Rebellion of 1810, many of their descendants did. By forming a demographically distinct presence in the region, these settlers, in concert with other British residents of West Florida not named on the Wilton map, constituted an early Anglo-American community that predated the Louisiana Purchase by a generation. If the settlers noted on the Wilton map of 1774 are typical (and this essay supposes that they were), all of the British West Florida grantees who stayed in the area across the shifting sovereignties of the late eighteenth century may well have been a decisive vanguard for the Anglo-Americanization of the lower Mississippi valley.

Notes

1. Luis de Unzaga to Marques de la Torre, February 22, 1772, Archivo General de Indias, Seville, Spain Audiencia de Santo Domingo, Legajo 1211. For the British side of these land grants, see Clinton N. Howard, *The British Development of West Florida, 1763–1769* (Berkeley: University of California Press, 1947), 84–92; and Robin F. A. Fabel, *The Economy of British West Florida, 1763–1783* (Tuscaloosa: University of Alabama Press, 1988), 6–21.

2. Julian de Arriaga to O'Reilly, May 28, 1772; and O'Reilly to Arriaga, June 5, 1772, Archivo General de Indias, Audiencia de Santo Domingo, Legajo 1211.

3. O'Reilly to Arriaga, June 5, 1772, ibid. For an overview of British interests in the lower Mississippi valley, see Cecil Johnson, *British West Florida, 1763–1783* (New Haven, CT: Yale University Press, 1943), 115–49; D. Clayton James, *Antebellum Natchez* (Baton Rouge: Louisiana State University Press, 1968), 13–19; Robin F. A. Fabel, *Bombast and Broadsides: The Lives of George Johnstone* (Tuscaloosa: University of Alabama Press, 1987), 43–57; and Robert R. Rea, *Major Robert Farmer of Mobile* (Tuscaloosa: University of Alabama Press, 1990), 63–79. A glimpse into everyday British life in these settlements is seen in the letter books of merchant John Fitzpatrick. *The Merchant of Manchac: The Letterbooks of John Fitzpatrick, 1768–1790*, ed. Margaret Fisher Dalrymple (Baton Rouge: Louisiana State University Press, 1978). See also Cecil Johnson, "The Distribution of Land in British West Florida," *Louisiana Historical Quarterly* 16 (October 1933): 539–53.

4. Stanley C. Arthur, *Old Families of Louisiana* (Baton Rouge: Louisiana State University Press, 1971), 189, 330, 352, 362, 390, 417; Emma K. Eaton, *Descendants of the New Jersey Settlers of Ogden's Mandamus, Kingston, Adams County, Mississippi* (Natchez: privately published, 1960), passim; Winston De Ville, *English Land Grants in West Florida: A Register for the States of Alabama, Mississippi, and Part of Louisiana and Florida, 1766–1776* (Ville Platt, LA: Polyanthos, 1986), passim.

5. The William Wilton map came to light in the 1930s during a New Deal–sponsored survey of federal-agency archives supervised by Louisiana historian Stanley C. Arthur. Arthur's project found the original manuscript of the map in the files of the Mississippi River Commission at Vicksburg. Copies of the map were made and placed in various Louisiana repositories, including the libraries at Tulane University and Louisiana State University. The map had apparently remained in the lower Mississippi valley when the British departed in 1781 and, by the early 1800s, became part of the files of the East Baton Rouge Parish surveyor. A private collector purchased the map in 1848 from that official, and by undetermined provenance, it eventually came into the possession of the Mississippi River Commission. Johnson, *British West Florida*, 141. The current location of the original manuscript map is unknown at this writing. Copies are located at the Mississippi Department of Archives and History at Jackson and at Louisiana State University, one at the Hill Memorial Library and the other at the Cartographic Information Center. For a physical description of the Cartographic Information Center copy, see Milton B. Newton Jr., "Mapping the Foundations of

the Old Natchez District: The Wilton Map of 1774," *Natchez before 1830*, ed. Noel Polk (Jackson: University Press of Mississippi, 1989), 81–84.

6. Newton, "Mapping the Foundations of the Old Natchez District," 75.

7. See Stanley C. Arthur, *The Story of the West Florida Rebellion* (St. Francisville, LA: St. Francisville Democrat, 1935); Mattie Austin Hatcher, *The Opening of Texas to Foreign Settlement, 1801–1821* (Austin, TX: University of Texas Press, 1927), 186–91; and David C. Weber, *The Spanish Frontier in North America* (New Haven, CT: Yale University Press, 1992), 297–300.

8. Fabel, *Economy of British West Florida*, 185; Dalrymple, *Merchant of Manchac*, 183, 187, 229–30. Wilton was himself a landowner in the region. In 1805, he attempted to have his British-era land grants reconfirmed by United States commissioners. See *American State Papers: Public Lands* (Washington, DC: Duff Green, 1834), 1:557, claim 2087.

9. The grantee listings of this map were published by Gordon M. Wells. See Wells, "British Land Grants—William Wilton Map, 1774," *Journal of Mississippi History* 28 (May 1966): 152–60. The name index used for this essay was taken from Wells's published listing. In addition, these names were cross-checked with other grantee maps for British West Florida located in the map collection of the Public Record Office, Kew Gardens, London. The following maps were consulted: CO 5/700, Florida 45, Florida 46, Florida 50, and Florida 55. Wells made two errors in transcribing his names for publication. He mistook Elias Burnford for Elias Durnford and William Ratcliff for William Ratliff, thus reducing my number of grantees by two from his total.

10. Elias Durnford was royal surveyor for British West Florida. His maps, rather than those prepared by Wilton, constituted the official grant recordings. In fact, two of his maps are especially important in pinpointing most of the grants in the province: CO 5/700, Florida 45, at the Public Record Office covers much of the area of the Wilton map but includes a larger geographic area into modern-day Alabama, while CO 5/700, Florida 38, provides additional detail. A third comprehensive Durnford map, located at the British Library Map Room (designated by the BL number K-CXXII/90), also provides detailed grantee information from Pensacola eastward to the Mississippi. However, for purposes of designating a group of settlers for demographic purposes, the Wilton map is as good as any other map of the region from the 1770s or 1780s. The research plan consisted of attempting to determine the "last date of documentary reference" for each person noted on the Wilton map. The "last date of reference" in the documentary record for each name on the Wilton map established a baseline for a particular person having remained in the lower Mississippi valley after the exit of Great Britain from the Floridas. Any appearance in the record that could not establish the physical presence of the individual as having been in the region was discarded in favor of a "last date of reference" that actually did so.

11. Most of the British-era land grants are found in CO 5/601 to CO 5/617, inclusive. CO 5/678 contains abstracts of early land grants. See Public Record Office, *Lists and Indexes, Number XXXVI: List of Colonial Office Records Preserved in the Public Record Office* (New York: Kraus Reprint, 1963), 14–15.

12. The standard guide to these papers is Roscoe Hill, *Descriptive Catalog of the Papeles Procedentes de Cuba* (Washington, DC: Carnegie Commission, 1913). The Hill guide, however, is often so general that it is of limited utility. A good, reliable listing of Spanish Louisiana census materials is contained in Antonio Acosta Rodríguez, *La población de Luisiana Española, 1763–1803* (Madrid: Ministerio de Asuntos Exteriores,, 1979), 483–90. It was this listing of census material that served as the basic finding aid for the material used in this study. Also useful as a finding aid, but less comprehensive, is Lawrence H. Feldman, *Anglo-Americans in Spanish Archives: Lists of Anglo-American Settlers in the Spanish Colonies of America—A Finding Aid* (Baltimore: Clearfield, 1991). Recent efforts to provide a microfilm set of the Papeles de Cuba located at the Historic New Orleans Collection and other repositories is described in Paul E. Hoffman, "The Cuban Papers Project and the National Endowment for the Humanities," *The Hispanic Experience in North America: Sources for the Study in the United States*, ed. Lawrence A. Clayton (Columbus: Ohio State University Press, 1992), 116–24. Additional Spanish Louisiana records of importance at the Historic New Orleans Collection are described in Alfred A. Lemmon, "Louisiana Materials from the Archive of the Indies," *Louisiana Library Association Bulletin* 55 (Summer 1992): 25–29. For an analogous study of Anglo-American settlement in British East Florida during this same time period, see Susan R. Parker, "Men Without God or King: Rural Settlers of East Florida, 1784–1790," *Florida Historical Quarterly* 69 (October 1990): 135–55.

13. For the full story of these papers, see Patricia Brady (Schmit), "Compromise Resolves Fate of Documents, Replevin Avoided," *Manuscripts* 37 (Fall 1985): 275–82; and Edward F. Haas, "Odyssey of a Manuscript Collection: Records of the Surveyor General of Antebellum Louisiana," *Louisiana History* 27 (Spring 1986): 5–26. See also Winston De Ville, *Louisiana and Mississippi Lands: A Guide to Spanish Land Grants at the University of Michigan: Properties at Ascension, Attakapas, Baton Rouge. . . .* (Ville Platte, LA: Polyanthos, 1985); and Henry Putney Beers, *French and Spanish Records of Louisiana: A Bibliographical Guide to Archive and Manuscript Sources* (Baton Rouge: Louisiana State University, 1989), 113–149.

14. The best concise guide to these records is Paul E. Hoffman, "La documentacion colonial en la Luisiana," *Archivo Hispalense*, nos. 207–8 (1985): 333–52. A listing of New Orleans notaries for the Spanish colonial era is found in *Gardiner's New Orleans Directory, 1869* (New Orleans, 1869), 27–28. The most useful guide to the New Orleans notary records is Sally Kittredge Reeves, "Spanish Colonial Records of the New Orleans Notarial Archives," *Louisiana Library Association Bulletin* 55 (1992): 7–12. The notary records for the Natchez area are today located in forty bound volumes of original manuscripts at the Office of the Clerk of Chancery, Adams County Courthouse, Natchez, Mississippi. A calendar of these records is May Wilson McBee, *The Natchez Court Records, 1767–1805: Abstracts of Early Records* (Baltimore: Clearfield, 1979). A similar class of records for the District of the Felicianas, which, after 1803, constituted Spanish territory south of the survey line (primarily West Feliciana, East Feliciana, and East Baton Rouge Parishes), are located in the East Baton Rouge Parish Courthouse, Baton Rouge, Louisiana. These colonial-era documents, which were translated and transcribed

as part of a Works Progress Administration project in the 1930s, are today called by the name "The Archives of Spanish West Florida," or more popularly "The West Florida Papers." An index to the translations is Stanley C. Arthur, comp., *Index to the Archive of Spanish West Florida, 1782–1810* (New Orleans: Polyanthos, 1975). An effort is currently underway to create a computerized database for Spanish Louisiana notary records specifically dealing with slave transactions, and undoubtedly, many Anglo-American residents will appear in this source. For information about this database project, see Gwendolyn Midlo Hall, "Africans and Afro-Creoles in Spanish and Early American Louisiana," *Louisiana Library Association Bulletin* 55 (Summer 1992): 13–17.

15. *American State Papers: Public Lands*, vol. 1. Various abstracts of these papers have been prepared; see, for example, Francis Igme and Carol Ericson, eds. *First Settlers of the Mississippi Territory* (Nacogdoches, TX: Ericson Books, 1982).

16. Bernard Bailyn, *Voyagers to the West: A Passage in the Peopling of America on the Eve of the Revolution* (New York: Knopf, 1986), 475.

17. W. B. Hamilton, "American Beginnings in the Old Southwest: The Mississippi Phase" (Ph.D. diss., Duke University, 1937), 9. Hamilton based his conclusions on the reports of the US land commission. The land commissioners denied many of these title reconfirmations because the applicants were not resident on their lands at the time of application for reconfirmation. Hamilton apparently interpreted these denials to mean that the applicants had never been residents on their grants, which in many instances was not the case.

18. This 26 percent is composed of those persons for whom no document other than the Wilton map could be located that noted that the person was actually resident in the colony. Logic would indicate that an undetermined number of the individuals in this category were actually in British Florida, but no documentary record of such presence has been discovered to date.

19. These ninety-two names were those for whom last dates of reference were located between December 1781 and 1810. In some cases, the last date of reference was an appearance in the historical record by heirs from the immediate family of the grantee who were clearly resident on the land noted by the Wilton map, even though the actual grantee might have been deceased. Prominent among the family names on the map were those of Philip Barbour; Robert Barker; Richard Barry; Rebecca and Jacob Blackwell; John and Alice Blommart; Ansel Blanchard; Isabella and James Bruce; Robert Callendar; John Campbell; William, Rachel, and George Canty; Richard and Caleb Carpenter; Daniel Clark (includes both the elder and the younger); Thomas and Phillips Comyns; William and Ann Escott; Ann Gauld; Jeremiah Green; Thomas Greer; Daniel Hickey; Sarah Holmes; Innes Hooper; Michael Hooter; Anthony, Thomas, and James Hutchins; William Joiner; Evan and James Jones; Alexander McCullough; James Martin; William Mill; William and Alexander Moore; Henry Nicholson; Amos Ogden; Mary Oliver; Daniel Perry; Jacob Phillipi; Oliver Pollock; Francis Poussett; William Ratliff; David Ross; Hezekiah Russ; Joseph Smith; John Stevenson; John Summers; Thomas Topham; George Urquhart; James Watkins; Daniel Ward; Benjamin Ward; William Welter; Jacob Winifree; and David Williams.

20. The computerized sort upon which these data are based was conducted using D-base II, with two index fields structured. One field consisted of an onomastic index containing either the name of a Wilton-map grantee or, in the absence of that individual's name, the name of a grantee's immediate family member in cases where genealogical research clearly substantiated actual permanent residence. In the instances when a family member's name was employed instead of that of the grantee, only one heir per family unit became part of the database. This avoided multiple appearance of the same grantee unit in the analysis category and the total number of 247 Wilton-map grantees. The other field consisted of the chronological last date of reference. Because of the imprecise nature of eighteenth-century records, however, the data presented in this essay are not purported to be statistically accurate. Instead, they are offered as support for general conclusions of interpretation.

21. For a discussion of loyalists in British West Florida, see J. Barton Starr, *Tories, Dons, and Rebels: The American Revolution in British West Florida* (Gainesville: University Press of Florida, 1976), 225–40; and J. Leitch Wright Jr., *Florida in the American Revolution* (Gainesville: University Press of Florida, 1975), 117–18.

22. For information about these particular Wilton-map grantees, see the following: George Johnstone: Fabel, *Bombast and Broadsides*, passim. Peter Chester: Starr, *Tories, Dons, and Rebels*, passim; Monforte Browne: Fabel, *Economic History of British West Florida*, 12–14, 59–60, 198–99; Frederick Haldimand: Alan Valentine, *The British Establishment, 1760–1784*, vol. 1 (Norman: University of Oklahoma Press, 1970), 399; Elias Durnford: Dalrymple, *Merchant of Manchac*, 79n; William Clifton: Johnson, *British West Florida*, 15, 27, 54–56; Alexander Dickson: John W. Caughey, *Bernardo de Gálvez in Louisiana, 1776–1783* (Berkeley: University of California Press, 1934), 171, 205–6; Philip Livingston Jr.: Johnson, *British West Florida*, 226–28; Charles Stuart: Rea, *Major Robert Farmer of Mobile*, 95–96; Edmond Rush Wegg: Francisco de Borja Medina Rojas, *José de Espeleta, gobernador de la Mobilia, 1780–1781* (Sevilla: Escuela de Estudios Hispanoamericanos, 1980), 614–17; Elihu Hall Bay: Johnson, *British West Florida*, 99, 228.

23. For information about these Wilton-map grantees, see the following: James Amoss: Fabel, *Economy of British West Florida*, 90, 185; Thomas Bentley: Dalrymple, *Merchant of Manchac*, 102n; John Falconer: McBee, *Natchez Court Records*, 355; Joseph Garriov: Fabel, *Economy of British West Florida*, 116, 201; John Gradenigo: Dalrymple, *Merchant of Manchac*, 62n; Charles Strachen: Fabel, *Economy of British West Florida*, 44–45, 85–86, 215; John Lorimer: Robert R. Rea and Jack D. L. Holmes, "Dr. John Lorimer and the Natural Sciences in British West Florida," *Southern Humanities Review* 4 (1970): 363–72; George Gauld: John D. Ware and Robert R. Rea, *George Gauld, Surveyor and Cartographer of the Gulf Coast* (Gainesville: University Press of Florida, 1982); Henry Fairchild: Fabel, *Economy of British West Florida*, 187, 214; and Walter Hood: Rea, *Major Robert Farmer of Mobile*, 142. The late date of reference for any of these persons was Census of Householders at the time of Capitulation, Archivo General de Indias, Papeles de Cuba, Legajo 200, f. 916. See also Feldman, *Anglo-Americans in Spanish Archives*, under various names noted.

24. For the activities of these ship captains, see Fabel, *Economy of British West Florida*, 45, 54, 72, 130, 141–42; Dalrymple, *Merchant of Manchac*, 120, 126; and McBee, *Natchez Court Records*, 54, 412, 488.

25. Harry L. Coles, *History of the Administration of Federal Land Policies and Land Tenure in Louisiana, 1803–1860* (New York: Ayer, 1970), 164–71; Ory G. Poret, *History of Land Titles in the State of Louisiana* (Baton Rouge: Louisiana State University, 1972); Harry L. Coles, "The Confirmation of Foreign Land Titles in Louisiana," *Louisiana Historical Quarterly* 38 (October 1955): 1–22. For a discussion of United States policy regarding British land claims, see Hamilton, "American Beginnings in the Old Southwest," 55–70.

26. James H. Helms Jr., "Land Tenure in Territorial Mississippi, 1798–1809" (M.A. thesis, University of Virginia, 1955), 112.

27. *American State Papers: Public Lands*, 1:557, claim no. 2096. For more information on Eglington, see Fabel, *Bombast and Broadsides*, 15, 47; and Fabel, *Economy of British West Florida*, 9, 158, 160.

28. His early career is explained in "Deposition of E. H. Bay," April 25, 1780, Public Record Office, CO 5/580, ff. 299–303. For last date of reference on Bay (1781) in West Florida, see Census of Householders at the time of Capitulation, Archivo General de Indias, Papeles de Cuba, Legajo 200, f. 916. For the Bay land claims, see *American State Papers: Public Lands*, 1:549, 574. Also, McBee, *Natchez Court Records*, 357. Late in his life, Bay returned to live his final years near Natchez. See Hamilton, "American Beginnings in the Old Southwest," 333.

29. *American State Papers: Public Lands*, 1:549.

30. Peter Zahendra, "Spanish West Florida, 1781–1821" (Ph.D. diss., University of Michigan, 1976), 22.

31. Ibid., 24.

32. Gilbert D. Din, "The Immigration Policy of Governor Esteban Miró in Spanish Louisiana," *Southwestern Historical Quarterly* 73 (October 1969): 156–57.

33. Ibid., 158–59. See also Caroline M. Burson, *The Stewardship of Don Esteban Miró, 1782–1792* (New Orleans: American Printing, 1940), 25.

34. Burson, *Stewardship of Don Esteban Miró*, 26. Jack D. L. Holmes, *Gayoso: The Life of a Spanish Governor in the Mississippi Valley, 1789–1799* (1965; repr., Gloucester, MA: Peter Smith, 1986), 50–51.

35. José Montero de Pedro, *Españoles en Nueva Orleans y Luisiana* (Madrid: Ediciones Cultura Hispánica, 1979), 109.

36. Newton, "Mapping the Foundations of the Old Natchez District," 79–80. Dalrymple, *Merchant of Manchac*, 123; Archives of Spanish West Florida, 9:83, 10:219, East Baton Rouge Parish Courthouse, Baton Rouge, La.

37. Grady Daniel Price, "The United States and West Florida, 1803–1812" (Ph.D. diss., University of Texas, 1939), 80.

38. Hickey's grants are noted in Public Record Office, CO 5/609, f. 219. His 1808 Last Will and Testament, along with probate materials, is found in the Archives of Spanish West Florida, 14:2, 62. For his Spanish land reconfirmation, see McBee, *Natchez Court Records*, 364. For a discussion of his early career, see Fabel, *Economy*

of British West Florida, 112. Also, "Hickey Family Genealogy," Philip Hickey Papers, Department of Archives and Manuscripts, Middleton Library, Louisiana State University, Baton Rouge. His son's role as a delegate to the West Florida convention and his work to maintain the validity of British-era land grants is discussed in Price, "United States and West Florida," 119.

39. Glenn Conrad, ed. *Dictionary of Louisiana Biography*, vol. 1 (Lafayette: Center for Louisiana Studies, 1988), 401–2.

40. He is listed in the Baton Rouge Census of 1782, Archivo General de Indias, Papeles de Cuba, Legajo 192, f. 327. See also Albert Tate Jr., "Spanish Census of the Baton Rouge District for 1786," *Louisiana History* 24, no. 1 (Winter 1983): 83–84. His will is located in the Spanish Judicial Records, Adams County Courthouse, Natchez, MS, Book C, 177. A synopsis is provided in McBee, *Natchez Court Records*, 107. Confirmation of his land grant by his heirs is in *American State Papers: Public Lands*, 1:787, dated July 22, 1805. Additional information about his lands is found in Archives of Spanish West Florida, 11:223.

41. For his early career, see Rea, *Major Robert Farmer of Mobile*, 94–95. Also, Dalrymple, *Merchant of Manchac*, 139n. Listed in Baton Rouge Census of 1782, Archivo General de Indias, Papeles de Cuba, Legajo 192, f. 327. See also Tate, "Spanish Census of the Baton Rouge District," 78.

42. For early merchant transactions engaged in by the Comyns brothers, see Public Record Office, CO 5/601, f. 333. For their impact on the colony as merchants, see Fabel, *Economy of West Florida*, 105; and Dalrymple, *Merchant of Manchac*, 64n. For an example of trading activities of this family during the Spanish period, see "Don Pablo Commyns solicitando extraer ciertos frutos del este puerto de Nuevo Orleans para el de Vera Cruz, 1798," Archivo General de Indias, Papeles de Cuba, Legajo 697-A.

43. Fabel, *Economy of British West Florida*, 44, 72, 103.

44. Dalrymple, *Merchant of Manchac*, 121–22; *American State Papers: Public Lands*, 1:51, 79, 151, 396, 550.

45. Tate, "Spanish Census of the Baton Rouge District," 81–82. See also Archives of Spanish West Florida, 2:306, 6:88, 7:306, 312, 8:34, 12:62, 13:45, 15:74, 112.

46. Hamilton Pollock Inventory, August 16, 1814, Probate File 86, Clerk of the Court Records, West Feliciana Parish Courthouse, St. Francisville, LA.

47. Light T. Cummins, "Oliver Pollock's Plantations: An Early Anglo Landowner on the Lower Mississippi, 1769–1824," *Louisiana History* 29 (Winter 1988): 35–48.

48. Testimony in these cases is contained in the Spanish Judicial Records, Adams County Courthouse, Book F, 109–12.

49. "Isabel Alexandre contra Luis Forneret," May 1793, Actos de Estevan Quinones, vol. 6, f. 134, Orleans Parish Notary Archives, Civil District Courts Building, New Orleans.

50. *Sarah Smith v. James Smith*, Spanish Judicial Records, Adams County Courthouse, Book E, 299–313.

51. Zahendra, "Spanish West Florida," 169–70.

CHAPTER 2

Anglo Merchants and Capital Migration in Spanish Colonial New Orleans, 1763–1803

The expansion of the United States into the Mississippi valley and Gulf coast is a development often associated in the historical literature with agriculture and the desire of English-speaking settlers to find fertile new lands for planting. In many studies, this expansion is considered to have begun in the decades after the American Revolution as a post-independence phenomenon of the young United States. In part, this chronology is not inaccurate because the late 1700s witnessed farmers and planters moving into the Ohio and Mississippi valleys. The settlements in Kentucky, growing from the 1778 founding of Louisville by Americans, blossomed in the 1780s and 1790s to the point that the territory became a state in 1792. Farther down the great expanse of inland waterways, colonists from the United States opened new lands for English-speaking settlement in places such as New Madrid and Potosi, both located within the present-day state of Missouri. Settlers from the new country also arrived during the 1780s in the former British colony of West Florida to populate the districts around Baton Rouge and Natchez, some locating in Spanish territory. By 1803, they had become successful farmers and planters who grew cotton, corn, sugar, and indigo while raising cattle and hogs. They made up the vanguard of the Louisiana Purchase.

These settlers seeking land in Spanish Louisiana during the late 1700s, however, were not the opening wedge of the Anglo-American advance into the lower Mississippi valley. Instead, merchants and traders constituted the first English speakers to establish themselves in this territory, coming from several places, including British West Florida, ports in the Caribbean islands, and major Atlantic Seacoast trading centers such as Philadelphia, New York, and Baltimore. These merchants engaged in their commercial activities as part of an expanding economic prosperity being experienced all across the Atlantic world. The mid-eighteenth century witnessed an increase in trade and commercial opportunities that ended the restrictive mercantile systems of Great Britain, France, and Spain, all founded earlier on imperial protectionism. The Spanish Free Trade Decree of 1778, for example, increased the number of ports with which New Orleans could conduct maritime commerce. English-speaking merchants had become well entrenched in that city by the time of the decree. The first of them arrived in 1763, when British West Florida provided them a base from which to establish connections with nearby New Orleans, where Spanish law permitted them to dock their boats on the riverbank. Even more arrived in Louisiana with the first Spanish governor, Antonio de Ulloa, and later with General Alexandro O'Reilly's appearance in 1769. The general brought with him several Irish merchants from Havana, including Oliver Pollock, who had already received clearance to trade in Spain's North American territories. Most of these Irish merchants were Roman Catholic and found ready acceptance with the colonial authorities for that reason. Even more English-speaking merchants came to the lower Mississippi valley after the Revolution, with many establishing themselves at New Orleans, drawn to the city because of its role as a commercial entrepôt during that conflict. These men came from the seaports of the United States, where trade with the lower Mississippi valley had become a feature of the revolt.

The essay that follows examines how the English-speaking merchants at New Orleans shifted trade patterns along the lower Mississippi valley in the late eighteenth century away from the previous commercial ties of that region while a French possession, reorienting this network toward the major port cities of the United States. They accomplished this in two ways. First, the goods that they furnished created a consumer demand in Spanish Louisiana while their exporting of Louisiana products created a profitable balance of trade. Second, besides their trading activities, English-speaking merchants engaged in creative financing that permitted Spanish New Orleans to take part in the system of capital migration that further enlaced it into the Atlantic-coast economy. This took place by manipulating bills of exchange in ways that permitted the collateralized loaning of money across great distances. In using bills of exchange in such a manner, New Orleans merchants also created a currency of sorts that provided monetary exchange with ports in the United States. English-speaking merchants in New Orleans and along the lower Mississippi in the late 1700s provided a stable foundation for the successful agrarian activities of settlers from the United States prior to the Louisiana Purchase of 1803. Daniel Usner's *Indians, Settlers, and Slaves in a Frontier Exchange Economy: The Lower Mississippi Valley before 1783*, published in 1992, provides an extensive analysis of Louisiana's economic development in the early stages of this process, with special attention given to the development of an internal trading economy in which residents of the region participated as part of their daily lives.

Light Townsend Cummins, "Anglo Merchants and Capital Migration in Spanish Colonial New Orleans, 1763–1803," *Gulf Coast Historical Review* 4, no. 1 (Fall 1988): 6–27.

HISTORIANS have long recognized the importance of New Orleans as a commercial center. Founded by the French in 1718, it had become a significant port by 1803. In spite of the fact that it suffered from restrictive trade policies during the time it existed as a French and Spanish possession, these mercantilistic policies were powerless to keep the city from eventually fulfilling its destiny as the entrepôt for a vast and rich hinterland that composed the entire middle section of the continent.[1] Although New Orleans experienced considerable economic difficulty during the late eighteenth century, including shortages of circulating specie, a local Spanish government that required subsidization from New Spain and Cuba, a barter economy that retarded external trade, and commercial disruption caused by war, the city underwent a sporadic net growth in external trade and commerce from the 1760s to the end of the century, with this expansion continuing well into the American period.[2]

The precise outlines of this general economic growth for colonial New Orleans have been difficult for historians to trace, with numerous scholars writing from different perspectives. All of these authors indicate that development took place, but they disagree on its rate, specific motivations, and causality.[3] Some of the reasons for this economic growth, however, are clear in retrospect. They include a liberalization of Spanish commercial restrictions as part of the imperial "Free Trade" policies of King Charles III and his ministers, the propagation in the lower Mississippi valley of staple crops such as indigo and tobacco, and the growth of extractive industries such as logging. As well, the Louisiana province witnessed a demographic movement that saw large numbers of settlers from the United States arrive in the lower Mississippi region to farm, thereby creating an increasingly stable economic base for the city's external trade with areas in the West Indies, the Atlantic coast, and various European ports.

A rarely considered aspect of New Orleans's mercantile economy during the Spanish period is the existence and steady growth of an Anglo merchant community in the city.[4] It was these merchants who opened colonial New Orleans to the larger trading network of the Atlantic basin. It had previously existed apart from the traditional, legal ports encompassed by the more geographically limited Spanish and French commercial systems. The Anglo merchants of New Orleans achieved this during the Spanish period by providing an important conduit for regular, ongoing capital migration in and out of New Orleans to ports in North America and the West Indies. This began in the 1760s and lasted for the rest of the century. Although some of this trade was technically smuggling, it fostered a capital migration that increasingly linked the formerly isolated Louisiana port with major commercial centers in Great Britain, the Atlantic coast, and the West Indies.[5] This essay will offer some general comments about the individual backgrounds of significant members of the Anglo merchant community, present a short analysis of the type of trade activities in which they engaged, and—in so doing—note the capital migration function that they performed in motivating the growth of the general trade economy of Spanish colonial New Orleans.

Up to the present time, historians have not studied the Anglo merchants in Spanish Louisiana in any organized fashion. The existing historical literature about colonial New Orleans also fails to address the phenomenon of capital migration. This is probably because there has been a basic problem regarding documentation for historians who wish to study the economic history of Spanish Louisiana: records of an economic nature are scattered, incomplete, and nonextant in many cases.[6] For example, few private business records from colonial New Orleans remain for the use of modern scholars. Moreover, the official documents contained in the Spanish archives must be used with care and circumspection by anyone who wishes to analyze New Orleans's economic growth since these records provide data only for legal commerce. Legal trade existed merely as one part of Louisiana's total economic activity because Spanish mercantile laws had a tendency to drive a significant amount of commerce underground into the realms of smuggling and contraband trade. The Spanish Judicial Records of colonial New Orleans do provide the historian with information on the nature of smuggling, but this important documentary source does not permit generalization because of selective enforcement of the contraband laws.

This study is based on two documentary sources that have been heretofore underutilized by historians of Spanish Louisiana: land records and notary acts. The systematic use of these records makes possible the historical study of the Anglo merchant community in Spanish New Orleans. The land grants and conveyances for the region, although they have been widely scattered since the late eighteenth century, are still accessible. The Spanish land grants and sale transactions can be found either as part of the conveyances in various Louisiana parishes or scattered among archival collections in the United States, including the state of Louisiana Land Office, the Library of Congress, the Historic New Orleans Collection, Louisiana State University, and the University of Michigan.[7] Many of these documents are easily consulted today because they came into the possession of either the government of the state of

Louisiana or of the United States after 1803, when landowners pressed for American reconfirmation of British and Spanish land titles. Since some parts of Spanish territory were included in West Florida prior to the American Revolution, historians can also consult the British-era land documents and grant maps at the Public Record Office in London.[8]

A second important source for the activities of Anglo merchants in New Orleans is the notarial acts of the city. These records have survived intact and provide the historian with a focused glimpse of the activities of all merchants in New Orleans regardless of a particular trader's citizenship or place of residence. Spanish law required that all transactions involving the transfer of real property (mostly land or slaves) or the execution of promissory notes be consummated before a notary. The records of these notaries contain land transactions, slave transfers, the creation of powers of attorney, mortgages, wills and testaments, and promises for future payment of debts executed by Anglo merchants during the Spanish period. Located today in the offices of the Civil District Court of Orleans Parish, the Spanish-era notary archives comprise some two hundred volumes of transactions that are rich for the study of economic history in colonial New Orleans.[9]

An examination of these materials indicates that, during the Spanish period, Anglo merchants generally came to New Orleans from three distinct trading backgrounds that were already linked to the major commercial networks of the British Empire and the Atlantic economy. First, a group of Anglo traders arrived on the lower Mississippi in the 1760s as residents of British West Florida. Although English citizens, they traveled freely between Spanish and English territory, sometimes maintaining residences in both provinces. Second, a number of Anglo traders, many of them Irish and Scottish Catholics, came to New Orleans from Havana in the 1760s and 1770s. Third, in the 1780s and 1790s, numerous Anglo-American merchants came to the lower Mississippi as part of the influx of United States citizens settling the region under Spain's defensive colonization policy.

The first group of Anglo merchants to trade extensively in Spanish New Orleans thus came from areas in West Florida settled by the British in the early 1760s. British West Florida and Spanish Louisiana shared a common boundary in the years between the Peace of Paris in 1763 and the end of the American Revolution, when the holdings of Great Britain became Spanish territory. Prior to 1783, the east bank of the Mississippi north of the Iberville River (located between Baton Rouge and New Orleans) was part of British West Florida. The entire west bank of the Mississippi and the Isle of Orleans, which included the city, along with land on the east bank south of the Iberville, belonged to Spain. The British authorities in the West Florida capital of Pensacola encouraged local merchants to trade with the Spanish. For example, West Florida's governor, George Johnstone, sent the provincial sloop to Havana in September 1767 to advertise the availability of goods in Pensacola, a trade patently illegal under Spanish law. Nevertheless, a Spanish merchant vessel soon thereafter called at Pensacola and purchased merchandise valued at thirty thousand *pesos fuertes*.[10] The following months saw the arrival of five or six additional Spanish ships, which illicitly traded their cargoes of bullion and logwood for British goods.[11]

This British desire for trade with the Spanish resulted in various individual merchants settling along the Mississippi, and if not in New Orleans itself, at the least in the British areas immediately to the north. These Anglo traders were not unmindful of the opportunity for quick profits, especially regarding the importation of slaves. For example, Robert Ross, who moved to New Orleans during this period, wrote the Spanish governor of Louisiana in 1767:

> Some of the principal Merchants in the Slave trade in Jamaica having desired me to inquire whether my Negroes, and what number of them, would be wanted at New Orleans on the establishment of the Spanish Government, and expressing at the same time a desire to contract for the supplying of them, I take the liberty of applying to your Excellency on that subject.

Ross suggested that slaves could be shipped from Jamaica to Pensacola, where potential buyers from Spanish Louisiana could take delivery.[12]

Although such a trade was illegal under Spanish commercial restrictions, an informal variation on Ross's proposal had developed by the late 1760s. The Treaty of Paris (1763) gave England the right to navigate the Mississippi in order to reach British settlements above New Orleans. British vessels could therefore anchor in the river in the vicinity of the city as long as they were not tied to the levee. Some of these ships evolved into floating warehouses and stores well known to historians of the province. These establishments ensured ample opportunity for residents of Spanish Louisiana to purchase goods and slaves directly from the British. In addition, these floating trade centers permitted easy resupply for the Anglo merchants resident in New Orleans.[13]

Thus, it is not surprising that the arrival of British merchants in West Florida marked the start of efforts to maintain a regular British trade between West Florida and the West Indies and New Orleans. A number of Anglo merchants established trading houses in the city, including William Barrow, Valens and Phillips Comyn, and Daniel Hickey.[14] Among these, the brothers Evan and James Jones were some of the first Anglo traders to open commerce between New Orleans and areas traditionally outside its established commercial patters. Evan Jones had been born in New England about 1739 and moved to the Mobile District of West Florida after the Treaty of Paris. He transferred to New Orleans in 1765, where he remained for the rest of his life. His brother James, in partnership with Evan, maintained a branch of their trading house at Pensacola. They routinely exchanged cargoes between the two cities. Evan became a Spanish subject while both the brothers conducted an active trade with Anglo-American ports along the Atlantic coast, specializing in the importation of flour while they exported furs and agricultural products.[15]

Another typical merchant of this group was Robert Ross, whose offer to sell slaves we have already noted. Along with his relation David, he arrived in the Mississippi valley in the 1760s. Of Scottish ancestry, Ross's commercial interests and activities made little distinction between British and Spanish territory. He traveled freely between West Florida and Louisiana, buying land in both colonies, trading in slaves, and dealing in indigo, tobacco, rum, and dry goods. Although he represented Pensacola in the West Florida provincial legislature, he also maintained a residence at New Orleans. He traded extensively with English merchants at

Jamaica, most notably Lewbridge Bright and David Duncomb. Siding with the royalists during the Revolution, he experienced difficulties with Spanish governor Bernardo de Gálvez, which eventually resulted in his leaving Louisiana.[16] Nevertheless, Ross can be seen as typical of many of these British merchants who came to New Orleans and maintained mercantile ties to the West Indies.

By the early 1770s, a growing number of Anglo merchants had established themselves either at New Orleans or in the upriver areas north of the city, where they traded in merchandise and slaves. Perhaps the most important of these individuals was John Fitzpatrick, significant not only due to his extensive mercantile operations but also because the letterbooks that detail his activities have been among the very few to survive as a source for historians.[17] Fitzpatrick maintained numerous commercial contacts throughout the region, in addition to correspondents in the West Indies, along the Atlantic coast, and in Europe. Weak enforcement of the Spanish commercial laws during the governorship of Antonio de Ulloa permitted these Anglo merchants in the lower Mississippi to prosper.[18] Most of them stayed, even when General Alejandro O'Reilly made a short-lived and ineffective attempt to expel them.

General O'Reilly's establishment of permanent Spanish government in Louisiana also marks the appearance of a second group of Anglo merchants in the lower Mississippi valley. These individuals initially had little to do with their counterparts who had ties to British West Florida. Instead, they were part of an Irish and Scottish trading community that had been established at Havana in the years after the Seven Years' War (1756–1763). Spain had long tolerated Irish and Scottish Roman Catholics in her realm, and some of them, including the family of Alejandro O'Reilly himself, had adopted Spanish citizenship and become culturally Hispanic. This Irish and Scottish merchant community in Havana in the 1760s prospered further when the *asiento* trading contract went to an Italian firm that maintained extensive non-Spanish commercial contacts throughout the Americas and Europe.[19]

The Irish merchants in Havana, in particular, traded extensively with the *asiento* while they profited from the Roman Catholic status that afforded them acceptance by the Spanish in Cuba. Irish priests maintained a school at Havana, which in addition to educating the Anglo-Irish children, served as a social center for these individuals, including Alexander Munro, Oliver Pollock, John Kelley, Bartholomew McNamarra, and Francis Murphy. General O'Reilly occasionally participated in events there and was a special friend of one of the priest, a Father Butler. It is therefore not surprising to learn that O'Reilly's mission to Louisiana in 1769 resulted in the expansion of Havana's Irish and Scottish merchant community into the lower Mississippi. These Anglo merchants also quickly forged commercial links between New Orleans and the traditional trading zones of the British system.

One of the most active of the new group was Bartholomew McNamarra. He regularly sold blacks imported into Louisiana to officials of the Spanish government, local residents, and other merchants. Between 1770 and 1775, he engaged in dozens of transactions before New Orleans notaries. Participating in similar trades as well were Irish merchants, including Oliver Pollock, Thomas O'Keefe, Patrick Morgan, and John Waugh. All of them purchased a great deal of real estate and property with their profits, both in Spanish Louisiana and West Florida. Maurice Conway, for example, traded extensively in residential property in New Orleans.[20] James McCarty came to New Orleans from Cuba and operated as a corresponding agent for the New York firm of Nicholas Low and Company. During 1783, he instructed Low to place an advertisement in the New York gazettes, which noted: "J. B. McCarty, merchant of New Orleans, informs the merchants of the United States that he will receive new flour on commission."[21]

Oliver Pollock probably ranks as the best-known Anglo merchant of Havana who came to New Orleans. His historical reputation rests upon his support for the rebel cause during the American Revolution. He had been an active member of Havana's Roman Catholic merchant community, which included Alexander Munro, Geronomo Enrile, and Geronomo LaChiapelli. All of these men were heavily involved in the slave trade.[22] In fact, Pollock's activities as a purveyor of slaves closely followed a general shift in such trade that came with the transfer of Louisiana from France to Spain. Traditional sources of slaves in the French West Indies were no longer available. Instead, Louisiana residents turned to

Anglo merchants for new slave shipments. These merchants had strong trade ties to most ports in the British commercial system. Many of them, including McNamarra, Munro, and Pollock, quickly dominated the importation of slaves into Louisiana. For this reason, they and their counterparts were readily accepted, even by General O'Reilly, who permitted many to stay in spite of his proclamation that legally expelled foreign merchants in 1770.[23]

Oliver Pollock's slave-trading transactions are typical of such commercial activities on the part of the Anglo merchants. For example, Pollock sold two house servants, Thomas and John, for the sum of 265 pesos fuertes in 1769. The purchaser of these two slaves from Pollock was none other than Alejandro O'Reilly himself.[24] Pollock also brokered slaves already in the colony. Members of the Spanish government and their families seemed to favor Pollock in these transactions. Bernardo de Otero, the colonial treasurer, bought three house servants from Pollock. Don Joseph de Peña, commander of Natchitoches post, sold Pollock a slave originally brought from the Red River post. In February 1776, he purchased a thirty-two-year-old mulatto woman named Teresa from Dona Luisa Gromel for 500 pesos. After almost eighteen months, Pollock sold Teresa to Andreas Reynaud for the amount originally paid.[25]

On April 6 and 8, 1778, Pollock sponsored a slave auction at which the Americans disposed of the majority of the blacks taken during an earlier military raid on the British. The rebel colonial officer James Willing had led the raid down the Mississippi to attack settlements in British West Florida. Most of the leading citizens of New Orleans attended and bought freely. In all, seventy-four slaves crossed the auction block, raising a total of 16,518 pesos for Pollock and Willing. Effort was made to keep slave families together during the sale. All slaves were blacks, except for a sixteen-year-old girl named Mariana, who was noted as being an Indian. Leading citizens of Spanish Louisiana, including Antonio de Marigny, Philipe de Mandeville, Gilbert Antonio St. Maxent, and Carlos Oliver, all purchased slaves, although in many cases cash money was not on hand to complete the sales. Pollock met this lack of specie by financing most of the transactions on promissory notes due the following first of January.[26]

The existence of these Anglo traders in New Orleans served as a catalyst for increasing the interest of additional merchants from the Atlantic coast and West Indies in the economic potential of the lower Mississippi valley. For example, Pollock motivated his business colleagues along the Atlantic coast to acquire land along the Mississippi. Robert Morris and Thomas Willing, the Philadelphia merchants for whom he served as corresponding agent, secured two grants on the Mississippi from authorities in Pensacola. Pollock organized these tracts as working plantations and hired a resident manager, Alexander Henderson, who operated the properties for the firm of Willing and Morris. Henderson had thirty-four slaves on these two tracts and successfully grew rice during most of the 1770s and 1780s. Pollock served as financial manager for this venture, keeping Willing and Morris's accounts and making local payments on their behalf.[27] These properties continued operation when Spain took possession of the region during the American Revolution.

The activities of the traders from Havana, coupled to the efforts of the merchants already trading in Louisiana from bases in West Florida, made for a large Anglo commercial community in New Orleans by the time of the American Revolution. Although they came to New Orleans from diverse backgrounds, several factors tied these Anglo merchants together into a community, although most of them as individuals did not recognize these commonalities. They established themselves in Spanish Louisiana or British West Florida (sometimes both) to trade in slaves and staples; many became landowners in the lower Mississippi valley both in British and Spanish territory; New Orleans became their significant trade depot; and a number of them eventually became citizens of the United States after the Louisiana Purchase, if not before. This is not to imply, however, that these early Anglo merchants cooperated among themselves or made attempts to share their common destiny, for such was certainly not the case. Most of them saw each other as major competitors and rivals, a situation exacerbated by the fact that some were rebels and others were loyalists during the American Revolution. Some, including Oliver Pollock, John Fitzpatrick, and James Rumsey, supported the rebel cause. Others, among them Anthony Hutchins, Robert and David Ross, John Campbell, and Bartholomew McNamarra, became loyalists. Nevertheless, the Anglo merchants formed a group apart from the Gallic and Hispanic residents of the colony.

The military successes of Bernardo de Gálvez during the Revolution swept the British from the Gulf coast and lower Mississippi, thereby extending Spanish rule to all areas of the former province of West Florida. Most of the Anglo merchants resident in the area remained and became Spanish subjects. They were joined during the 1780s and 1790s by a new group of merchants, Anglo-Americans who moved to the region as part of a general immigration from the United States into the region. This Anglo immigration into Spanish Louisiana has been the subject of a considerable amount of scholarly investigation. Most of these efforts have concentrated on analyzing the immigration policies or entrepreneurial schemes that attempted to bring Anglo settlers into the colony after the American Revolution.[28] Although the scholars who conducted these studies have added immeasurably to our knowledge of Spanish Louisiana, they have been unable to agree on the number of Anglos who actually came to the province. For example, Mattie Austin Hatcher, taking various contracts with immigration agents at face value, noted that the population of lower Spanish Louisiana grew tremendously between 1769 and 1798. "All authorities agree," she wrote in 1921, "that this unquestionably represented, for the most part, a large immigration of Americans." According to Hatcher, Anglo immigrants had by 1803 clearly become the dominant group. Gilbert C. Din, however, estimated that Anglo-Americans came in a much smaller influx. "When the United States acquired Louisiana," he observed, "the colony still had not been overwhelmed by the Anglo-Americans, although their numbers were growing steadily."[29]

Nevertheless, the land records and notary transactions do contain ample evidence of a large number of Anglo merchants new to the region, with most of them resident in New Orleans. James Mather, Daniel Clark the elder and his nephew Daniel the younger, James Jordan, Thomas Acklin, Thomas Patterson, Richard Clark, and others all founded successful New Orleans merchant houses in the decade after the American Revolution. Of these, Daniel Clark the younger ranks as an individual who amassed one of the greatest fortunes in colonial New Orleans. A native of Sligo, Ireland, he had gone at an early age with his family to the Philadelphia area, where he established himself with the merchant firm there led by Daniel Coxe. In 1786, young Clark journeyed to New Orleans, where he joined his uncle of the same name in mercantile ventures. In addition to his import and export operations, he invested heavily in land along the Mississippi and, like other Anglo merchants, engaged in slave trading. He acquired massive amounts of land during the 1790s in the districts north of New Orleans, including a tract of some 200,000 acres along the Ouachita River.[30]

By the 1780s, Anglo merchants were firmly established in New Orleans, and they were propelling the trade of the city into new international trade patterns. The land records and notarial acts reveal several common sorts of transactions among the Anglo merchants, which enable historians to judge their significance in the economic development of the port of New Orleans. On the surface, they certainly engaged in the normal sorts of exchanges that were routine for any nonspecialized, port-city merchant. They imported and exported commodities and staples, traded in slaves, and brokered in land. At first glance, most of them did not appear to be overly successful when compared to their counterparts in the major port cities of the United States, especially since the economic system under which they operated in Spanish Louisiana was primitive by the standards of the times. As historian John Clark has noted:

> Specialization in business was rare in New Orleans through the Spanish period and into the early American era. . . . Moreover, brokerage, banking, and insurance services among others were unknown in New Orleans until the transfer to the United States. Insurance was obtained elsewhere. Credit was extended from one firm or individual to another as a personal service and not on the basis of the borrower's reputation for business integrity, rather than on any objective measurement of his assets. Investment opportunities outside of traditional sectors of trade and land were almost nonexistent.[31]

Although this simple economy at times worked hardships on the Anglo merchants of New Orleans, at the least, when compared to commercial practices on the Atlantic coast, its relatively primitive nature also provided those who had imagination and business creativity various additional opportunities for profit. For example, since colonial New Orleans usually suffered from a shortage of circulating specie, local merchants sometimes found themselves hampered by a lack of currency with which to complete their transactions. The Anglo merchants felt this impediment more acutely than the Hispanic and Gallic trading community since much of their commerce rested on business dealings with trading houses outside the credit structures of the Spanish and French colonial systems. So Anglo merchants developed a complex strategy by which they manipulated bills of exchange in order to create a means of currency in Louisiana for use in financing their transactions. These bills of exchange, in providing local Anglo merchants with a means of currency, also had the unanticipated byproduct (which at the time went unrecognized by the Anglo merchants themselves) of providing a direct, continuous financial link between New Orleans and major credit centers in Great Britain and the United States for the first time. The Anglo merchants thus became the masters of the basic system of capital migration upon which the city's commercial economy would eventually rest.

The notary records and land conveyances of New Orleans contain numerous instances of Anglo merchants engaged in transactions whose primary purpose was to create negotiable bills of exchange. The creation of bills of exchange by New Orleans's Anglo merchants on their corresponding merchant houses in Great Britain and along the Atlantic coast eventually provided rudimentary banking services in Louisiana for all merchants engaged in foreign trade.[32] Spanish and French merchants did not need a similar system since they conducted their commerce with port cities in Europe and the West Indies customarily a part of the Spanish and French credit network.

The negotiation of bills of exchange for use as currency may be seen in many of the legitimate business transactions that were consummated by Anglo merchants before the various notaries public of New Orleans. Many of these merchants favored the notary Don Andres Almonaster y Rojas for such purposes, apparently because he was a businessman who engaged in foreign trade in addition to his official duties. Oliver Pollock often appeared before Almonaster. Pollock especially favored the strategy of lending money by means of bills of exchange drawn for eventual payment on his accounts at Philadelphia merchant houses. In 1773, he loaned Francisco Mainard one thousand pesos, requiring in return collateral of a farm, the house on it, five horses, twenty-six cows, and the maize crop produced that year. Pollock bought a house on present-day Royal Street during December 1777, paying for it with a bill of exchange. James Harris bought the property three months later with another bill of exchange that redeemed the first bill.[33] Pollock purchased a great deal of land during the 1770s in both British and Spanish territory. All of these transactions were financed with bills of exchange drawn on Philadelphia merchants.[34] In the face of limited circulation of specie in Louisiana, these bills of exchange became local currency that sometimes passed through many hands before being presented for final payment at maturity.[35] Local merchants dealing with Pollock thus profited by receiving negotiable instruments with which they financed other transactions. Pollock's Philadelphia partners Willing and Morris profited in two ways. First, they made profits by trading in goods. Second, Willing and Morris also profited in Pennsylvania from manipulating the exchange rates between bills of exchange negotiated in New Orleans and their discounted price on the Philadelphia credit market. Meanwhile, in New Orleans, Pollock again profited when the local Anglo merchants with whom he dealt reciprocated in similar trades with their respective roles reversed.[36]

All of these dealings, and many others like them, were based upon actual transactions, that is, they actually involved the notarized transfer of property from one owner to another. The Anglo merchants of New Orleans also developed negotiable instruments by means of what they called a "dry exchange." Such dry transactions were not the product of actual commerce or trading in goods or services. Instead they were fictional business dealings consummated by willing participants before notaries public under the guise of being actual commercial transactions. Their primary purpose was to circumvent the restrictive Spanish commercial laws by manipulating the unsuspecting notary public into creating a legally enforceable bill of exchange that could be used as a financial instrument in lieu of circulating specie.[37] These dry trades also had the additional advantage of enabling merchants to mask the payment of interest for money loaned.[38]

Anglo merchants seem to have favored notarized slave trades as the most popular method of procuring a dry exchange. Like other transfers of titled property, the law required all slave sales to be notarized. Unlike real estate, a slave transaction involved a highly mobile commodity, which made it difficult for a notary suspecting a dry transaction to prove the transfer was one that the participating traders never really intended to be consummated.[39] Dry transactions worked in the following manner, although there were numerous variations that involved third or fourth parties. Merchant "A" of New Orleans desired a loan of money to engage in commercial activities. He would approach local merchant "B" for the loan. The second merchant would agree to purchase a slave from "A," the price of which was equal to the desired amount of the loan plus interest payable to "B." Merchant "B" would thus draft a bill of exchange drawn on his foreign corresponding merchant house payable to "A's" foreign correspondents at a specified date in the future. Both merchants appeared before a New Orleans notary to transact the slave sale in order to make their execution of the bill of exchange into a legal contract enforceable under Spanish law. Merchant "A" thereafter financed his other business dealings with the bill of exchange written by merchant "B" as payment for the slave. This bill might pass through the hands of numerous other traders in a chain of commerce traced back to "A." At the time stipulated for final payment noted in the bill, merchants "A" and "B" met once again before the notary and performed the sale of the same slave in reverse, thus cancelling the bill created in the first transaction. Merchant "A" had thus secured a loan of capital value. As an unwritten part of the process, the two merchants agreed to repeat a similar cycle of transactions in the future with their roles reversed should merchant "B" ever desire a loan.

It may be that a major importance of Anglo merchants in Spanish New Orleans lay in their unique ability to create negotiable capital instruments, especially bills of exchange, which routinely found their way into the mainstream of the Atlantic commercial-credit network. Unlike their Spanish and French counterparts in Louisiana who lacked such commercial connections, the Anglo merchants came to New Orleans as correspondents of trading firms in London, Halifax, New York, Baltimore, Philadelphia, Charles Town, Kingston, St. Eustacius, and other major trading centers outside the Spanish and French mercantile systems. In the course of their trade and commerce, these Anglo merchants established for the first time a regular channel for capital migration by means of negotiable financial instruments between Spanish New Orleans and important Atlantic ports, especially those of the United States. In so doing, the Anglo merchants of Spanish Louisiana made an important contribution to the development of New Orleans as a significant commercial center by the time of the Louisiana Purchase in 1803.

Notes

1. John G. Clark, *New Orleans, 1718–1812: An Economic History* (Baton Rouge: Louisiana State University, 1970), 299.

2. The barter economy has been recently analyzed by Daniel H. Usner Jr., "The Frontier Exchange Economy of the Lower Mississippi in the Eighteenth Century," *William and Mary Quarterly*, 3rd ser., 44 (April 1987): 165–92. The best exposition of this city's early growth by a study using quantitative methods in assessing trade is Jesus Lorente Miguel, "Commercial Relations between New Orleans and the United States, 1783–1803," in *The North American Role in the Spanish Imperial Economy, 1760–1819*, ed. Jacques Barbier and Allen Kuethe (Manchester, UK: Manchester University Press, 1984), 177–91.

3. For studies of New Orleans and its economy during the Spanish era, see Light T. Cummins, "Spanish Louisiana," in *A Guide to the History of Louisiana*, ed. Light T. Cummins and Glen Jeansonne (Westport, CT: Greenwood, 1982), 17–26. The classical study of the New Orleans economy during the Spanish period is Jack D. L. Holmes, "Some Economic Problems of Spanish Governors in Louisiana," *Hispanic American Historical Review* 42 (November 1962): 521–43.

4. The term "Anglo" as used in this essay is broadly employed to mean a person of non-Hispanic extraction who appears to have been of British or British American descent, whose native language is English, and who is culturally Irish, Scottish, or English.

5. Leland Hamilton Jenks, *The Migration of British Capital to 1875* (1927; repr., London, 1963), 11. The modern definition for capital migration is "The flight of capital as expressed primarily in shifting bank funds and credits resulting from international trade, as well as in net gold movement, from one country to another." Glenn C. Munn, *Encyclopedia of Banking and Finance*, 8th ed., rev. F. L. Garcia (Boston: Banker's, 1983), 161. For standard works dealing with the phenomenon of capital migration, see W. Stanley Jenons, *Money and the Mechanism of Exchange* (New York: Nabu, 1965), esp. 186–89; William J. Schultz and M. R. Cairo, *Finan-*

cial Development of the United States (New York: Prentice Hall, 1937), esp. 240–50; Roland I. Robinson, *Money and Capital Markets* (New York: McGraw-Hill, 1964); and Simon Kuznets and Elizabeth Jenks, *Capital in the American Economy: Its Formation and Financing* (Princeton, NJ: Princeton University Press, 1961).

6. The only published study that touches upon these merchants is Robin F. A. Fabel, "Anglo-Spanish Commerce in New Orleans during the American Revolutionary Era," in *Anglo-Spanish Confrontation on the Gulf Coast during the American Revolution*, ed. William S. Coker and Robert R. Rea (Pensacola: Gulf Coast History and Humanities Conference, 1982), 25–53. This study is based almost entirely on the records in the Public Record Office, Kew Gardens, London. For a discussion of archival materials available to historians interested in the economic history of colonial New Orleans, see Paul Hoffman, "La documentacion colonial en la Luisiana," *Archivo Hispalense*, nos. 207–8 (1985): 333–52.

7. Although there is no one guide to these diverse Spanish-era land records, the following provide an introduction to the locations of significant collections: Glenn R. Conrad and Carl A. Brasseaux, *A Selected Bibliography of Scholarly Literature on Colonial Louisiana and New France* (Lafayette: Center for Louisiana Studies, 1982), 6–7; Winston De Ville, *Louisiana and Mississippi Lands: A Guide to Spanish Land Grants at the University of Michigan: Properties at Ascension, Attakapas, Baton Rouge. . . .* (Ville Platte, LA: Polyanthos, 1985); and Hoffman, "documentacion colonial en la Luisiana," 335–44. A set of Louisiana land records, popularly known as the Trudeau Survey Papers, has been the recent object of a replevin controversy, during which various archival repositories disputed the present-day ownership of these documents, which include numerous Spanish-era land surveys and related manuscripts. These papers are currently in the possession of the Historic New Orleans Collections in New Orleans. For both sides of the ownership controversy and a description of the documents, see Patricia A. Schmit, "Spanish Land Documents at the Historic New Orleans Collection," *Manuscripts* 37 (Fall 1985): 275–82; and Edward F. Haas, "Odyssey of a Manuscript Collection: Records of the Surveyor General of Antebellum Louisiana," *Louisiana History* 27 (Winter 1986): 5–26.

8. For descriptions of these land purchases, see State Land Office, Baton Rouge, *Greensburg Land Claims*, Book 2, pt. 2:69, 94, 109–10; and *American State Papers: Public Lands* (Washington, DC: Duff Green, 1834), 3:46, 4:313. The British land-grant ledgers and conveyances are contained in the Public Record Office, Kew Gardens, London, CO 5/601–17. There are also detailed grantee maps in the PRO. The Library of Congress has copies of most of them in its Geography and Map Division. The State Land Office of Louisiana in Baton Rouge also has a random selection of copies made in the early nineteenth century.

9. Guy Wootan, *A Manual of Every-Day Procedure in the Notarial Archives, 1867–1973* (New Orleans: privately published, 1973). For a listing of all notaries public who acted in New Orleans between 1735 and 1869, see "Notaries Public," in *Gardner's New Orleans Directory* (New Orleans: C. Gardner, 1869), 413–14.

10. John B. Born Jr., "Governor Johnstone and Trade in British West Florida, 1764–1767," *Bulletin of Wichita State University* 75 (May 1968): 8.

11. Cecil Johnson, *British West Florida, 1763–1783* (New Haven, CT: Yale University Press, 1943), 63–64.

12. Robert Ross to Antonio de Ulloa, April 29, 1767, Archivo General de Indias, Seville, Spain (hereafter referred to as AGI), Papeles Procedentes de Cuba, Legajo 187.

13. John W. Caughey, "Bernardo de Gálvez and the English Smugglers on the Mississippi, 1777," *Hispanic American Historical Review* 12 (1932): 46–58.

14. For these transactions of Anglo merchants and others, see Actos de Andres Almonaster y Rojas, August 18, 1768–April 1782, vols. 1–16, Orleans Parish Notarial Archives, Civil District Courts Building, New Orleans (hereafter cited as Orleans Notary Archives).

15. Margaret Fisher Dalrymple, ed., *The Merchant of Manchac: The Letterbooks of John Fitzpatrick, 1768–1790* (Baton Rouge: Louisiana State University Press, 1978), 121.

16. This sketch of Ross is based upon a discussion of him in Fabel, "Commerce in New Orleans," 40–41.

17. Dalrymple, *Merchant of Manchac.*

18. Holmes, "Economic Problems of Spanish Governors," 521–43.

19. The Cuban *asiento* was a private business organization that enjoyed a government trade monopoly for the exclusive importation of slaves into Spanish colonies of the region. As well, it traded in foodstuffs, regularly sending ships to French and British colonial ports in the Americas. Some merchant houses, including Willing and Morris of Philadelphia, sent corresponding agents to Havana in order to deal with the *asiento.*

20. For examples of slave sales, see Actos of Andres Almonaster y Rojas, vol. 2, May 6, 1772, August 20, 1772, Orleans Notary Archives. For Conway's real-estate transactions, see Actos of Andres Almonaster y Rojas, vols. 1–4, ibid.

21. Clark, *New Orleans,* 272.

22. James A. James, *Oliver Pollock: The Life and Times of an Unknown Patriot* (New York: Appleton-Century, 1937), 4–6; Horace E. Hayden, *A Biographical Sketch of Oliver Pollock* (Harrisburg, PA: Lanes, Hart Printers and Binders, 1883), 6–19; William Henry Egle, *Notes and Queries, Historical and Genealogical, Chiefly Relating to Interior Pennsylvania* (Harrisburg, PA: Harrisburg Publishing, 1894), 1:475–81.

23. Alejandro O'Reilly to Marquis de Grimaldi, October 17, 1769, AGI, Papeles de Cuba, Legajo 560.

24. For Pollock's sale of slaves to O'Reilly, see Actos of Andres Almonaster y Rojas, vol. 1, February 9, 1770, f. 50, Orleans Notary Archives.

25. Actos of Juan Baptista Garic, vol. 4, March 10, 1773, f. 73, Orleans Notary Archives; David Hodge to Oliver Pollock, February 14, 1775, Peter Force Collection, Library of Congress; Actos of Andres Almonaster y Rojas, vol. 3, September 1, 1773, f. 225, vol. 6, February 6, 1776, Orleans Notary Archives; Actos of Juan Baptista Garic, Book 7, February 1, 1776, f. 32, vol. 8, November 25, 1777, f. 437, ibid.

26. Actos of Juan Baptista Garic, vol. 9, April 6–8, 1778, ff. 202–24, Orleans Notary Archives.

27. "Proceeding instituted by Don Olivero Pollok for the purpose of settling certain accounts with his principals through an arbitration board," April 27, 1782, Spanish Judicial Records of Louisiana, Louisiana Historical Center, Louisiana State Museum, New Orleans. For a synopsis of this case, see *Louisiana Historical Quarterly* 11 (1935): 230.

28. For a survey of this literature, see Mattie Austin Hatcher, *The Opening of Texas to Foreign Settlement, 1801–1821* (Austin, TX: University of Texas Press, 1927); Hatcher, "The Louisiana Background of the Colonization of Texas, 1763–1803," *Southwestern Historical Quarterly* (hereafter referred to as *SHQ*) 24 (January 1921): 169–95; Gilbert C. Din, "Colonización en la Luisiana espanola; proyectos de emigración en la Luisiana del siglo XVIII" (Ph.D. diss., University of Madrid, 1960); Din, "The Immigration Policy of Governor Esteban Miró in Spanish Louisiana," *SHQ* 73 (October 1969): 155–75; Din, "Spain's Immigration Policy in Louisiana and the American Penetration, 1792–1803," *SHQ* 76 (January 1973): 255–76; William S. Coker, "The Bruins and the Formulation of Spanish Immigration Policy in the Old Southwest, 1787–88," in *The Spanish in the Mississippi Valley, 1762–1804*, ed. John Francis McDermott (Urbana: University of Illinois Press, 1974), 61–71; and C. Richard Arena, "Land Settlement Policies and Practices in Spanish Louisiana," ibid., 51–60.

29. Hatcher, "Louisiana Background," 194; Din, "Spain's Immigration Policy," 275.

30. Many of Clark's land acquisitions are contained in Actos de Francisco and Narciso Broutin, vols. 1–23, Orleans Notary Archives. See also the Trudeau Survey Papers, Historic New Orleans Collection, New Orleans. The best recent study of Clark is Michael S. Wohl, "A Man in Shadow: The Life of Daniel Clark" (Ph.D. diss., Tulane University, 1984). For additional sketches of Clark, see Grace King, *New Orleans: The Place and the People* (New York: Macmillan, 1902, 104–29; Daniel Clark, *Proofs of the Corruption of General James Wilkinson, and of his connextion with Aaron Burr . . .* (Philadelphia: Wm. Hall, Jun. & Geo. W. Pierie, 1809); and Nolan B. Harmon Jr., *The Strange Case of Myra Clark Gaines* (Baton Rouge: Louisiana State University, 1946), 1–156.

31. Clark, *New Orleans*, 273.

32. The local practice in this regard at New Orleans was consistent with similar events throughout the Atlantic trading network of the late eighteenth century. See Stanley Chapman, *The Rise of Merchant Banking* (London: Routledge, 1965), 1–15.

33. Actos of Andres Almonaster y Rojas, vol. 23, March 4, 1773, f. 45, vol. 4, March 7, 1774, f. 68, vol. 8, February 15, 1777, f. 130, Orleans Notary Archives; Actos of Juan Baptista Garic, vol. 5, July 30, 1774, f. 143, vol. 8, July 8, 1777, f. 280, ibid.

34. This was common practice on the part of merchants loaning money in countries with medieval-based usury laws. See Sidney Homer, *A History of Interest Rates*, 2nd ed. (New Brunswick, NJ: Rutgers University Press, 1977), 77.

35. Such transactions were a form of converting debt into currency. See Charles Carroll, *Organization of Debt into Currency and Other Essays*, ed. Edward C. Simmons (Princeton, NJ: Princeton University Press, 1964), 87.

36. No hard data exists for the exchange rate between Philadelphia and New Orleans in the late Spanish period. John J. McCusker has provided general figures for Havana and continental Europe based on notations in the journals of Anglo merchants in Cuba. These indicate a ratio of 177.78 Cuban currency to 100 pounds sterling. Although McCusker does not address the question of hidden interest, it can be assumed the 177.78/100 ratio of exchange (current in the early 1780s) comprehends both the discount rate and an amount of obscured interest. See John J. McCusker, *Money and Exchange in Europe and America, 1600–1775* (Chapel Hill: University of North Carolina Press, 1978), 300.

37. Such transactions seem to have been fairly common practice in many parts of the Spanish Indies, with enterprising merchants routinely engaging in variations according to local circumstances. For example, in colonial Mexico City, silver merchants manipulated the exchange rates of specie in order to mask the payment of interest for money loaned. See Victoria Hennessey Cummins, "The Church and Business Practices in Late Sixteenth Century Mexico," *The Americas: A Quarterly Review of Inter-American Cultural History* 44 (April 1988). Indeed, some European merchants had routinely manipulated bills of exchange for the purpose of creating currency and masking the payment of interest as early as the late Middle Ages. This is noted in Raymond de Roover, *The Rise and Decline of the Medici Bank, 1397–1494* (Cambridge: Cambridge University Press, 1963), 10–11; Richard Ehrenberg, *Capital and Finance in the Age of the Renaissance*, trans. A. N. Lucas (1928; repr., New York: A. M. Kelley, 1963); and Raymond de Roover, "New Interpretations of the History of Banking," *Cahiers d'histoire mondiale* 2 (1954–55): 48–50.

38. Spanish law prohibited usury, which was defined to include charging interest on money loaned. This is a variation of a method common to the eighteenth century. See the discussion of bills of exchange in Malachy Postlethwayt, *The Universal Dictionary of Trade and Commerce*, 4th ed. (London: Printed for W. Strahan et al., 1774), vol. 1.

39. The Notary Acts of colonial New Orleans contain numerous examples of incomplete sale transactions that were never signed and promulgated. Nonetheless, Spanish law required the notary public to save these incomplete documents and file them along with those acts that had been consummated. It may be that at least some of these incomplete transactions represent attempts at dry trades that the notary stopped in process because he suspected that they did not involve real property and, hence, were ineligible for notarization.

CHAPTER 3

The Gálvez Family and Spanish Participation in the Independence of the United States of America

The American Revolution marked a significant turning point in the English-speaking influx into the lower Mississippi valley and Gulf coast. This demographic movement had already started by the time of Lexington and Concord. Spanish authorities in Havana and New Orleans had been watching the growing dissatisfaction being manifested by the British colonists along the Atlantic coast. Soon after becoming governor of Louisiana in the early 1770s, Luis de Unzaga y Amezaga sent periodic reports to his superiors in Spain regarding the growing unrest in British North America. The captain general of Cuba, the highest-ranking military administrator in the region, which included Louisiana, also followed the unfolding dissent in the English-speaking colonies to the north. These Spanish authorities redoubled their intelligence efforts once the actual rebellion began in 1775. Rebels coming down the Ohio and Mississippi Rivers to secure needed supplies at New Orleans gave the Louisiana governor additional information about the revolt. Unzaga dispatched New Orleans merchants to Philadelphia under the guise of undertaking commercial activities to collect information about the revolt. Authorities in Madrid also paid close attention to the Revolution through the diplomatic channels available to them. The Spanish court coordinated some of these efforts with the French government, which also manifested a marked interest in the Revolution, since both nations were centuries-old British rivals.

During the first three years of the American Revolution, two rival factions in the government in Madrid differed with each other regarding the policy Spain should follow in response to the British colonial revolt. The chief minister of state, the Conde de Floridablanca, counseled neutrality in case the rebel Americans lost. Should that happen, and such appeared a possibility until late 1777, the entire bellicose might of an active British military force in the Americas could then be turned against Spain's possessions there if Madrid supported the defeated Continental Congress. The other faction, led by José de Gálvez, favored a more bold course of action, at least openly supporting the American rebels if not eventually declaring war against Great Britain. Gálvez would serve as minister of the Indies, the chief colonial officer of the Spanish government. His influence grew across 1776 and 1777 as the warlike opinions he recommended gained support with the king and his court. José was one of four members of the Gálvez family who had emerged as important figures in the government both at home and in the Americas. His brother Matías commanded the military forces of Spain in Central America, while after late 1776, his nephew Bernardo held a key post as governor of Spanish Louisiana. On the Iberian Peninsula, Matías headed the Council of War in Madrid, the chief administrative arm of the Spanish military. The Gálvez family played a more significant role in crafting and implementing Spain's response to the American Revolution than almost any other then in government service. The Gálvez family advocated using Spain's colonies bordering on the south of English America as supply depots to assist the Americans in securing war materials. Bernardo had great success in such efforts, working in concert with merchants in New Orleans, including Oliver Pollock. Later, when Spain declared war on Great Britain in 1779, Bernardo led a series of successful military campaigns against the British along the lower Mississippi River and Gulf coast, sweeping them from the region by 1780. Matías won similar victories over the British in Central America. In Spain, brothers José and

Miguel worked to ensure that Great Britain would not win the larger War of American Independence, which by then involved France and Spain as combatants allied with the American rebels.

The support for the Continental Congress and the American cause, which became the hallmark of the Gálvez family during the Revolution, had an unintended consequence: the expanding Anglo-American interest in the lower Mississippi valley and Gulf coast. The merchants animated by Bernardo de Gálvez established firm commercial ties between Atlantic-coast ports and New Orleans. His military victories received much attention and positive notice in the new country, thus becoming a factor that would increase interest of citizens of the United States in these areas. The essay below provides in summary fashion a survey of the activities of the Gálvez family in support of the United States during the American Revolution. It is logical to assume that without the members of this influential family in Spain, the American rebels might never have won the victory that created the United States. Kathleen DuVal's *Independence Lost: Lives on the Edge of the American Revolution* (2015) examines the Revolution along the Gulf coast and the western regions, employing a biographical approach that includes a chapter dealing with Oliver Pollock and his relations with Bernardo de Gálvez.

Light Townsend Cummins, "The Gálvez Family and Spanish Participation in the Independence of the United States of America," *Revista Complutense de Historia de America* 32 (2006): 179–96.

Introduction

SPAIN'S ROLE in the American Revolution is of great importance in assessing the history of that struggle, especially regarding the Spanish military operations that occurred throughout the Americas.[1] Spanish victories at Baton Rouge, Mobile, and Pensacola represented important contributions to Great Britain's defeat in North America. Moreover, the campaigns of Spain's armies in Central America, naval successes in the Bahamas, Crillon's victories in the Minorcan Islands, and even the siege of Gibraltar all had a significant impact on the eventual military resolution of the Revolution.[2]

These military events had a tremendous subsequent influence on the westward expansion of the United States. After 1783, the young United States of America faced a Spanish colonial empire that spanned the entire northern coast of the Gulf of Mexico, westward across most of the Mississippi valley, and into the midcontinent reaches of North America.[3] One particular Spanish family, the Gálvez clan from the province of Malaga, played an important and determined role in the struggle. Indeed, the contribution of these scions of "La Familia de Gálvez" to the independence of the United States of America constitutes one of the great stories of the American Revolution.[4] Although some historians have stressed the role of Bernardo de Gálvez in Louisiana, their participation in the American Revolution was a family affair and must be seen as such. Indeed, it is almost impossible to overestimate the Gálvez family's interrelated role in collectively setting and implementing Spanish military policy regarding the American Revolution.

Spain's role in the American Revolution grew out of international forces set in motion during the period of intercolonial warfare that lasted from 1689 to 1763. Spain, along with its traditional ally France, was intermittently at war with Great Britain for almost a century. During this time, it fought the British in four major conflicts: The War of the League of Augsburg, which lasted from 1689 to 1697; the War of Spanish Succession, which was fought from 1701 to 1713; the War of Austrian Succession, which began in 1744 and ended in 1748; and the Seven Years' War, which saw fighting from 1756 to 1763.[5]

In the Seven Years' War, which was the great contest for colonial empire in the Americas, Great Britain definitively defeated France and Spain. The Spanish, in this war, lost Havana and Manila to invading British armies. By early 1763 and the end of fighting, both France and Spain were at the peace table in Paris, where they were forced to accept a humiliating defeat in the signing of a treaty. The Peace of Paris, signed in that year, was a resounding international embarrassment for Spain. By its provisions, France gave Canada to the British while Spain ceded the Floridas to King George III. In addition, the French king gave Louisiana to Spain since the British did not want it for themselves. The Spanish monarch, King Charles III, and his ministers stewed in rage over the

Peace of Paris and waited for the chance to work revenge against Great Britain.[6]

The American Revolution provided them with the opportunity for which they waited.[7] Spanish aid and assistance to the American rebels, especially for the army led by George Washington, would help set in motion events that would weaken Great Britain and the British Empire. Indeed, by the time of Lexington and Concord in April 1775, Spain had long been following events in North America by dispatching espionage agents and observers to locations scattered throughout the region.[8] These persons provided a steady stream of information and served as initial points of both diplomatic and commercial contact between the governments of the infant United States and Spain.[9] The information provided by these observers allowed King Charles III and his ministers to set their own goals for reacting to the American Revolution. In short, the American Revolution would provide Spain with an unsolicited but effective weapon by which the British Empire might be humbled, if not destroyed. Spain hoped that a weakened and defeated Great Britain would allow a return of Gibraltar to Spanish control. Spain could also regain the Floridas, clear the British from the lower Mississippi valley and the Gulf of Mexico, and remove the British from the logwood coasts.

The Gálvez Family and Spanish Policy

Various factions at the Spanish court had different opinions about the military role that Spain should play in the conflict. This was especially the case from the spring of 1776 until Spain entered the war during the summer of 1779. Two powerful groups of Spanish ministers at court vied with one another in setting Spain's policy regarding the British colonial revolt in North America. A bellicose group, known as the *Aragoneses* because they desired Spain's immediate intervention in the conflict, advised Spanish intervention during 1776 as soon as news of fighting in North America arrived in Europe.[10] Taking a more cautious approach, a second group, including the politically powerful Gálvez family, preferred to wait until an opportune time in order to enter the conflict so that Spain's military machine in the Americas and Europe could be fully mobilized. This second faction, which included two successive ministers of state in the persons of the Marqués de Grimaldi and Conde de Floridablanca, therefore cautioned neutrality in the contest between Great Britain and her recalcitrant colonists well into 1779.[11] Both the *Aragoneses* and the moderates united in common national purpose when Spain finally declared war against Great Britain in June 1779. Differences of opinion between them continued thereafter, however, when the Spanish king and his advisors attempted to identify and articulate specific military goals to be achieved in the war. Some ministers at court, especially the *Aragoneses*, favored placing primary military emphasis on European-based objectives, including the retaking of Gibraltar, the restoration of Spanish control over Minorca, and gaining greater diplomatic independence from France.[12] Others, including Minister of the Indies José de Gálvez, desired that Spain focus on American-based war goals, namely, the elimination of British settlements from the lower Mississippi valley and northern coast of the Gulf of Mexico, along with the removal of the British establishments on the eastern coast of Central America. Minister Gálvez also wanted the reassertion of Spanish control over East Florida.[13]

Hence, by 1775 and 1776, Spanish colonies bordering on English America, especially Louisiana and Cuba, became important centers by which Spain could animate the American rebels, thereby hoping to destroy the international power of the British Empire.[14] This consideration was especially the case for Louisiana, which shared the lower Mississippi valley and Gulf coast region with British West Florida after 1764.[15] This brings us to a consideration of the Gálvez family, one of the most prominent in the court of King Charles III. In spite of humble origins in the Spanish province of Malaga, the generation of Gálvez brothers born in the tiny village of Macharaviaya during the 1710s and 1720s rose to high positions in the Spanish government during the mid-eighteenth century. All men of talent and ability, the Gálvez brothers individually distinguished themselves either as career military officers or as university-trained governmental administrators. The eldest brother, Matías de Gálvez, served as viceroy of New Spain, the vast territory that contained most of colonial Mexico and Central America, while his brother José de Gálvez enjoyed a long career as a minister at court and advisor to the king of Spain. During the era of the American Revolution, their brother Antonio commanded the Coast Guard force at the major Spanish port of Cadiz, the nation's major port of entry and exit to the Americas. Another brother, Miguel de Gálvez, served as chief military advisor of the Spanish court and held a seat on the Council of War, Spain's highest military policymaking body. By the 1760s, as well, a younger generation of individuals from the Gálvez family had also risen to prominence in Spanish military circles. Matías's son, Bernardo de Gálvez, served as governor of Louisiana during much of the American Revolution.[16]

José de Gálvez and the Revolution

Of the members of the family, José de Gálvez was arguably the most important. He had daily contact at court with the king from 1776 until his own death in 1786. Born in the province of Malaga at Macharaviaya in January 1720, José de Gálvez attended the University of Salamanca and became a lawyer. He rose to be a successful member of Spain's *letrado* bureaucracy and advanced rapidly in the civil service.[17] He served as an advisor at the Spanish embassy in Paris before going to New Spain as visitor general in the 1760s and 1770s.[18] There he reorganized the administrative structures of the vice-regal government, motivated the founding of Spanish California, set in motion the creation of the Provincias Internas, and enacted other important reforms.[19] As minister of the Indies (Spain's colonial secretary), he had complete administrative responsibility for the Spanish empire in the Americas. José de Gálvez clearly saw the American Revolution as an opportunity to end British international and territorial influence in the Gulf of Mexico (the Seno Mexicano) and northern Caribbean. He pushed aggressively at court for material assistance and supplies for the American rebels to be sent by way of Spanish military centers at Havana and New Orleans.[20] Largely because of his efforts, Spain began sending shipments of blankets, gunpowder, medicines, weapons, and other supplies to the American rebels.

As minister of the Indies, José also set in motion, along with Minister of State the Marqués de Grimaldi, an espionage and observer network in the Americas that was designed to provide the court in Spain with news and information about the revolt in British North America.[21] These observers and agents sent a steady stream of news and information about the revolt and also served as initial points of both diplomatic and commercial contact between the governments of Spain and the United States.[22] The captain general of Cuba and his military subordinate, the governor of Louisiana at New Orleans, superintended Spain's surveillance activities.[23] The captain general enlisted ship's masters in the commercial fishing fleet based in Cuba to provide regular observation of British maritime movements. The Cuban commander also corresponded secretly with Luciano de Herrera, a Spaniard living in St. Augustine, who became a spy for the Spanish. Herrera provided regular reports from British West Florida about military affairs in English America.[24] The governor of Louisiana sent Juan Suriret and Bartolome Beauregard, an ancestor of the American Civil War general, to New York and Philadelphia under the guise of being private merchants. Both men talked with leaders from both sides of the revolt. In particular, Beauregard visited with leaders of the Continental Congress and George Washington.[25]

The most important observers were Juan de Miralles and Francisco Rendon, who went to Philadelphia to serve as contact points between the rebel leadership and the Spanish government. Miralles departed first, arriving in Philadelphia in 1779. The success of Juan de Miralles as the first permanent Spanish observer at the site of North American government provided for open, yet unofficial, diplomatic relations between Spain and the United States. Even though his arrival was for the secret purpose of sending news and information under the cover of being a merchant, Miralles's responsibilities soon developed a diplomatic character. He became personal friends with George Washington, Henry Laurens, John Jay, and other important leaders of the United States government.[26] Upon his death in 1780, he was replaced by Francisco Rendon, who remained in Philadelphia as a link between the two governments until the establishment of formal diplomatic relations in 1786. What Miralles and Rendon did while serving as observers for José de Gálvez and the Spanish court constituted the beginnings of diplomatic and commercial relations between the United States of America and Spain.

Matías de Gálvez in Central America

José's brother Matías also played an important role in Spain's participation in the American Revolution.[27] Born in Malaga in 1717, Matías followed a military career. He married Joséfa Gallardo in October 1745. Their son, Bernardo de Gálvez y Gallardo, was born in 1746. Matías de Gálvez served with distinction in the Canary Islands, where he commanded the castle at Paso Alto.[28] In 1778, the king named him as the inspector general of royal troops in Guatemala, a position that made him second in command of the troops in that Spanish colony. In actuality, his promotion to this post came as a result of his brother José's influence. The king of Spain had been monitoring the British colonial revolt in North America with growing interest, and thereafter he began military preparations in 1778. Although the Spanish court decided against military participation in the revolt during 1776, Charles III decided to increase preparedness throughout the Indies. In the fall of 1777, José de Gálvez accordingly sent additional troops to Central America in order to protect Spain's colonies there and prepare for a possible attack on British establishments at Belize and on the Black River. Minister of the Indies Gálvez decided to dispatch his brother Matías to oversee these military preparations. Matías arrived at the great Spanish presidio of Omoa in present-day Honduras in July 1778. As inspector general of all Spanish forces in the region, General Gálvez reformed the militia structure of the region and improved the readiness of the infantry and cavalry corps under his command.[29] In April 1779, he was promoted to the position of president of the Audiencia and captain general of Guatemala.[30] By that time, the possibility of war with Great Britain had increased tremendously. José de Gálvez had already sent orders in March 1779 that warned: "prepare for imminent war with England." Matías de Gálvez did just that. He spent several months thereafter planning attacks against the British posts in the region, augmenting his supplies and forces, and training his officers and men. When Spain formally entered the war, General Gálvez commanded 30,000 troops, along with the fortress at Omoa that existed as one of the largest fortified military positions in the Western Hemisphere.[31]

The plans laid by General Matías de Gálvez for his campaign against the British positions at Belize were made moot by an attack launched by Commodore John Luttrell and Captain William Dalrymple against the Spanish fort at Omoa, commanded by Simon Desnaux, a Spanish officer of Italian origin. This attack, made by a combined land-and-sea expedition, resulted in the fall of the fort during late October 1779.[32] Meanwhile, Matías de Gálvez had mustered an army of reinforcements upon hearing initial reports about the start of the British campaign against the fort. During October, General Gálvez personally led one of the most daring forced marches of the wars of the American Revolution. At the head of over 1,000 men, Gálvez led his men through the jungles of Central America, across the rough terrain of the mountain ranges, and down to the coast of Omoa, where he laid siege to the British forces then ensconced there.[33] Gálvez thereupon turned his attention to fortifying the defenses in Nicaragua, especially at Omoa where he retook the fortress on November 28, 1779, thereby restoring the region to Spanish control. He established his headquarters at Granada, created a naval patrol from Lake Nicaragua, and coordinated the defensive arrangements at Fort Inmaculada, the military stronghold that guarded the San Juan River that flowed from the great inland lake. The British soon attacked Inmaculada, commanded by Gálvez's subordinate Juan de Ayssa. Matías de Gálvez mobilized his troops for the defense of the province. He constructed a new fort, San Carlos, near to the point where the lake flows into the San Juan River. Entrenched at this second line of defense, he augmented naval forces on the lake and mobilized local militia units. Ayssa, however, was unable to hold Fort Inmaculada and it fell to the British in April 1780. Undaunted by this setback, Gálvez laid careful plans to retake Inmaculada, which was accomplished without great loss of life because of his meticulous planning.[34]

The successful retaking of Omoa and Inmaculada then freed Matías de Gálvez to launch his long-anticipated attack against the British positions along the Gulf coast of Central America at Black River in Nicaragua. He organized a massive campaign that included additional Spanish troops from Spain, Cuba, and Peru, along with an extensive supply effort. He began his campaign in May 1782. The Spanish settlement at Trujillo became the port from which Gálvez launched his concerted assault against the British at Roatan. After several days of bombardment, the English commander surrendered. Matías de Gálvez emerged from these conquests very much a hero for Spain. King Charles III rewarded him by appointing him as viceroy of New Spain, where he governed from 1783 until his untimely death the following year. Spain's military actions in the West Indies during the Revolution also enjoyed some success. Field Marshal Juan María de Cagigal engineered a bloodless victory for Spain when his army invaded New Providence Island in the Bahamas. In early May 1782, Cagigal signed a capitulation by which the British turned over to Spain all of the Bahamas Islands.[35]

Bernardo de Gálvez in Louisiana

Of the Gálvez men, however, Bernardo de Gálvez enjoys the most important role as a true hero of the American Revolution, for he was the greatest Spanish general of the conflict and, as an individual, worked the hardest to ensure the independence of the United States. Like his uncle and his father, he was a native of the province of Malaga, where he was born in 1746. From a very early age, he expressed a desire for a career in military service. After training as a cadet, he was promoted to the rank of lieutenant and fought in Portugal in 1762 during the Seven Years' War. Later, he went to New Spain while his uncle was visitor general and served on the northern frontier, where he commanded Spanish troops fighting against the Apache Indians. There, he was wounded several times. In 1772, he returned to Spain and took part in the disastrous Spanish invasion of Morocco in 1775, a debacle that ranked as one of Spain's greatest military failures of the era. Nonetheless, he served with valor and bravery in this expedition, once again having been wounded in the line of duty a second time. He later served as a professor at the Spanish military academy at Avila before being promoted to the rank of colonel in 1776. Shortly thereafter, he was posted to New Orleans as commander of the Spanish military garrison there. On January 1, 1777, Bernardo de Gálvez became governor of Spanish Louisiana. His role as governor of Louisiana ensured partiality at Spanish New Orleans toward the rebel Americans.[36] Gálvez and American partisan Oliver Pollock formed a partnership of cooperation that placed New Orleans squarely center stage as a major supply base for the armies of George Washington. Starting in 1777, boatload after boatload of crucial supplies went up the Mississippi and the Ohio Rivers to the American base at Fort Pitt, and then across Pennsylvania to the Continental Army. Many of these vessels that carried vital shipments flew the Spanish flag while they sailed on the inland waterways of North America in order to avoid British harassment.

This aid to the American rebels was increased as a result of a meeting in Spain during 1777 between Arthur Lee, the representative of the Continental Congress, and the Marqués de Grimaldi, the Spanish minister of state. As a result of their discussions, Grimaldi promised Lee that Spain would continue sending supplies to the colonies. Shortly thereafter, the Bilbao merchant Diego de Gardoqui began shipping large amounts of military supplies from Spain to Havana, and then on to New Orleans, where they were delivered to representatives of the American congress. In addition, the Spanish minister arranged for loans of money to be made directly to the accounts of the Continental Congress at various European banking houses. Spain, throughout the remainder of the American Revolution, loaned a tremendous amount of money to the rebels. The American diplomatic historian Samuel Flagg Bemis estimated that the total amount of this assistance for the entire course of the Revolution amounted to almost $1 million, including some $175,000 loaned to John Jay, who served as American envoy to Spain in the early 1780s.[37]

In addition to setting into motion the events that resulted in Spain furnishing material aid to the American rebels, Bernardo de Gálvez also assisted the cause of the Continental Congress by supporting American military expeditions that attacked the British in the Illinois country and in the Mississippi valley. The first of these was the military expedition commanded by the Continental Army captain James Willing in the spring of 1778.[38] James Willing, the brother of a prosperous Philadelphia merchant, commanded a small expedition of Americans as they floated down the Mississippi River, plundering the holdings of British

West Florida planters. Willing and his men took valuable prizes, including a large number of slaves from the British settlements. Oliver Pollock interceded with Governor Gálvez to have Willing and the American troops granted the freedom of New Orleans and safety from British retaliation.[39] This Gálvez did, permitting the Americans to sell their plunder in the Spanish colony.[40] Later, when a British navy vessel appeared at New Orleans to protest Spanish support for the Willing expedition, Governor Gálvez maintained his position without provoking hostilities from the neighboring British colony.[41]

Spanish support for the American cause continued in 1778 and 1779, when Bernardo de Gálvez permitted New Orleans to serve as a supply base for the military conquests of George Rogers Clark in the Ohio valley. Clark, at the head of a troop of Virginians, took Vincennes, Kaskaskia, and Cahokia from the British. Cut off from regular sources of supplies east of the Appalachians, Clark turned to Oliver Pollock in New Orleans. Not only did Governor Gálvez permit Pollock to arrange large shipments of needed materials and foodstuffs for Clark, but the Spanish governor also continued to loan money to the congressional agent.[42] It is clear, therefore, that the rebel conquest of the Ohio River valley would have been impossible except for the assistance afforded the rebels by Gálvez at New Orleans.

The Campaigns of Bernardo de Gálvez

In spite of assistance to the rebels, Spain remained neutral in the American Revolution from the time of Lexington and Concord until the summer of 1779. It had numerous reasons for doing so, ranging from a cautious distrust of the American rebellion—which, after all, was a rebellion against the concept of monarchy—to a fear of angering Great Britain and provoking a British military retaliation. Nevertheless, during 1777 and 1778, the Spanish government accelerated the amount of material support sent to the Americans, and by 1779, Spain had become an unofficial, de facto ally with the United States in the cause against Great Britain. By the summer of 1779, the time for a Spanish declaration of war against England seemed right; but even when this happened, Spain decided not to ally formally with the United States. King Charles III and his advisors, especially the Conde de Floridablanca, who had replaced the Marqués de Grimaldi as minister of state in 1777, worried that the young United States might replace Great Britain as Spain's territorial and commercial rival in North America.

Nonetheless, Spain decided to enter the war for a variety of reasons: several years had been devoted to preparing the Spanish military; a long-planned offensive against the Portuguese in South America had come to an end; France had already been at war against England for over a year; and an attempted peace negotiation sponsored by the Conde de Floridablanca had failed.[43] Hence, Spain declared war on Great Britain on June 21, 1779. On the whole, Spain enjoyed military success in the war—and her campaigns assisted the United States by distracting and diluting British attentions away from the rebel Americans in the South Atlantic, the Gulf of Mexico, and the Caribbean.[44] Bernardo de Gálvez undertook a series of bold initiatives that would eventually win for Spain most of the lower Mississippi valley and the entire northern coast of the Gulf of Mexico. In so doing, he also forged a stronger link between Louisiana and Spanish Texas; Gálvez permitted the importation of Texas cattle in order to supply his troops.[45]

Bernardo de Gálvez undertook three important and crucial campaigns against British West Florida between 1779 and 1781.[46] The first of these occurred in the fall of 1779 soon after the declaration of war. Governor Gálvez, having been given advance notice of the Spanish declaration by way of his uncle José in Madrid, had already planned a surprise invasion of the English posts along the Mississippi River. Then, just as he was ready to launch his attack in late August, a destructive hurricane struck New Orleans, dashing his army, ruining its supplies and provisions, and demoralizing many of his troops.[47] Nevertheless, the young governor rallied his men with exhortations to patriotism, pride, and love of country to attack anyway. After capturing Fort Bute at Manchac, some 770 bedraggled men marched northward up the Mississippi River, where Gálvez laid siege to the British post at Baton Rouge. After three hours of an intense artillery barrage, Baton Rouge fell to the Gálvez army on September 21, 1779.[48] Shortly thereafter, the English post at Natchez surrendered before the Spanish could attack it.[49] By this one bold campaign, Gálvez captured over one thousand British troops, took possession of eight British vessels then on the Mississippi, and added some 520 squared leagues of territory to Spanish Louisiana.

The following year, Bernardo de Gálvez commanded a successful Spanish expedition against Mobile. In January, he left New Orleans at the head of some 2,000 Spanish soldiers in fourteen ships. By March, his men had laid siege to the town, cutting it off from reinforcement from the sea.[50] By mid-March, Mobile surrendered, and Gálvez turned his attention to the conquest of Pensacola.[51] Another hurricane, however, badly damaged his fleet and forced him to delay his expedition against the largest British naval station on the Gulf coast. He traveled to Havana, where in consultation with the captain general of Cuba and the commander of the Spanish naval squadron, he planned a massive assault against Pensacola for 1781. King Charles III sent a personal emissary, Francisco de Saavedra, to Cuba for the purpose of working with Gálvez in planning a successful assault. Saavedra and Gálvez quickly became a highly effective team. Gálvez's confident manner, aggressive forcefulness, and ready enthusiasm for command blended with Saavedra's grasp of strategy and logistical planning.[52]

Gálvez's campaign against Pensacola, which began in the spring of 1781, is deservedly the most important exploit of his career.[53] Upon the arrival of the Spanish fleet off Pensacola, the Spanish admiral in command of the fleet refused to sail his ships across the bar from the Gulf of Mexico into the bay while under the guns of the British Fort George, which overlooked the seaward approaches. Gálvez valiantly took affairs into his own hands with a display of bravado. He took personal command of a frigate and its crew and sailed it through the artillery gauntlet. This shamed the Spanish admiral into following with the rest of the fleet. For this feat, Gálvez was later ennobled, being named the Conde de Gálvez by King Charles III, and, on his coat of arms, was emblazoned the escutcheon "Yo Solo" (I Alone) in commemoration of his courage in sailing his lone ship into Pensacola harbor. Once the Spanish troops had gained the harbor, Gálvez's army made camp across the bay from the British fort and began a siege that lasted for several weeks. Shortly after three o'clock on the afternoon of May 8, 1781, a lucky grenadier's shot hit the main British powder magazine, and a roaring explosion of deadly impact convinced the English commander to surrender. Bernardo de Gálvez had won his greatest victory. This was a major victory for the Spanish. Great Britain had some 3,000 regular troops on the field, and their losses were large compared to the Spanish. There were 382 British wounded and 105 dead. The Spanish, who had twice as many men on the field, lost only 74 dead and had 198 wounded after the battle.[54]

The Siege of Pensacola and Gálvez's victory there was one of the last major military victories for Spanish arms during the long history of Spain's colonial empire in the Americas. It was also of significance in resolving the War of Independence in favor of the United States. Occurring only months before the American victory at Yorktown, the resounding British defeat at Pensacola weakened the British military and deprived Lord Cornwallis of potential reinforcements. Even so, many historians of the United States have largely ignored this important chapter of American history. Indeed, the campaigns of Bernardo de Gálvez have yet to receive their full due attention from American historians concerned with the military history of the American Revolution.

Conclusions

The successful campaigns of Bernardo de Gálvez also marked the start of official diplomatic relations between Spain and the United States at the court in Madrid. In September 1779, the Continental Congress sent the first accredited United States envoy to Spain, the New York lawyer John Jay.[55] His purpose was to negotiate a treaty of alliance with the government of King Charles III. Jay remained in Spain from January 1780 until May 1782. Although he failed for a wide variety of reasons in fulfilling his goal to draft a treaty, he did establish a good working relationship with the Conde de Floridablanca, the foreign minister.[56] Because Spain did not desire formal diplomatic relations with the United States until after the war was concluded, Jay was never received as ambassador. His presence, nonetheless, was useful to Floridablanca, who was still hoping to coerce Great Britain into an eventual peace settlement that gave Gibraltar back to Spain. Indeed, by the early 1780s, the combined French and Spanish siege of Gibraltar had become the largest military operation of the war, and one that was destined to fail for Spain. Floridablanca did, however, discuss diplomatic relations with Jay, in addition to giving him a several-hundred-thousand-dollar loan for the United States.

It was not until after the Treaty of 1783 that Spain decided to recognize the United States. Francisco Rendon continued in Philadelphia as Spanish observer. He continued to superintend Spanish concerns regarding relations with the United States.[57]

The disputed boundary between Georgia and Spanish Florida, along with navigation rights on the Mississippi River, consumed much of his attention. He also wrote long memorials on the financial and governmental structure of the United States in an effort to help the Spanish minister at court understand the new nation.[58] Finally, Diego de Gardoqui was appointed in 1785 as Spain's first accredited envoy to the United States. His mission in Philadelphia began the long period of formal diplomatic relations between Spain and the United States that has continued to the present day.

Three of the important Gálvez men, however, did not live to appreciate the full import of Spain's military participation in the American Revolution. José, ennobled as the Marqués de Sonora in reward for his services during the Revolution, died at Aranjuez in 1787. Matías, appointed viceroy of New Spain, served only a year before he died in office during 1784. His son, Bernardo, replaced him in this high office and soon followed his father's fate. After an auspicious beginning, during which he implemented various reforms and undertook a constructions program in Mexico City, Bernardo took sick with a mysterious fever, worsened, and died in 1786. He is buried in the Iglesia de San Fernando in Mexico City.[59] He never lived to understand the role he played to create an independent United States.

The military victories of Bernardo de Gálvez in the Gulf of Mexico and the Caribbean, the establishment of diplomatic foundations in Philadelphia by Juan de Miralles and Francisco Rendon, and the attainment of Spanish war goals at the peace table in 1783—with the important failure of Spain to regain Gibraltar—left Spain feeling justified for participating in the American Revolution.[60] By 1783, King Charles III had seen the British Empire defeated, the flag of Spain flying over the entire Gulf of Mexico, and a restoration of Spanish international prestige. Although some ministers in Madrid, including Minister of State Floridablanca, fretted that that newly independent United States would supersede Great Britain as an irksome New World rival to the Spanish Indies, their concern did not seem compelling in the years immediately following the Peace of Paris of 1783, which ended the Revolution.[61] Largely because of the Gálvez family, the American Revolution was the occasion of Spain's final flash of military glory in North America.

Notes

1. Thomas Chávez, *Spain and the Independence of the United States: An Intrinsic Gift* (Albuquerque: University of New Mexico Press, 2002); Eric Beerman, *España y la independencia de Estados Unidos* (Madrid: Editorial Mapfre, 1992), 297–303; Light Townsend Cummins, *Spanish Observers and the American Revolution, 1775–1783* (Baton Rouge: Louisiana State University Press, 1992), 209–22; Cummins, "Spanish Historians and the Gulf Coast Campaigns," in *Anglo-Spanish Confrontation on the Gulf Coast during the American Revolution*, ed. William S. Coker and Robert R. Rea, 194–205 (Pensacola: Gulf Coast History and Humanities Conference, 1982); Robert Middlekauff, *The Glorious Cause: The American Revolution, 1763–1789* (New York: Oxford University Press, 1982).

2. Light Townsend Cummins,"Spain in the American Revolution," in *The American Revolution, 1775–1783: An Encyclopedia*, by Richard L. Blanco, 3:1555–60 (New York: Garland, 1993); Don Higginbotham, *The War of American Independence: Military Attitudes, Policies, and Practice, 1763–1789* (Bloomington: Indiana University Press, 1971); Piers Mckesy, *The War for America, 1775–1783* (Cambridge, MA.: Harvard University Press, 1965).

3. Mario Hernández Sánchez-Barba, *La ultima expansion Española en América,* (Madrid: Instituto de Estudios Políticos, 1957), 3–6; Elena Sánchez-Fabres Mirat, *Situación histórica de las Floridas en la segunda mitad del siglo XVII (1783–1819), los problemas de una region de frontera* (Madrid: Ministro de Asuntos Exteriores, 1977), 87–109.

4. John W. Caughey, *Bernardo de Gálvez in Louisiana, 1776–1783* (Berkeley: University of California Press, 1934).

5. Carlos Martínez de Campos, *España bélica en el siglo XVIII* (Madrid: Aguilar S. A., 1965), 17.

6. Mario Rodríguez, *La revolución Americana de 1776 y el mundo hispáanico: ensayos y documentos* (Madrid: Editorial Técnica, 1976), 19–21.

7. Manuel Conrotte, *La Intervención de España en la independencia de los Estados Unidos de la América del Norte* (Madrid: V. Suárez, 1920), 3–10; L. Angel García Melero, *La independencia de los Estados Unidos de Norteamérica a través de la prensa Española ("Gaceta de Madrid" y "Mercurio Histórico y Político")* (Madrid: Ministerio de Asuntos Exteriores, 1977), 24.

8. Light Townsend Cummins, "Spanish Espionage in the South during the American Revolution," *Southern Studies* 19 (1980): 39–49.

9. Marqués de la Torre to José de Gálvez, July 13, 1777, Archivo General de Indias, Seville, Spain (hereafter referred to as AGI), Audiencia de Santo Domingo, 1598-a.

10. Vincente Rodríguez Casado, *La política marroquí de Carlos III* (Madrid: Consejo Superior de Inestigaciones Científicas, 1946), xiii–xv.

11. Rafael Olaechea, *El Conde de Aranda y el "partido aragones"* (Zaragoza: Universidad de Zaragoza, 1967); Juan J. F. Yela Utrilla, *España ante la independencia de los Estados Unidos*, 2 vols. (Lérida: Gráficos Academia Mariana, 1925), 2:192–93.

12. Yela Utrilla, *España ante la independencia de los Estados Unidos*, 2:208–9.

13. Yela Utrilla, *España ante la independencia de los Estados Unidos*, 201–4.

14. B. Parker Thomson, *La ayuda Española en la Guerra de la independencia norteamericana* (Madrid: Ediciones Cultura Hispánica, 1967), 22, 43–45.

15. Joseph P. Sánchez, *A Selected Bibliography of the Florida-Louisiana Frontier with References to the Caribbean, 1492–1819* (Albuquerque: Spanish Colonial Research Center, University of New Mexico, 1991).

16. Beerman, *España y la independencia de Estados Unidos*, 203, 217, 292–93, 296; Jack D. L. Holmes, "Bernardo de Gálvez," in *The Louisiana Governors: From Iberville to Edwards*, ed. Joseph G. Dawson III (Baton Rouge: Louisiana State University Press,1990), 52–56; José Montero de Pedro, *Españoles en Nueva Orleans y Luisiana* (Madrid: Ediciones Cultura Hispánica, 1979), 34–44; Lorenzo G. Lafarelle, *Bernardo de Gálvez: Hero of the American Revolution* (Austin, TX: Eakin, 1992).

17. Angeles Rubio Argüelles, *Un ministro de Carlos III, D. José de Gálvez y Gallardo Marqués de Sonoro* (Málaga: Diputación Provincial de Málaga, 1949), 1–6.

18. Herbert I. Priestley, *José de Gálvez, Visitor-General of New Spain, 1765–1771* (Berkeley: University of California Press, 1916); Luis Navarro García, *José de Gálvez y la comandancia general de las provincias internas* (Sevilla: Escuela de Estudios Hispanoamericanos, 1964), 156–68.

19. Harry W. Crosby, *Antigua California: Mission and Colony of the Peninsular Frontier, 1697–1768* (Albuquerque: University of New Mexico Press, 1994), 387–93; Ignacio Del Río, "Utopia in Baja California: The Dreams of José de Gálvez," *Journal of San Diego History* 18 (1972): 1–13.

20. José de Gálvez to Luís de Unzaga, December 24, 1776, AGI, Audiencia de Santo Domingo, 2596.

21. José de Gálvez to the Marqués de la Torre, June 22, 1776, AGI, Papeles de Cuba, 1143.

22. Kathryn T. Abbey, "Efforts of Spain to Maintain Sources of Information in the British Colonies before 1779," *Mississippi Valley Historical Review* 15 (1928): 56–68.

23. Instrucción que V. M. manda guardar y observer a Don Diego Joséf Navarro, Mariscal del Campo, January 6, 1777, AGI, Audiencia de Santo Domingo, 1598-a.

24. Marqués de la Torre to Luciano de Herrera, September 6, 1776, AGI, Papeles de Cuba, 1227.

25. Noticias Adquiridos de los vecinos colonias ingleses por Mr. Suriret vecino de Punta Cortada, November 2, 1777, AGI, Papeles de Cuba, 1146; Bernardo de Gálvez to José de Gálvez, March 21, 1777, no. 26, AGI, Audiencia de Santo Domingo, 2547.

26. Cummins, *Spanish Observers and the American Revolution*, 113–39.

27. Wilbur E. Meneray, "The Kingdom of Guatemala during the Reign of Charles III, 1759–1788" (Ph.D. diss., University of North Carolina, 1975).

28. 1968, Mariana Rodríguez del Valle and Ángeles Conejo Díez de la Cortín, "Matías de Gálvez (1783–1784)," in *Virreyes de Nueva España (1779–1787)*, ed. José Antonio Calderon Quijano, 2 vols. (Sevilla: Escuela de Estudios Hispano-Americanos, 1968), 2:224–26.

29. Troy S. Floyd, *The Anglo-Spanish Struggle for Mosquitia* (Albuquerque: University of New Mexico Press, 1967), 128–29.

30. Rodríguez and Conejo, "Matías de Gálvez," 2:226–29.

31. Floyd, *Anglo-Spanish Struggle for Mosquitia*, 130–31.

32. Matías de Gálvez to José de Gálvez, January 12, 1780, AGI, Papeles de Cuba, 2.

33. Floyd, *Anglo-Spanish Struggle for Mosquitia*, 140.

34. Floyd, *Anglo-Spanish Struggle for Mosquitia*, 151–52.

35. James A. Lewis, *The Final Campaign of the American Revolution: Rise and Fall of the Spanish Bahamas* (Columbia: University of South Carolina Press, 1991).

36. Lawrence Kinnard, "The Western Fringe of Revolution," *Western Historical Quarterly* 7 (1976): 253–70.

37. Samuel F. Bemis, *The Diplomacy of the American Revolution* (1935; repr., Bloomington: Indiana University Press, 1957), 91–93.

38. J. Barton Starr, *Tories, Dons, and Rebels: The American Revolution in British West Florida* (Gainesville: University Press of Florida, 1976), 78–121; John W. Caughey, "Willing's Expedition down the Mississippi, 1778," *Louisiana Historical Quarterly* 15 (January 1932): 5–36.

39. Robert V. Haynes, "James Willing and the Planters of Natchez: The American Revolution Comes to the Southwest," *Journal of Mississippi History* 27 (1975): 38–40.

40. Kathryn T. Abbey, "Intrigue of a British Refugee against the Willing Raid, 1778," *William and Mary Quarterly*, 3rd ser., 1 (1944): 397–404.

41. Kathryn T. Abbey, "Spanish Projects for the Reoccupation of the Floridas during the American Revolution," *Hispanic American Historical Review* 9 (1929): 265–85.

42. Light Townsend Cummins, "Oliver Pollock and George Rogers Clark's Service of Supply: A Case Study in Financial Disaster," in *Selected Papers from the 1985 and 1986 George Rogers Clark Trans-Appalachian Frontier History Conferences*, ed. Robert J. Holden (Vincennes, IN: National Park Service, 1988), 1–16.

43. Yela Utrilla, *España ante la independencia de los Estados Unidos*, 2:253–54.

44. J. Leitch Wright Jr., *Anglo-Spanish Rivalry in North America* (Athens: University of Georgia Press, 1971), 134.

45. Robert M. Thonhoff, *The Texas Connection with the American Revolution* (Austin, TX: Eakin, 1981), 50–53; Robert S. Weddle and Robert M. Thonhoff, *Drama and Conflict: The Texas Saga of 1776* (Austin, TX: Madrona, 1976), 176; Jack Jackson, *Los Mesteños: Spanish Ranching in Texas* (College Station: Texas A&M University Press, 1986), 195–97.

46. Albert W. Haarman, "The Spanish Conquest of British West Florida, 1779–1781," *Florida Historical Quarterly* 39 (1960): 103–34.

47. Manuel Serrano y Sanz, *Documentos Históricos de la Florida y la Luisiana, Siglos XVI al XVIII* (Madrid: V. Suárez, 1912), 44.

48. Henry P. Dart, "West Florida. The Capture of Baton Rouge by Gálvez, September 21, 1779, from Reports of the English Officers," *Louisiana Historical Quarterly* 12 (1929): 255–65; Jack D. L. Holmes, *The 1779 "Marcha de Gálvez": Louisiana's Giant Step Forward in the American Revolution* (Baton Rouge: Baton Rouge Bicentennial Commission, 1974).

49. Robert V. Haynes, *The Natchez District in the American Revolution* (Jackson: University Press of Mississippi, 1976): 124–25.

50. Diario de la Expedición contra Mobilia por Bernardo de Gálvez, Panzacola, May 12, 1781, AGI, Papeles de Cuba, 2351.

51. Francisco de Borja Medina Rojas, *José de Espeleta, gobernador de la Mobilia, 1780–1781* (Sevilla: Escuela de Estudios Hispanoamericanos, 1980), 8–30.

52. Francisco Morales Padrón, *The Journal of Don Franciso Saavedra de Sangronis, 1780–1783* (Gainesville: University Press of Florida, 1989), xxx–xxxvii.

53. Carmen de Reparaz, *Yo solo: Bernardo de Gálvez y la toma de Panzacola en 1781: una contribución española a la independencia de los Estados Unidos* (Madrid: ICI, 1986), 29.

54. J. Leitch Wright Jr., *Florida in the American Revolution* (Gainesville: University Press of Florida, 1975), 84–86; James A. Padgett, "Bernardo de Gálvez's Siege of Pensacola in 1781 (as Related in Robert Farmer's Journal)," *Louisiana Historical Quarterly* 26 (1943): 11–29; Nixon Orbin Rush, *The Battle of Pensacola: Spain's Final Triumph over Great Britain in the Gulf of Mexico* (Tallahassee: Florida State University, 1966).

55. Richard B. Morris, *John Jay: The Winning of the Peace, Unpublished Papers, 1780–1784*, 2 vols. (New York: Harper and Row, 1980), 2:225–34.

56. Richard B. Morris, *The Peacemakers: The Great Powers and American Independence* (New York: Harper and Row, 1965), 305.

57. Relación de los meritos y servicios de Don Francisco Rendon, AGI México, 3189.

58. Memoria sobre las finanzas de los Trece Estados Unidos de America Seteptrional, April 20, 1782, AGI, Audiencia de Santo Domingo, 2598; Primera y segunda parte de la memoria sobre las producciones exportaciones e Importaciones y modo de hacer el comercio con los Estados Unidos: Que Don Francisco Rendon remite al Eximo Señor Don J. de Gálvez, September 8, 1783, ibid.

59. Caughey, *Bernardo de Gálvez in Louisiana*, 256–57.

60. Cummins, "Spanish Historians and the Gulf Coast Campaigns," 194–205.

61. Arthur P. Whitaker, *The Mississippi Question, 795–1803: A Study in Trade, Politics, and Diplomacy* (1934; repr., Lexington, KY: Peter Smith, 1962), 254–67; Whitaker, *The Spanish American Frontier: 1783–1795, the Westward Movement and the Spanish Retreat in the Mississippi Valley* (1927; repr., Lincoln: University of Nebraska Press, 1969), 4–14.

CHAPTER 4

Oliver Pollock and George Rogers Clark's Service of Supply

A Case Study in Financial Disaster

The American Revolution in the Mississippi valley and Gulf coast has been a secondary chapter in the history of that conflict. The exploits of the two generals who won singular victories in those regions, George Rogers Clark and Bernardo de Gálvez, have failed to attract as much scholarly attention as better-known commanders on the Atlantic Seaboard. This seems all the more remarkable because the successful campaigns led by Clark and Gálvez not only contributed to the American victory but also influenced postwar territorial settlements in a substantial manner. Clark's defeat of the British in the Illinois country expanded the reach of the infant United States into the Ohio River valley and down the Mississippi to New Orleans. Bernardo de Gálvez created a second front along the Gulf coast from Baton Rouge to Pensacola, thereby diluting British military strength along the Atlantic coast. The territories taken by both generals also set in place conditions that would encourage the expansion of the young republic into the areas where their campaigns took place.

Clark's military victories rested on the activities at New Orleans of Oliver Pollock, who also played a role supporting the campaigns of Gálvez. Because of his efforts, the Crescent City became an important supply depot for the American rebels. Starting soon after Lexington and Concord, Pollock shipped supplies and military goods up the Mississippi and Ohio Rivers to Fort Pitt, from where they made their way to the Continental Army. His role as the supply agent at New Orleans had escaped notice by scholars until the early years of the twentieth century. In the 1930s, historian James A. James wrote a biography of the New Orleans merchant, a man he called "an unknown patriot of the American Revolution." James, initially interested in researching Clark, had learned much about Pollock while gathering information on the life of the conqueror of the Illinois country. Having completed his biography of Clark in 1928, James turned his attention to Pollock.

His biography of Pollock, however, had weaknesses beyond his ability to correct. All of these relate to the fact that James worked from a restricted documentary base due to the loss of the New Orleans merchant's papers during the Civil War when a Union gunboat shelled and burned his grandson's plantation on the Mississippi River north of Baton Rouge. James thus had access only to the official papers of the Continental Congress, materials that documented Pollock's activities solely from the viewpoint of the young government. He also relied on a packet of written materials the merchant had furnished the US Congress in the 1780s and 1790s while seeking to have his wartime expenditures reimbursed. My research, conducted a half-century later, located documentary collections that had been unavailable to James. These included Spanish documents in the Archive of the Indies in Spain and transactions in the notary records in the municipal archives of the City of New Orleans. These collections contained previously unexamined correspondence, leger books, accounts, and bills of exchange that shed much light on how Pollock raised money and secured supplies. Materials from these sources enabled me to reconstruct his personal finances at a level of detail far beyond that accomplished by earlier scholars. This permitted a reassessment of an observation James made about Pollock: namely, that he was a wealthy person who committed his own resources to the American cause. The essay that follows presents a more complete analysis of Pollock's finances than James A. James could provide. I presented this study at the 1985 George Rogers Clark Conference held at Vincennes, Indiana, sponsored by the National Park Service with the support of the George Rogers Clark National Monument and Vincennes University. The most recent published study is William R. Nester's *George Rogers Clark: I Glory in War* (2012). It presents a full analysis of the Illinois-country campaigns and examines Pollock's role as supply agent. It also offers the reader an extended evaluation of Clark's complex personality.

Light Townsend Cummins, "Oliver Pollock and George Rogers Clark's Service of Supply: A Case Study in Financial Disaster," *Selected Papers from the 1985 and 1986 George Rogers Clark Trans-Appalachian Conference*, ed. Robert J. Holden (Vincennes, IN: Vincennes University Press, 1988), 1–16.

OLIVER POLLOCK'S activities during the American Revolution are well known to students of that history. His role as the congressional agent at New Orleans has earned him a deserved reputation as "The Financier of the Revolution in the West."[1] He arranged shipments of gunpowder from Spain and Cuba to George Washington's army in 1776 and 1777. He is best known, however, for his supply efforts that provisioned the military expedition of James Willing down the Mississippi River and his substantial financial support of George Rogers Clark, this latter in large measure enabling that American commander to hold the Illinois country.

Pollock's financial contributions to the Revolution have been the subject of investigations by two historians in particular: James A. James and J. G. Randall.[2] These scholars, making extensive use of the ledger books of George Rogers Clark and the records of the Continental Congress, have provided an accurate account of the tremendous amount of money and supplies that Pollock advanced for the American cause. This is only part of the story. It does not explain how Pollock raised the money to support Willing and Clark. This essay will address that issue.

The documents and financial records upon which James and Randall based their studies of Pollock were not the contemporary accounts kept by the merchant. Pollock's personal papers, including his financial records, were destroyed by fire when a Federal gunboat shelled his family's plantation at Bayou Sarah, Louisiana, during the Civil War.[3] Lacking these, all historical investigations of Pollock until this date have been based upon a variety of legal records, claims papers, and memorials that were presented after the fact to various authorities either by Pollock or his creditors during the 1790s or early 1800s. These documents provide general information about the money owed to the New Orleans merchant by the United States or the state of Virginia, but they do not permit the historian to reconstruct Pollock's personal finances on a transaction-by-transaction basis during the American Revolution.

My investigations in the archives of Spain and the notarial records of the City of New Orleans, however, have located a relatively large holding of previously unused materials directly related to Pollock's personal finances during the 1770s and 1780s. Research in these documents supports the basic conclusions offered by historians such as James and Randall regarding the total amount of support that Pollock advanced for the American cause. It also sheds new light on the merchant's personal financial situation during the revolt. Their studies characterized Pollock as a wealthy merchant of substantial fortune with ample case reserves, but my review of the methods that he employed to finance the American expeditions in the West suggests otherwise. An overview of the strategies by which he raised money highlights a previously unconsidered side of Pollock. What emerges is a portrait of an undercapitalized middle-class merchant of limited means struggling with short-term deficit financing in order to support the American cause.

An understanding of Pollock's activities as a general merchant specializing in the Latin American trade is important in assessing the nature of his personal wealth. Born in Ireland, Pollock moved to the Pennsylvania frontier as a young man. By the late 1750s, he had become a resident of Philadelphia, where he forged lasting bonds with successful merchants, including Robert Morris. After a short time, Pollock moved to Havana, where he represented the firm of William and Morris in Cuba. There he joined in the activities of Havana's Irish and Italian Roman Catholic merchant communities, which included Alexander Munro, Geronimo Enrile, and Geronomo LaChiapelli. These individuals, including Pollock, were heavily involved in the slave trade, a commerce permitted foreign merchants by the laws of Spain.[4]

In 1769, Pollock went to New Orleans, following on the heels of the military expedition sent from Cuba to assert Spain's control of Louisiana. General Alejandro O'Reilly, its commander, awarded Pollock a contract to supply New Orleans with flour. This contract provided Pollock with the firm base upon which he established a successful merchant house in Louisiana.[5] Pollock quickly opened a profitable trade between Spanish New Orleans and Philadelphia by way of the Gulf of Mexico and the Atlantic Ocean. Still acting as agent for Willing and Morris, he invested in plantation lands along the Mississippi for his backers. Between 1772 and 1776, Pollock bought four large plantations along the Mississippi and Amite Rivers in British West Florida. Most of the capital for these land investments came from profits that he earned in the slave trade. One parcel thirteen miles above Manchak on the Mississippi, for example, was bought from Phillip Comyn in direct exchange for slaves.[6]

In fact, much of Pollock's operating capital seems to have been generated by trading in slaves, both in Spanish Louisiana and in British West Florida. His first major sale came in March 1773, when he imported eighty blacks. All of them were apparently recent arrivals in the New World since the bills of sale described them as "brutish males, females, and children who were not baptized." In 1774, Pollock undertook a trip to the Atlantic coast, returning with "a good number of Negroes." News of this shipment caused considerable interest along the Mississippi valley as planters in West Florida and Louisiana contacted Pollock about selling slaves.

Pollock also brokered slaves already in the region. Members of the Spanish government in Louisiana and their families seemed to favor Pollock as a supplier of slaves. Bernardo de Otero, the colonial treasurer, bought three house servants from Pollock. Don Joseph de Peña, commander of Natchitoches post, traded Pollock a slave originally brought from the Red River. Although Pollock showed a profit in most of these transactions, there was always an element of risk. In February 1776, for example, he purchased a thirty-two-year-old mulatto woman named

Teresa from Doña Luisa Gromel for 500 pesos. After almost eighteen months, Pollock finally sold Andreas Reynaud for the amount originally paid.

Pollock's other commercial transactions rested on a wide variety of commodities besides slaves, although these did not produce as much income for him. As a merchant, he traded in goods imported into the Mississippi valley from the Atlantic coast or England. During 1772, Pollock took Thomas Willing's brother James as a partner in the operation of trading posts at Natchez and Manchac. The Willings were one of Pennsylvania's best-established mercantile families. Pollock operated as a correspondent all along the river for the parent firm of Willing and Morris. He seems to have specialized in the importation of flour and manufactured goods to the Mississippi valley. Exports of wood, peltry, and some tobacco ensured profits for him in return.[7]

As well, Pollock engaged in private banking, especially dealing in bills of exchange. As part of these services, he loaned money at interest. A typical transaction was his loan to one Francisco Mainard of the Arkansas Post for a thousand pesos. In return, Pollock required of Mainard collateral of a farm, the house on it, five horses, twenty-six cows, and the maize crop produced during 1773. Pollock also traded in real estate. He bought a house on Royal Street in New Orleans at public auction in December 1777, reselling it to James Harris less than three months later. Pollock increased his personal land holdings in West Florida and bought land along the Mississippi.[8] By 1776, Oliver Pollock had emerged as a prosperous merchant in New Orleans. He also invested in lucrative ventures and had capital for various business transactions. Much of this wealth, however, existed in the form of land investments, thereby limiting its liquidity. Other than the regular sale of slaves, he engaged in other commercial activities that generated large amounts of specie.

The American Revolution had an immediate impact on the lower Mississippi valley because of the proximity of British West Florida to Spanish Louisiana.[9] Oliver Pollock quickly became a partisan of the American cause. Largely through his efforts, envoys of the Continental Congress and the Virginia state militia were welcomed in New Orleans by the Spanish government. By 1776, Pollock had become an unofficial agent and spokesman in lower Mississippi valley for the American rebels. In early 1778, he received an official appointment from the Continental Congress as its agent in Louisiana. He also received a similar commission from the governor of Virginia on behalf of that state. For the next four years, he steadfastly supported the American cause by arranging for supplies and money to meet rebel needs.[10]

Pollock's first major opportunity to fulfill his commission came with his efforts to supply the American force led by James Willing.[11] These activities, although not related directly to the George Rogers Clark expedition, assume some importance for understanding later events. The methods of generating cash (especially the sale of slaves and the issuing of bills of exchange) that Pollock later employed for Clark in the Illinois country were first used by the New Orleans merchant to underwrite Willing. Unlike in the later case of George Rogers Clark, these efforts on behalf of Willing were successful.

James Willing had been a personal associate of Pollock prior to the Revolution. Unable to prosper in Spanish Louisiana, he returned to Philadelphia at the start of the revolt. Willing thereupon petitioned Congress for permission to lead a military expedition against West Florida. By the early spring of 1778, he was commanding a small force of Americans as they floated down the Mississippi River, plundering the holdings of West Florida planters.[12] Willing and his men took valuable prizes, including a large number of slaves. Upon arriving at New Orleans, Pollock interceded with the Spanish governor to have Willing granted the freedom of the city and the right to sell the expedition's prizes. Governor Bernardo de Gálvez, primarily because of Pollock's support, permitted the Americans to dispose of their plunder, but only after an investigation ensuring that the prizes had been obtained according to the customs of war. In some cases, Willing could not establish such. For example, the governor ordered the return of a slave belonging to George Ross, the boat *Neptune*, the goods of Stephen Shakespear, slaves belonging to Pansset and Marshall, and bateaux belonging to a Mr. Rapicault. Willing, however, was permitted to sell most of the seized goods, including the majority of the slaves.[13]

On April 6 and 8, 1778, Pollock sponsored a public auction at which the Americans disposed of the majority of the slaves taken during the

Willing raid. In all, seventy-four slaves crossed the block, raising a total of 16,518 pesos for Pollock and Willing. Leading citizens of Spanish Louisiana, including Antonio de Marigny, Philipe de Mandeville, Gilbert Antonio St. Maxent, and Carlos Oliver, all purchased slaves, although in many cases cash money was not on hand to complete the sales. Pollock met this lack of specie by financing most of the transactions on promissory notes due the following January first.[14]

It was only a few months after this auction that Pollock received his first requests for financial support from Lieutenant Colonel George Rogers Clark. The Committee of Commerce of the Continental Congress had earlier instructed Pollock to support Clark's expedition and purchase in New Orleans any supplies that it required. Aware of this, Clark wrote to the Louisiana merchant on July 18, 1778, informing him that "I have succeeded agreeable to my wishes and am necessitated to draw bills on the state and have reason to believe that they will be accepted by you, the answering of which will be acknowledged by his Excellency, the Governor of Virginia."[15] The support provided by Pollock came in two forms: the bills of exchange, which Clark gave to Illinois-area merchants drawn on Pollock, and actual materials purchased in New Orleans for shipment north up the river system. Pollock kept careful record of these amounts, noting both the bills that he received and the supplies that he purchased.

The successful slave sales that financed the Willing raid impressed Pollock with the additional profits that could come to the American cause by raiding British slaveholders in West Florida. Pollock's men thus captured British sympathizer David Ross's schooner, the *Dispatch*, in the late summer of 1778. It had aboard some fifty slaves and one hundred barrels of flour. Although Ross requested restoration of his property from the Spanish government, his solicitations were in vain. Pollock sold the captured slaves and used the money to purchase goods and supplies for Clark.[16]

These profits convinced Pollock to regularize this source of income. Willing's men had earlier captured a small British vessel on the Mississippi. Pollock outfitted this vessel as an American privateer, naming it the *Morris* in honor of his Philadelphia associate. He commissioned

William Pickles as her captain. The *Morris* immediately began raiding English plantations along Lake Pontchartrain and the Mississippi Sound. The taking of slaves to finance the American cause seems to be one of its primary motivations. In October 1779, Pickles arrived in New Orleans with a prize of thirteen blacks whom he had taken from a British subject living on the coast near Mobile. Pickles petitioned Martin Navarro, the acting governor in Bernardo de Gálvez's absence, for permission to sell the slaves at public auction. After examining the cargo, Navarro approved the sale. Two government appraisers fixed the value of the slaves at 1,260 pesos. At noon on October 12, the slaves captured by the *Morris* were offered at public auction under the direction of Navarro. Eight of the slaves were purchased, but the remaining five went unsold. It took two additional sales before the remainder of the slaves found buyers. Even with the paucity of purchasers on the first day, the total sale netted the Americans almost 600 pesos over the presale appraisal.[17]

These slave sales provided an initial fund of money that could be diverted easily to the American cause. Pollock was thus able to meet fully Clark's initial requests for assistance and, in so doing, perhaps unintentionally gave the American commander and his subordinates the impression that ample support was to be had on his behalf. The following year witnessed the arrival in New Orleans of a continuing series of bills drawn on Pollock by American commanders in the Illinois region.[18]

In many cases, Pollock had no prior knowledge of these bills until the time at which creditors presented them to him for payment. By the end of 1779, his ability to pay these bills had been outstripped both by the lack of cash on hand and his inability to raise funds. His chances to sell slaves had been seriously curtailed by several factors: the Revolution had reduced routine slave trading in the Gulf of Mexico and the Caribbean Sea; his earlier successes in capturing slaves from neighboring English subjects had diminished the supply; and the military victories of Louisiana governor Gálvez in British West Florida during 1779 and 1780 brought the region, including its residents, under the protection of Spain, an informal ally of the Americans.

Pollock therefore resorted to four additional measures that he hoped would generate cash for Clark and Illinois posts. First, he borrowed money from the Spanish government. In all, Governor Bernardo de Gálvez lent the American agent more than 74,000 pesos. Second, Pollock borrowed freely from individual merchants in New Orleans, creating an almost thirty-thousand-dollar debt guaranteed by his personal assets.[19] Third, he enlisted the assistance of other merchants, who sold him supplies on credit against eventual repayment by the American government. He received, for example, numerous supplies from the New Orleans merchant Daniel Clark, an Anglo trader not related to Colonel Clark. The merchant Clark kept a detailed accounting of the various materials furnished. Fourth, Pollock began transferring the bills of exchange to other investors who were willing to purchase them at discount against future repayment at face value. Some of the investors in this latter funding-raising attempt were Louisiana residents Martin Navarro, Narciso Alba, Mario Olivares, and Santiago Beauregard.[20]

New Orleans investors were willing to purchase these bills as speculative ventures largely because of the public support given Pollock by Thomas Jefferson, who then served as governor of Virginia. Jefferson had earlier written the governor of Louisiana, noting that the state of Virginia had created a trust account with the French firm of Penet, Da Costa, and Feres to cover bills of exchange written by George Rogers Clark and his subordinates. Virginia, through the congressional agents in Europe, would be selling tobacco and other products to maintain these accounts. Jefferson subsequently instructed Pollock to present bills from the Illinois country for payment to the French firm. Based upon this information, Pollock instead transferred the bills to local New Orleans investors in an effort to increase his short-term cash reserves. Santiago Monlon, the Creole planter and merchant, became the heaviest investor in these bills.[21]

In early 1781, Pollock's ability to finance the American debt without sufficient cash on hand or collateral came to an end. In January of that year, Lieutenant Robert George, the American commander at Fort Jefferson, drew a bill of exchange on Pollock in the total amount of $237,320, a sum greater than all of Pollock's personal assets.[22] As well, the debt that the New Orleans merchant had already created in the name of the state of Virginia and the Continental Congress was considerable. He owed the government of Louisiana some 74,087 pesos, which had been borrowed in the name of the Continental Congress. In addition, he was a debtor in the additional amount of 29,440 pesos to various New Orleans residents, including Bernardo de Otero, Joseph Foucher, Narciso Alba, Luís Toutant Beauregard, Juan Prieto, and others.[23] Pollock's ability to maintain solvency ended when the French merchant firm of Penet, Da Costa, and Feres refused to honor the bills of exchange supported by the state of Virginia. That state had failed to make deposits to its account. Since Pollock had already renegotiated these French bills of exchange with local residents in Louisiana, he rather than Virginia became personally liable for them with his creditors. The refusal of the French bills left him penniless. Bankruptcy was his only recourse.

Pollock embarked on a full-scale selling of his personal possessions in an effort to reconcile with his creditors. In January and February 1782, Pollock liquidated his holdings. On January 29, he began to sell his slaves at auction. He owned half interest in four slaves with William Henderson, who purchased Pollock's half interest. Francisco Bouligny, lieutenant governor of Louisiana, bought a slave couple for 602 pesos. Joseph Porell, Julian Vienna, Patrick Conway, and Maurice Conway were among the other buyers. In all, Pollock sold a full interest in fifteen slaves.[24]

Pollock sold his residential property in New Orleans, along with some of his upriver lands. These transactions were not without their legal difficulties. In one case, Pollock sought to sell two estates that he had been managing for Willing and Morris. The plantation manager, Alexander Henderson, brought suit against him in New Orleans courts in an effort to stop the sale proceedings. Henderson contended that Pollock owed him unpaid salary, had failed to reimburse for expenses incurred in buying supplies, and that Pollock's accounts were in error. In return, Pollock charged Henderson with improperly paying carpenters and jobbers on the plantation, not accounting for two years' worth of rice crops, squandering a year's hire of thirty-four slaves who were supposedly kept in idleness, and incurring unnecessary medical expenses for the slaves. This dispute was submitted to a board of arbitration following Spanish legal custom. The court appointed two arbitrators who examined the claims.

They were unable to reach a decision and recommended that the matter be referred to Willing and Morris in Philadelphia.[25]

Pollock, however, did not wait for a complete resolution of his failing business matters in New Orleans. In late April 1782, he requested a passport from Governor Esteban Miró in order to leave Louisiana and return to the Atlantic coast. Pollock saw this as the only successful way to convince Congress to pay the loans he had negotiated in New Orleans on its behalf. He thus left for Philadelphia and what he hoped would be an end to his financial troubles. His absence from Louisiana would last six years, take him to a Cuban prison, and see both Congress and the state of Virginia question his claims for reimbursement.[26] He did not receive full compensation for his debts from the state of Virginia until 1813.

The story of Pollock's subsequent career is well known to the readers of studies by James A. James and J. G. Randall. It needs little elaboration here. What does emerge from a study of Pollock's personal finances of the Revolutionary era, however, indicates that he was not the person of considerable financial substance as portrayed by his biographers. Although a person of comfortable means, Pollock was still building his fortune when the American Revolution came to the Mississippi valley. A review of his liquidated assets indicates that he was not wealthy, especially when his holdings are compared to those of New Orleans residents Luís Toutant Beauregard and Santiago Monlon, who enjoyed such reputations. Aside from landholding and slaves amounting to approximately thirty thousand dollars, his prosperity instead rested on profits from trade and commerce. As long as he was able to engage in these mercantile activities, especially slave trading, Pollock could generate the capital necessary to support the American cause. When the Revolution diminished this trade, Pollock resorted to various means of short-term financing in order to maintain cash on hand. Such measures proved inadequate, and his efforts resulted in a financial disaster that would take him the rest of his life to rectify.

Notes

1. The best biographical treatment of Pollock is James A. James, *Oliver Pollock: The Life and Time of an Unknown Patriot* (New York: Appleton-Century, 1937). See also John W. Caughey, *Bernardo de Gálvez in Louisiana, 1776–1783* (Berkeley:

University of California Press, 1934); and William F. Mullaney, "Oliver Pollock: Catholic Patriot and Financier of the American Revolution," *Historical Records and Studies of the US Catholic Historical Society* 28 (1937): 164–236.

2. The classic study of Pollock's supply efforts on behalf of the military forces in the Illinois country is J. G. Randall, "George Rogers Clark's Service of Supply," *Mississippi Valley Historical Review* 8 (1921): 250–63. See as well an earlier study on this subject, Margaret B. Downing, "Oliver Pollock: Patriot and Financier," *Illinois Catholic Historical Review* 2 (October 1919): 196–207.

3. Horace E. Hayden, *A Biographical Sketch of Oliver Pollock* (Harrisburg, PA: Lanes, Hart Printers and Binders, 1883), 6.

4. James, *Oliver Pollock*, 4–6; Hayden, *Biographical Sketch of Oliver Pollock*, 6–19; William Henry Egle, *Notes and Queries, Historical and Genealogical, Chiefly Relating to Interior Pennsylvania* (Harrisburg, PA: Harrisburg Publishing, 1894), 1:475–81.

5. Oliver Pollock to the Captain General of Cuba, June 22, 1796, Archivo General de Indias, Seville, Spain (hereafter referred to a AGI), Papeles de Cuba, Legajo 1469; Pollock to Luís de las Casas, July 14, 1796, ibid. Pollock's contract was for the supply of flour. For the Cabildo deliberations on the scarcity of this commodity, see Actas del Cabildo. New Orleans, October 5, 1770, August 2, 16, 1771, 1:20, 32, 33, WPA Transcripts in Spanish on Microfilm, New Orleans Public Library, New Orleans.

6. For Pollock's land purchases, see State Land Office, Baton Rouge, *Greensburg Land Claims*, Book 2, pt. 2:69, 94, 109–10; *American State Papers: Public Lands* (Washington, DC: Duff Green, 1834), 3:46, 4:313; Acts of Andres Almonaster y Rojas, vol. 9, March 5, 1778, f. 176, Orleans Parish Notary Archives, Civil District Courts Building, New Orleans (hereafter referred to as Orleans Notary Archives). The Geography and Map Division of the Library of Congress contains several maps by British cartographers that note lands owned by Pollock. See *Map of the Mississippi River from the Mount of the Yazoo River to the Southern Part of Louisiana, 1774*, and *Plan of the Rivers Mississippi, Iberville, Mobile and Bay of Pensacola in the Province of West Florida, September 1772*; and Phillip Comyns to Oliver Pollock, January 21, 1774, Peter Force Collection, Library of Congress.

7. "Partido de Nueva Orleans," June 15, 1778, AGI, Papeles de Cuba, Legajo 191; John Blommart to Oliver Pollock, January 29, 1775, Force Collection; Oliver Pollock to General Frederick Haldimand, December 1, 1772, Haldimand Papers, pt. 4, mss. 21729, Division of Manuscripts, Library of Congress..

8. Acts of Andres Almonaster y Rojas, vol. 23, March 4, 1773, f. 45, vol. 4, March 7, 1774, f. 68, vol. 8, February 15, 1777, f. 130, Orleans Notary Archives; Acts of Juan Baptista Garic, vol. 5, July 30, 1774, f. 143, vol. 8, July 8, 1774, f. 280, ibid.

9. J. Barton Starr, *Tories, Dons, and Rebels: The American Revolution in British West Florida* (Gainesville: University Press of Florida, 1976), 87–88; Caughey, *Bernardo de Gálvez*, 112–13.

10. James, *Oliver Pollock*, 113–14.

11. Robert V. Haynes, *The Natchez District and the American Revolution* (Jackson: University Press of Mississippi, 1976), 62–66, 73.

12. John W. Caughey, "Willing's Expedition down the Mississippi, 1778," *Louisiana Historical Quarterly* 15 (January 1932): 5–36.

13. Bernardo de Gálvez to José de Gálvez, March 11, 1778, nos. 130 and 131, AGI, Audiencia de Santo Domingo, Legajo 2547, ff. 445–57, 461–62. For a list of prizes returned, see ibid., f. 546.

14. Acts of Juan Baptista Garic, vol. 9, April 6–8, 1778, ff. 202–24, Orleans Notary Archives.

15. James, *Oliver Pollock*, 140; James A. James, *George Rogers Clark Papers, 1771–1781*, vol. 3 (Springfield: Illinois State Historical Library, 1912), 55.

16. David Ross to Bernardo de Gálvez, April 11, 1778, Public Record Office, Kew Gardens, London, CO 5/631.

17. "Presa hecha por el Corsario la Corbetta de la Fragta. La *Moreis* de los Estados Unidos de America Capn. Guillermo Pickles," no. 116, 1779, AGI, Papeles de Cuba, Legajo 701.

18. For examples of these bills, see Acts of Leonard Mazange, vol. 5, February 5, 1781, f. 72, Orleans Notary Archives.

19. "Lista de los creditos que contra si tiene en la Luisiana Don Olivero Pollock," February 19, 1789, AGI, Audiencia de Santo Domingo, Legajo 253, f. 627.

20. Acts of Rafael Perdomo, vol. 13, May 5, 1789, ff. 230–50, Orleans Notary Archives.

21. Thomas Jefferson to Bernardo de Gálvez, November 8, 1779, AGI, Papeles de Cuba, Legajo 2370; *Santiago Monlon v. Oliver Pollock*, April 20, 1782, Spanish Judicial Records of Louisiana, Louisiana Historical Center, Louisiana State Museum, New Orleans.

22. Robert George to Oliver Pollock, January 1, 1781, in James, *George Rogers Clark Papers*, 3:496.

23. "Resolution Setting Forth the Value of Oliver Pollock's Services as US Commercial Agent at New Orleans during the Revolution and Urging a Settlement of His Accounts," October 22, 1782, E. A. Parsons Collection, Humanities Research Center, University of Texas at Austin; Acts of Rafael Perdomo, vol. 13, January 16, 1789, f. 19, Orleans Notary Archives; Acts of Leonard Mazange, vol. 3, February 1781, f. 66, ibid.

24. For representative liquidations, see Acts of Andres Almonaster y Rojas, vol. 13, February 5, 1782, f. 99, Orleans Notary Archives; Acts of Leonard Mazange, vol. 2, August 7, 1780, f. 621, vol. 3, March 3, April 11, 1781, ff. 171, 248, vol. 4, November 6, 1781, f. 495, and vol. 5, January 28, February 4, 1782, f. 102, 136, ibid.

25. "Proceedings Instituted by Don Olivero Pollock for the Purpose of Settling Certain Accounts with His Principals through an Arbitration Board," April 27, 1782, Spanish Judicial Records of Louisiana, Louisiana Historical Center.

26. Oliver Pollock to Esteban Miró, April 27, 1782, AGI, Papeles de Cuba, Legajo 2370.

CHAPTER 5

"Her Weary Pilgrimage"

The Remarkable Mississippi River Adventures of Anne McMeans, 1778–1782

The movement of Anglo-Americans from the Atlantic-coast colonies into unsettled regions of the interior occurred because of individual families seeking new lands upon which to establish themselves and farm. Such was a model of settlement that began as early as the seventeenth century in places such as Virginia and continued later in the Carolinas, Pennsylvania, New York, and even the New England colonies. By the time of the American Revolution, English-speaking settlements existed in the middle to upper Ohio River valley and had started to move toward the Mississippi River. The 1780 establishment of Fort Jefferson and nearby Clarksville was the first attempt by Anglo-Americans to create a town on the banks of the Mississippi as part of this demographic movement. Settlers arrived in the area during the early months of that year by coming down the Ohio. By the spring of 1781, however, both the fort and the town were in dire straits, with most of the soldiers and inhabitants having departed. Serious supply difficulties for the military garrison, coupled to several disastrous Indian raids, spelled their end by June 1781. During subsequent decades, however, thousands English-speaking migrants would float down the Ohio and Mississippi Rivers past the long-abandoned site of Fort Jefferson. It is doubtful if any of them had any awareness of the historic role the vanished fort and Clarksville had nonetheless played as a vanguard of their efforts, the first Anglo-American settlement in the Mississippi valley established by citizens of the United States.

Professor Kenneth C. Carstens of Murray State University in Kentucky has spent most of his career studying Fort Jefferson and Clarksville. A historical archeologist, Carstens has undertaken over recent decades extensive research initiatives and on-the-ground efforts both to determine the exact location of the fort and to reconstruct the historical events that occurred there. His excavations and documentary research have enriched our knowledge about this settlement. I first learned of his work in the mid-1980s, when we both made presentations at a scholarly conference dealing with the American Revolution in the West. The settlement effort at Fort Jefferson and Clarksville piqued my interest because of my research on Oliver Pollock and his relationship to the fort as its supply agent at New Orleans. Turning my attention to documentary sources on Fort Jefferson, I encountered the narrative of Anne McMeans, whose memoir constitutes the only known firsthand account of someone who lived there. Published in abbreviated form in the 1820s as a religious tract, few people other than descendants and specialized scholars knew about this reminiscence. The essay below tells her story as completely as permitted by the extant documentation, making extensive use of a handwritten version of this memoir I read while conducting research on a related topic at the Newberry Library in Chicago; I may have been the first historian to read this version because a cataloging error indicated that it was written by someone else. In looking at it, I determined that it was a more complete and thorough copy of McMeans's narrative than had previously been known to historians, containing much new information about her residence at Fort Jefferson and Clarksville. I thereupon resolved to conduct additional research on her. Kenneth C. Carstens's *George Rogers Clark's Fort Jefferson, 1780–1781: Kentucky's Outpost on the Western Frontier* (2005) will long remain the definitive study of this topic.

Light Townsend Cummins, "'Her Weary Pilgrimage': The Remarkable Mississippi River Adventures of Anne McMeans, 1778–1782, *Louisiana History* 47, no. 4 (Autumn 2006): 389–415.

IN APRIL 1782, Anne McMeans, a bedraggled yet tough-minded woman in her late thirties, arrived at New Orleans aboard a boat carrying a load of flour from Pennsylvania. This vessel had floated down the Ohio and Mississippi Rivers with a cargo that would undoubtedly command a high price in the Louisiana capital. Thomas White, a merchant sometimes associated with Oliver Pollock, served as this vessel's master. Pollock, the New Orleans commercial agent for the Continental Congress, had organized several years earlier a very profitable trade between Spanish New Orleans and Fort Pitt on the western Pennsylvania frontier. White served as one of the boat captains in this commerce, which supplied military goods sent to the Continental Army from Spain to Pennsylvania by way of New Orleans, while, in return, merchants in Spanish Louisiana received vital foodstuffs, especially milled white flour, at New Orleans from the middle states of the infant United States.[1]

Anne McMeans, however, had nothing to do with this mercantile activity. She had not traveled all the way from Pennsylvania with White and his crew. Instead, she and her surviving children had boarded the vessel at Natchez as it passed through on its voyage down the river. Anne, financially broke and without possessions, hoped for passage down to New Orleans, where she prayed it would be possible to catch an oceangoing packet bound for Pennsylvania, her original home to which she and the children yearned to return. They had been living in a succession of places in the Ohio and Mississippi valleys during the previous four years. Thomas White took Anne and the children as passengers aboard his flour boat at Natchez. He had known her years earlier in Pennsylvania, and, indeed, he had been keeping a wary eye for her as he traveled down to New Orleans on his voyages during the early 1780s. They found each other at Natchez. White took great pause when Anne told him the remarkable story of her adventures on the great western waters. He immediately volunteered to carry her and the children to New Orleans from Natchez free of charge. He even offered to pay their passage back to Philadelphia himself, with profits from the sale of his flour, if no other means could be found to fund the remainder of their trip. Such, however, would not be necessary. Once at New Orleans, Anne learned that only one ship in the Louisiana port city prepared to sail for Philadelphia. When she told her compelling story to its master, the Pennsylvania packet captain seemed as moved as White had been several weeks earlier. Not only did the captain give Anne and her brood free passage to Pennsylvania on his vessel, but he also put ashore several other passengers in order to make room for them.

The essay that follows tells, for the first time in historical context, the remarkable story that Anne told these men during April 1782.[2] Her exploits, however, are not completely unknown to specialists of the American Revolution in the Mississippi valley because a publisher in Philadelphia printed an edited version of her narrative in 1824 as a little-known religious tract in which the tale of "her weary pilgrimage" brought her Mississippi River adventures to the attention of a small readership.[3] Today, Anne's exploits on the Mississippi River constitute a little-known story of high adventure and profound tragedy during the American Revolution.[4] It began in the upper Ohio valley and ended in Spanish Louisiana. The story of Anne McMeans constitutes an extraordinary experience that speaks directly to the reservoirs of courage and determination that can often be found in the most ordinary of people. Beyond that, Anne's experiences on the Mississippi River are much more than the account of a resolute and religious woman who made great sacrifices, both for herself and her family, in order that they might live. It is also the larger epic of the first attempt to plant a settlement of frontier folk from the young United States on the banks of the Mississippi River. As such, Anne can be counted among the first resolute citizens of the United States who took the initial steps in a movement that would eventually open the entire Mississippi valley to the frontier expansion of the new nation. Although these initial efforts ended in failure, Anne's personal resolve and strength of character, in the direct face of adversity and hardship, constituted a presage to the spirit of determined fortitude that would serve as a hallmark of that powerful demographic movement. As well, her pronounced and committed religious values also proved to be a significant wellspring of personal strength that further bolstered her resolve. Anne McMeans survived the hostilities of a very dangerous frontier. In short, her largely unknown story is part and parcel of the early chapter in the Anglo-American settlement of the Mississippi valley.[5]

Anne McMeans's remarkable story of determined survival on the Mississippi River during her voyage through Spanish Louisiana began years earlier with her birth in the southern colonial backcountry of the British colonial frontier. Born in the western part of Maryland during 1744, Anne grew up as the second daughter of James Willson and Susannah Alexander.[6] Anne's mother had been born in 1719 in western Pennsylvania, while James, her father, had emigrated from Northern Ireland. Both sides of her family could trace their roots back to seventeenth-century Scotland and to the plantation settlements of Ireland.[7] As young people, her parents had migrated to the Scotch Irish settlement belt that lay to the west of the tidewater region of the British North Atlantic colonies. Like other families along the western backcountry, the Willsons moved several times over the course of their lives as they sought better opportunities on the frontier. By the 1760s, they had moved to Pennsylvania, settling near Lancaster, where young Anne married Andrew McMeans, who would be her partner during her later Mississippi River adventures. Like his new wife, Andrew also had deep roots in the Scotch Irish society that flourished beyond the western mountains of the mid-Atlantic colonies. His father, James McMeans, had come to the British colonial frontier from Northern Ireland as one of six brothers who sought new lives in the backcountry wilderness. His son, Andrew, had been born in the Maryland colony, although he was a few years older than Anne since his birth occurred in 1740. Anne and Andrew married in Lancaster, Pennsylvania, on October 25, 1762. As a young married couple, the McMeans struck out on their own and moved to the very edge of the colonial Atlantic-coast settlement line as it then existed. They choose a rural area south of Fort Pitt as the location for their new home. The newlyweds now lived in raw and unsettled country that served as the object of a territorial dispute between the colonies of Pennsylvania and Virginia. The colonial government at Williamsburg considered the area south of Fort Pitt to be part of its Yohogania County, while Pennsylvania instead believed it to be inside its own colonial borders.[8] Territorial sovereignty meant little to the McMeans family as they set up housekeeping at a small settlement where the Youghiogheny River flows into the Monongahela River at a place then known as the "Forks of the Yough," the site of present-day McKeesport. There they settled a tract of some 224 acres.[9] Andrew began to farm while he and Anne started a family. Children came in regular succession, with the birth of Mary in May 1764, James three years later, Jane about twelve months thereafter, followed by John in 1771, Isaac two years later, and Robert in 1776.[10]

The year of the infant Robert's birth in 1776 saw the fervor of the American Revolution sweep the backcountry as some Virginians began to consider the Ohio River valley as a gateway to the West and the British Illinois country. One of them, Governor Patrick Henry of Virginia, dispatched an expedition to New Orleans from Fort Pitt under the command of George Gibson, who had as his objective to secure badly needed supplies and munitions from the Spanish government in Louisiana.[11] Gibson's expedition produced additional, larger schemes in the backcountry to open commerce with Spanish Louisiana and the lower Mississippi by way of the Ohio River. The first of these expeditions fell to the command of James Willing, who spent late 1777 at Fort Pitt organizing a force to harass the British province of West Florida.[12] Willing's expedition left Pennsylvania in January 1778, floated down the Ohio River to the Mississippi and eventually attacked the British settlement at Natchez in West Florida. Although ultimately unsuccessful, the James Willing expedition quickly became a harbinger of continuing rebel interest in the Mississippi valley. It would be a sturdy Virginia frontiersman, however, who would bring the full-scale American Revolution to the West: George Rogers Clark, an intrepid soul who came of age in the Virginia plantation belt as a childhood neighbor of Thomas Jefferson. By 1778, Clark had already visited the western areas that would become Kentucky. While James Willing descended the Mississippi with his expedition, Clark also considered an invasion of British posts in the West; namely, the Illinois country that lay north of the great confluence of the Ohio and Mississippi Rivers. Clark desired to bring this rich agricultural territory under the control of his native Virginia. In 1778, he traveled to Williamsburg, where he laid his plans before Governor Henry and the Burgesses, all of whom approved. Clark thereafter hurried back to the upper Ohio region, where he and his agents began enrolling recruits for the proposed expedition to conquer British Illinois. It would be both a military force and a settlement effort. Clark and his officers concentrated their recruitment efforts in the disputed area of Pennsylvania and Virginia, the region where the McMeans family resided.[13] Andrew and Anne McMeans became aware of Clark's plans, which influenced their subsequent decision to move to Kentucky. Indeed, they had already thought about moving their young family to South Carolina; but, instead, probably because of the enthusiasm created by Clark's recruiting agents, they opted for Kentucky.

Andrew and Anne, however, were unable to complete all necessary arrangements in time to depart with Clark, who had recruited about two dozen civilian families to settle at the Falls of the Ohio in Kentucky, the site of modern Louisville. Clark and his expedition left Redstone on May 12, 1778, and arrived at the Falls of the Ohio two weeks later. There they set up a base camp on Corn Island while Clark assigned parcels of land for settlement to the families who had accompanied him. Once these arrangements had been completed, Clark and his military force sailed down the river for the Illinois country during late June in order to attack the British posts, leaving behind the settlers and a few troops to guard the area. Additional settlers continued to arrive in the vicinity of Corn Island during the remainder of the year. The settlement zone quickly expanded from Corn Island onto the south shore of the Ohio, where new arrivals began clearing farms in the vicinity of Beargrass Creek. A steady stream of new settlers continued to arrive in the region from the upper Ohio during the entire period that George Rogers Clark and his men engaged in their military conquests during 1778 and 1779. Some estimates hold that as many as 300 families, including the McMeans, came down the Ohio into Kentucky during the two-year period between 1778 and 1780.[14]

In September 1778, the McMeans sold their Pennsylvania farm to Thomas Applegate and left for Kentucky. Although no specific account survives of their journey down the Ohio, it is probable that Andrew, Anne, and the children arrived in the vicinity of the Falls of the Ohio sometime in the autumn of 1778. Their arrival may have coincided with that of a Virginian named John Floyd, an old friend of George Rogers Clark.[15] Floyd led a group that included many of his family members and friends to the Beargrass Creek area on the south bank of the Ohio across from Corn Island. He constructed there a small fort, where the McMeans family mostly likely first set foot on the soil of Kentucky. Andrew soon signed on with a group of men who departed this location for the interior in order to establish a small settlement on the Wilderness Road that would connect the Beargrass region with Harrodsburg to the south. They followed "an old buffalo path" through a place called Blue Lick Gap until they came to the Salt River at its junction with a smaller stream known as Floyd's Fork.[16] At this location, they commenced to build a small fort and settlement first known as Brashear's Station, later called Floyd's Fork Station. This community quickly constituted some twenty "resedenters," including the McMeans family.[17] Andrew used the proceeds from the sale of his Pennsylvania farm to purchase 1,200 acres at the Floyd's Fork settlement.[18] Anne and the children arrived soon thereafter and set up housekeeping, bringing with them a new baby, little Anne, who had been born several months earlier. Andrew planted a corn crop and probably also engaged in salt production, which fast became the primary economic activity at the new settlement.

The small community at Floyd's Fork, however, did not prosper to the extent that the McMeans had hoped. Most of the families along the Salt River in the spring of 1780 thus began considering a new colonization scheme that had presented itself: the founding of a military fort and civilian community to be established much farther to the west near the confluence point of the Ohio and Mississippi Rivers. Anne later wrote in her narrative that there existed "much confusion in the rights of land in this Country and, having fine proposals made to us to go settle on the Mississippi," they decided to do so.[19] This venture, organized under the auspices of the state of Virginia, would be commanded by George Rogers Clark, with his military subordinates serving as the organizers and implementers. Plans for this settlement had been discussed as early as 1777, when Clark first suggested to Virginia authorities that a settlement on the Mississippi River could serve as a bulwark to ensure Williamsburg's claim to that region, hinder the British from supplying their Indian allies in the area, and become an important trading station with Spanish Louisiana.[20] Finally, in January 1780, Virginia governor Thomas

Jefferson authorized construction of the fort, which would soon bear his name, along with its accompanying civilian settlement named in honor of Clark. Once authorized, plans for Fort Jefferson and Clarksville moved forward quickly. Jefferson dispatched surveyors Daniel Smith and Thomas Walker to the proposed location of the new fortification in order to ensure its location would fall within the declared far western boundaries of Virginia. In addition, the governor reminded Clark that the founding of a civilian community near the fort would be essential in order to provide foodstuffs for the garrison. Jefferson also mistakenly ordered Clark to purchase land for the fort from the Cherokees, not understanding that the site of this new establishment actually fell within the tribal lands of the Chickasaw. This later proved to be a fatal error since the Chickasaw operated as British allies against the rebels during the entire American Revolution, especially in the Mississippi valley.[21]

While these organizational efforts took place at the new site on the Mississippi, some of Clark's lieutenants began recruiting families for the town of Clarksville. They identified families living at the Falls of the Ohio, and at the nearby interior stations, as the chief prospects for this enterprise. In early 1780, James Piggott, one of Clark's lieutenants who would later be a trustee of Clarksville, appeared at Floyd's Fork Station, where he apparently had little trouble in recruiting almost all of the residents of that settlement for the new venture on the Mississippi.[22] The McMeans family heard Piggott's presentation about the new community of Clarksville and deemed it a fine proposal. They decided to join the expedition, which included all of the families in the region, except for two who professed pro-British, tory sentiments. The first wave of settlers departed, while Andrew McMeans traveled to Harrodsburg to transact business related to his impending move to the Mississippi. This left Anne and the children alone at Floyd's Fork, where they experienced various hardships in his absence. Most of the other families were already at the Falls of the Ohio, where they had joined with parties assembling for the trip to found Fort Jefferson and Clarksville. Andrew left Anne and his family in the care of a friend. This person "did his utmost, but as our provision depended upon the good success of the hunter in killing buffalo," Anne later recalled, "he could not wherewith supply our wants."

Lacking food and supplies, Anne reported that "although my husband wrote me not to move until his return, I was however under the necessity to do the best I could for my children who began to suffer as I could get nothing but nine pounds of meat to live on for three days." Finally, Eleanor Piggott, the wife of Captain Piggott, brought Anne and the children plenty of meat. This relieved the children and "stayed their crying." The Piggotts, however, pressured Anne to leave for the Mississippi without Andrew, who had not returned from his trip to Harrodsburg. Piggott wanted the entire party from the Floyd's Fork settlement to depart immediately. Anne did not wish to do so without her husband. Happily for her, Andrew reappeared just as they prepared to leave. However, McMeans now had reservations about joining the expedition to the new settlement on the Mississippi and shared his concerns with his wife. "He intended not to go down the river," Anne noted, "but as he had added his name to the paper and had been detained by being in cloudy weather ten days longer than he would have been, and that he thought there was a hand of providence in this, he therefore would not draw back."[23] The McMeans therefore left Floyd's Fork in order to rendezvous with Clark's main party at the settlement on the Ohio River near Corn Island.

A spirit of optimism prevailed as the remainder of Clark's military expedition and his civilian settlers gathered at the Falls of the Ohio in preparation for the main trip down to the new settlement. Once at the falls, the McMeans found some of their relatives who had also signed on for the venture, including Andrew's two sisters with their own families. Like Andrew, they had probably been drawn to the new settlement venture because of Clark's liberal land provisions. Each family would be granted a land warrant in the amount of 650 acres. Additionally, all male settlers would serve in a militia regiment at the fort, which would be commanded by Captain George Owens. In early April 1780, the group departed from the Falls of the Ohio. Clark, his officers, and approximately 250 persons, including both soldiers and civilians, floated down the Ohio, passed by the great confluence of the rivers, and landed at a place known as the Iron Banks on the east bank of the Mississippi River, approximately five miles south of the point where the two rivers joined.[24] Here they established Fort Jefferson and the town of Clarksville in the name of the state of Virginia and by the authority of its governor, Thomas Jefferson.

The soldiers who went with the expedition busily set about constructing the fortification. By early June 1780, construction of the fort had been completed while the settlers had also finished building their homes and planting their crops. "We built a fort and called it Fort Jefferson," Anne later wrote in her narrative, "and made great proficiency in clearing land, planted corn," and seemed to be in a prosperous way of making a comfortable settlement during the summer. In spite of this industriousness, however, the fort and the community soon had great difficulty raising enough food to supply its needs. The numbers of people arriving at the fort placed great strain on provisions and the food supply. In June, additional troops from George Rogers Clark's Illinois Battalion arrived to expand the size of the garrison. The following month, sixty-five Kaskaskia Indian allies came to the fort along with another company of soldiers. Captain Robert George, the fort's commander, put the Kaskaskia Indians to work as hunters in order to supply the fort and the settlement with fresh meat. Nonetheless, a situation quickly developed that Clark and Captain George eventually could not resolve: namely, there were never enough supplies for the number of persons at the fort, and the Clarksville settlement could not supply them. Captain George had no choice but to begin the tedious and expensive purchase of foodstuffs from merchants at New Orleans, especially Oliver Pollock, who continued to serve as the authorized commercial agent of the Continental Congress in Spanish Louisiana.[25]

The difficulty of provisioning Fort Jefferson, however, paled in comparison to the threat of depredations and violence from the neighboring Native Americans, a worry that quickly consumed the attentions of Clark, Captain George, and the entire garrison. They belatedly realized that the site of Fort Jefferson clearly fell within the tribal lands claimed by the Chickasaw, who actively supported the British. The summer of 1780 not surprisingly witnessed three attacks against the fort and the settlement. On June 7, 1780, a party of Chickasaw warriors ambushed a small group of Clarksville militiamen who were foraging beyond the settlement, killing several of them. Then, on July 17, the Chickasaw moved against Clarksville directly in an attack that seemed more of a test of defenses than a full-scale assault. Little damage occurred. This skirmish, however, only prepared the way for a larger attack the following month, when a group of warriors estimated at about 150 in number moved against the fort. This action, a sizeable and well-planned event, initiated a battle that would last over four days, from August 27 until August 30. Those in the fort and at the settlement held their ground, and the Chickasaws eventually withdrew. This battle, although a victory for the Americans, had particularly devastating consequences for the settlement. Anne lamented that "the Indians attacked us three times, the third time they killed four persons and took one prisoner, killed all the cattle they could catch and cut down the corn, which was eating ear, so that there was no prospect for our support."

Indeed, the following months at Fort Jefferson saw a steady accumulation of problems related to these attacks, as it became increasingly obvious that there would not be enough food available for the coming winter. As well, neither the state of Virginia nor George Rogers Clark had effective strategies to provide such supplies. Captain George, as the post commandant, eventually overextended his credit with Oliver Pollock. He could no longer look for a reliable source of supplies from New Orleans.[26] Accordingly, George Rogers Clark officially abandoned Fort Jefferson and Clarksville on June 8, 1781, thus ending the first attempt to establish a community of settlers coming directly from the United States on the banks of the Mississippi River. The McMeans family, however, did not remain to witness the formal closing of the fort. The August 1780 Chickasaw raid that had lasted four days had proven to be the deciding factor for them in leaving the settlement, especially since they had reservations about the whole enterprise even before they had left Kentucky. The McMeans were not alone in this decision. By September 1780, approximately half of the forty families living at Clarksville had already departed, either ascending the Ohio River or floating down the Mississippi to the English-speaking settlement at Natchez.

"We heard there was a number that agreed to go to the Natchez," Anne later remembered, "with a view to winter there and in the spring to come round by water to their old habitations" along the western frontier of the mid-Atlantic states. Accordingly, Anne and Andrew McMeans, along with Andrew's two sisters and their families, decided to become part of this exodus and joined a party of settlers bound for Natchez. Anne's strong religious faith also showed through into this decision when she learned that "God in mercy prevented the Indians from destroying our boats." In that regard, the various families who decided to leave Clarksville for the lower Mississippi in the late summer of 1780 had seven boats between them. "In these," she noted, "we embarked with all the property we could take, designing, if possible, to reach Natchez." These families, including the McMeans and the families of Andrew's two sisters, selected this location because of its recent conquest by the Spanish. They obviously knew that English-speaking Natchez, formerly a part of British West Florida, had fallen to the control of a friendly power. Spain had entered the Revolution during the summer of 1779 as an American ally. General Bernardo de Gálvez had thereafter successfully embarked on a series of successive military conquests against British posts along the lower Mississippi valley and the Gulf coast.[27] Indeed, American merchant Oliver Pollock, a familiar name to them since he served as one of the chief supply agents for Fort Jefferson, had personally negotiated the British surrender of Natchez.[28]

Accordingly, the small flotilla of refugee families set sail from Fort Jefferson on September 13, 1780. The McMeans, along with the families of the two sisters, filled all of one boat. There were nineteen persons aboard: Andrew and Anne McMeans, his sister Margery and her husband James Young, and an older sister of Andrew composed the adults, while there were a total of fourteen children, including the seven McMeans youngsters. All of the children were McMeans cousins. Indeed, Anne specifically noted that "there were some three families containing nineteen persons in our boat among whom only two men." The voyage down the Mississippi River got underway without much difficulty. For three days, the entire compliment of seven boats remained together and all seemed uneventful. On the third day out, however, problems began to develop. Some of the travelers had taken sick, this especially being the case in the McMeans boat. Anne's narrative provides a clear exposition of the specific symptoms that she and her family experienced. Reviewing these, it may be noted that most likely everyone in the McMeans boat suffered from malaria.[29] This seemed all the more probable since the region of the Mississippi valley through which they passed had a well-deserved reputation for infestation by mosquitoes and resultant outbreaks of malaria.[30]

With so many people in their boat not feeling well, the McMeans could not keep up with the rest of the vessels. Although all of them had agreed to keep together in order to avoid being attacked by Indians, Anne later recalled, "the third morning after we set out, they all left our boat, and said that as soon as they would kill some meat, they would wait for us." The McMeans party had no choice but to agree with this plan of action. They soon found themselves alone on the river in a solitary boat as the rest of the flotilla sailed away down the river. She remembered that "all in our boat was sick so that we could not sail," especially since a high wind had come up that further increased their difficulties. Now separated from the other boats in the Fort Jefferson refugee flotilla, malaria began to take its toll on the adults in the McMeans vessel. Margery Young, Andrew's sister, had been hit hard by the sickness, and her condition continued to worsen rapidly. She died several days after the McMeans had been abandoned by the rest of the flotilla. Illness also ravaged Anne, although she seemed to have a milder case, noting that "I was not able to help myself, but it pleased the Lord to recover me so that I could sit up and walk with support."

By the time of Margery Young's death, the McMeans boat was also suffering from an increasingly dangerous lack of provisions and foodstuffs since everyone aboard was too sick to hunt game on the riverbank. James Young did manage to shoot a buffalo on shore from the boat, but when they attempted to land in order to collect the meat, the strong current snagged the vessel against a sandbar. Here they remained stranded for almost a week, unable to free the vessel. Further tragedy struck the beleaguered group at this time. Andrew McMeans died, leaving Anne a widow with their seven children remaining in her care under the most difficult of circumstances. Then, as an additional blow, Andrew's elder sister died the following day, leaving Anne and her brother-in-law, James Young, as the only two surviving adults in the boat. With both of the two surviving adults still sick and attempting to recover, their vessel remained snagged on the sandbar for two additional weeks before they could free it.

"By this time," Anne remembered, "our provisions was all done, all but one peck of flaxseed, which we parched, and heated to meal in a pot, so as to make a soup." They also had some animal skins of elk, bear, and buffalo, which Anne roasted into a crude and unpalatable jerky that they chewed to relieve their hunger. "We had not anything to live on for three weeks," Anne remembered, "except when we saw anything on the shore that we could eat such as grapes, greenbriers, honey locust pods, muskatines [*sic*], a fruit like fox grapes, a wild kind of rough small peas, and wild tongue grass which was the plentiest [*sic*] of anything we could get." Not surprisingly, the symptoms of prolonged nutrient deprivation and starvation, coupled to their preexisting malarial condition, began to affect them profoundly. "What flesh I had left after two months of sickness wore off faster than I ever knew it to fall off with one sickness," Anne worried. She also had special concern for the children, who understandably bore the brunt of the suffering since the two remaining adults could barely manage the boat and care for themselves. At night, they usually pulled to shore in order to camp on the riverbank. While ashore, Anne permitted the children to leave the boat while it was beached so that they could forage for food. One such evening, while "the children all went up the bank to look for something to eat," Anne's seven-year-old son, Isaac, remained in the boat because he was too weak to leave the vessel. The boy seemed very lethargic. Anne later recalled, "I was then eating a piece of roasted skin which I divided with him," but still he fretted. The other children soon thereafter returned to the boat with some grapes they had found, which they offered to share with Isaac, who was too sick to eat them. The next day, Isaac's condition improved enough that he got up from the boat in the morning, went ashore in order to urinate, and returned to his place before they cast off. However, Anne was unable to get him to drink water. Anne recalled that "he strove to eat but there was nothing that would quench his poor heart." Isaac "continued striving to eat until the sun was about an hour high, and then he lost his senses and lay quite [*sic*] for about two hours and departed this life." They put the boat ashore. Anne and her oldest daughter, Mary, dug a shallow grave in the sand along the bank and laid Isaac to rest just a few feet from the waters of the great river.

Isaac's death raises troubling questions about the maladies suffered by those in the boat. Indeed, the desperate foraging that the children depended upon for their survival made worse their plight since it appears that they unknowingly ingested a poisonous substance that contained a toxin.[31] The McMeans children, and perhaps the adults as well, had fallen into the trap of eating Moonseed fruit, a toxic plant sometimes mistaken for edible wild grapes, and this caused the children's death.[32] The significant clue to this tragedy can be found in the "Beavis" narrative of the McMeans journey because it contains a longer and more complete listing of the foraged foods they ate. In this more detailed version, Anne noted that the children gathered and ate three kinds of grapes: Muscadine, Fox, and a third variety whose name she did not know, calling it simply "a fruit like fox grapes."[33] Given the symptoms of illness manifested by the children in the boat and the ecosystem through which they passed, there is a very high probability that the grape whose name Anne did not know was a plant commonly known as Moonseed today. There are two related species of toxic fruits similar to wild grapes that range in eastern North America: Canadian Moonseed (*Menispermum canadense*) and Carolina Moonseed (*Cocculus carolinus*), both members of the Menispermaceae family.[34] The first of these two plants has a marked similarity to wild fox grapes, and in the fall season throughout the mid-Mississippi valley, Moonseed bears clusters of showy fruit that closely resemble the edible variety of grapes. Although birds are able to eat menispermum, humans cannot without becoming sick, with sometimes fatal consequences, due to the fruit's alkaloid content. One modern authority on the plant has noted: "the fruits are dangerous due to the presence of isoquinoline alkaloids, including dauricine, a compound with curare-like action; they can be mistaken for grapes and deaths have been reported."[35] Even if the adults could recognize Moonseed, and it is not clear that they did, the problem for the McMeans group lay in the fact the children foraged alone on the bank without supervision. Moonseed poisoning is still seen today in younger patients who cannot discern the subtle differences between menispermum and edible grapes, although with medical treatment, it seldom has fatal consequences.[36] As well, Moonseed is even today more toxic to the children who ingest it than adults because a child's lesser body mass makes a smaller ingestion potentially more lethal than that experienced by an adult.[37]

Given this, it was not entirely surprising that the youngest McMeans child, two-year-old Anne, had also been unusually sick and took a bad turn for the worse in the days after Isaac's death. Still a toddler, she had been born after the family had left Pennsylvania for the Kentucky frontier. The day after her older brother's passing, little Anne clearly began exhibiting symptoms of extreme distress similar to those experienced by Isaac. Little Anne clearly also suffered from Moonseed poisoning. She was very lethargic and often unresponsive, although at times she appeared to revive. Her mother gave her some broth made of the few coffee beans they still had on hand. This temporarily revived the young girl, and she seemed somewhat better for almost two days thereafter. At night, however, young Anne would scream and writhe as if she were in great pain. Her mother remembered that the child "would scream out as if some sharp things stabled her to the heart." During one such episode, the two-year-old cried until almost midnight, at which time she became limp and silent. She died shortly after sunrise. Once again, Anne and her oldest daughter, Mary, conducted an impromptu funeral on the riverbank. Clearly exhausted and filled with anguish, Anne later recalled almost clinically that "my oldest daughter and myself buried her in the bank of the river; the warm rays of the sun was very helpful to digging her grave by drying the mud and causing it to open almost wide enough to let her in between three and four foot deep."

These tragic events also had a numbing effect on James Young, who had clearly descended into obtunded thinking, if not some special sort of madness. "He would not so much as touch or come near the dead or dying," Anne complained, "while it was possible to avoid it." Although Young, like the others, was sick, he apparently did little to assist Anne or to deal with their plight. Anne complained that "it is true that he was unwell and weakly, but with all he was able to go about and appeared to be the strongest person in the boat." Nonetheless, Young fell into a mental lethargy and refused to hunt for food or attempt to shoot game. "He was a good marksman and had been a good hunter," she observed, "yet such was his stupidity that he would not use the least endeavor to procure anything that way, nor would he let his own son go out to hunt." At one point, Anne and her oldest son landed the boat because they saw two deer on the shore. Young would not shoot them. All the while, however, Young complained of hunger.

It was at this point that the plight of those in the boat, especially the children, increased dramatically. Shortly after Anne had buried her young daughter, "James Young proposed that one of the children should be put in a lottery," she later recalled. The child selected in the lottery would be killed and eaten by the rest of the party. Young wanted the name of the younger children written on chits of paper and put into the drawing. "I told him," Anne said, "that it was us that brought those innocent children to suffer and I thought that if any was to die to save life, that he or me was the proper objects of this dreadful madness, but I thought it was best to wait for Devine disposal." Young, however, persisted over the next several days, saying it would not be a sin to kill and eat one of the children in order that the rest might live. He finally decided to act. Young wrote the names of the four youngest children in the boat on slips of paper, including those of his own children. He then placed the slips into a hat, along with another one upon which was written a single word: "death." Stricken to the bone, Anne prayed silently as she watched in horror while Young made preparations for the lottery. "Then by his orders," Anne recalled of this gruesome undertaking, "the tickets was drawn and given to me to read." Young's own daughter Mary proved to be the unlucky child. Anne later painted a poignant picture of the scene that followed. Anne watched in a stupor, remembering for the rest of her life the reaction of young Mary to her fate. "As soon as she heard the lot fell on her," Anne remembered that Mary jumped out of the boat "and scarce able to walk, she made her way along the shore." She cried out over and over: "O, Daddy, will you kill me? O, Daddy will you kill me?" Anne watched this horrible scene. "I sat confounded and silent," she noted, but then began to "entreat that he would spare her life till tomorrow, who knows but the land will provide something for our relief."

"Just at this instant," Anne later recalled, to the astonishment of everyone in the boat and to little Mary on the shore, "we heard two dogs bark, a gunfire, and a person speak to the dogs." The shock of these unexpected sounds broke the moment of high tension as all of them began yelling and crying in order to attract the attention of whoever had fired the shot. Pulling the boat to the bank, they soon encountered a Native American man who was out hunting with his family. He explained that he had noticed their boat some hours earlier and had been shadowing it from the bank as it floated down the river in order to determine their intentions. Having witnessed the recent lottery, he understood their circumstances and had fired the shot. He gave them a supply of food, including a quarter of a small bear, along with its heart, lungs, and other entrails. He also provided them with some dried venison. The starving party in the boat ate all of this food in one meal, so the hunter gave them more the following day before he departed. This stayed their starvation for a number of days and made moot the children's lottery, but it did not end their afflictions.

Restored by this unexpected event, Anne and her party resumed their solitary journey southward on the waters of the Mississippi. Young, however, continued his erratic and unpredictable behavior, which increased when they once again ran short of food. Hunger returned to plague those in the boat. One morning, Young renewed his threat to kill and eat one of the children. Anne's oldest daughter told her mother that she had heard Young musing to himself that he would murder one of the children if only he could find a way not to bloody the boat and its contents. Again, however, a chance encounter resolved the desperate situation of the moment. That evening, as they put to shore, they spied a group of Native Americans encamped nearby. The natives drew closer, and this caused some panic in the boat since they clearly belonged to a tribe hostile to Americans, most likely the Chickasaw. To Anne's surprise, they acted friendly and gave them some bear meat. Later that evening, they brought even more meat to the camp of the hapless travelers, but not without a price. The Native Americans robbed them of all their possessions, except for the clothes they were wearing and the boat. Anne noted that "they took our pewter, knives, and forks, and everything they could find that suited them." Left in such destitute circumstances, it was little wonder that Anne once again found herself in a deep depression. Her deep religious convictions were no doubt again reinforced when, at this very time of deepest desperation, relief once more appeared unexpectedly on the scene in the person of Captain Phillip Barbour, a merchant who was routinely engaged in the Mississippi River trade. Barbour was a partner in a Natchez merchant firm. He was carrying a load of badly needed supplies from New Orleans destined for Fort Jefferson and Clarksville, the very place from which the McMeans family had departed weeks earlier. The cargo had been consigned to Barbour for billing to the New Orleans merchant Oliver Pollock.[38] Barbour and his men readily provided those in the boat with biscuits, hominy, and rice in large-enough quantities to forestall any future worries about starvation. He also gave them the welcome news that two of the boats from whom they had become separated weeks earlier lay only a few days below them on the river.

Fortified with food and renewed hope, Anne made haste to catch up with her fellow refugees from Fort Jefferson. Even so, navigating the boat proved to be very difficult. James Young was no help whatsoever, refusing to assist her. Thus, the exhausted party continued on the journey "disconsolate, heartless, and hapless," as Anne later recalled. She did all the work and also tended to the children. The trip still did not go smoothly, again because of Young. One night, James's five-year-old son, who was still sick, fell asleep in the bottom of the boat, lying in the bilge water that had collected there. Young refused to move him, and Anne's efforts to do so were unsuccessful. The boy died soon thereafter. This latest tragedy, however, did not destroy Anne's resolve to rejoin her former traveling companions in the other boats below them on the river. About fourteen days after having been provisioned by Captain Barbour, Anne and the survivors came upon them and happily rejoined the small flotilla of refugees that had earlier departed from Fort Jefferson. Salvation had come. "We were a surprising sight to beholders," Anne noted, and the families with whom they had caught up "thought we could not possibly recover." Now, at last, they had plenty of food, and although they were still on the river over a hundred miles north of Natchez, their hope was completely renewed. They enjoyed a rich larder for the first time in many weeks. This proved to be the downfall for James Young, whose inaction and erratic behavior had been the cause of so much misery for Anne McMeans. At their first Sunday dinner after rejoining the group, Anne recalled, James Young ate such a large meal of bear meat and pumpkins that he became very ill. Within an hour, he was speechless and in great distress. His companions put him to bed, and after a few days of lying in a coma, he died. One of the other families took Young's surviving children as their own. Others in the party cared for Anne McMeans and the remaining youngsters while the group continued their journey down the Mississippi.

Once at Natchez, it took Anne McMeans many months to recover from her ordeal. She recalled of that time: "I was there three months before the color of blood appeared in my hands or feet; nine months before the least sensible impression of either love or hatred was felt in my breast." She credited her eventual recovery to her strong religious faith. Anne took a position as a housekeeper on a plantation in the countryside near Natchez. Her children lived with her. Periodically, she visited Natchez to inquire about boats that might be passing through from Pennsylvania. Anne hoped that eventually she "could find a chance of conveyance" back to her original home near the Forks of the Yough, although she had no funds for the trip. One day in the spring of 1782, she heard that a vessel from Fort Pitt had landed at Natchez. "I went along with the rest to hear the news," she related, "and as soon as I came to the place, I found an old acquaintance by the name of Thomas White." Captain White, she learned, "had heard of my distress and was making enquiry for me." He agreed to take Anne and the children to New Orleans, from whence they would be able to book passage for Philadelphia. She and the children thus found their way back to Pennsylvania from New Orleans during the summer of 1782. They settled in the same region of Pennsylvania from which she and Andrew had departed in 1778. Eventually, she remarried, and all of her surviving children began families of their own as adults. One son eventually returned to Kentucky, where he resettled the land at Floyd's Fork that had been pioneered many years before by his parents at the start of their remarkable adventure.

The gripping historical narrative that Anne later provided of her Mississippi River adventures raises unresolved questions of veracity in the light of modern historical analysis. Is the story of her trip down the Mississippi truthful? Does she embellish her tale with extra drama and exaggerated hyperbole? In short, can she be believed by a modern person who considers the events of her personal story, many details of which cannot be corroborated by separate, independent sources? The publication of the edited version of her narrative in 1824 anticipated these questions. The publisher, Joseph Patterson of Pittsburgh, provided a certification on the title page of the pamphlet containing her narrative that noted: "I have been acquainted with the narrator more than forty years, and believe her to be of excellent character for truth, prudence and piety." He further noted that "she earnestly desired me to publish the narrative of God's dealing with her, during five years of her weary pilgrimage, that her numerous offspring and others might be excited to acknowledge God in all their ways."[39] The basic nature of this pamphlet as a self-conscious religious tract, quite naturally, does permit the possibility of embellishment and ex post facto interpretation on the part of Anne McMeans, especially since research has been unable to date the actual writing of the narrative in chronological relationship to the events it relates. Nonetheless, many of the people and events that Anne does describe in her narrative touching on the settlement of Louisville, the building of Fort Jefferson, and the events that occurred there can be clearly substantiated by numerous other extant historical sources, many of which would not have been available to a writer living in the early nineteenth century. One can thus absolutely assert without question that Anne McMeans really existed, as did her family, and that they indeed participated in many of the events that are accurately noted in her narrative. Such assertions, however, cannot prove per se the veracity or accuracy of the particular events noted about "her weary pilgrimage" on the Mississippi except for one event. Her meeting with Captain Philip Barbour remains as indisputable evidence of her voyage. Although Barbour apparently never mentioned meeting her in any extant documents, independent sources can be mustered to substantiate that he was indeed sailing north on the Mississippi at the very time he provided

Anne and her party with food and supplies.[40] It thus falls to each person who contemplates Anne's remarkable story to decide for himself the full truth of the sad events noted in her narrative of the voyage.

Beyond such judgments, however, Anne's experiences on the Mississippi River during the American Revolution do give a personal dimension to the efforts that hundreds of frontier folk made in settling the Ohio and Mississippi River valleys during the late eighteenth and early nineteenth centuries. Her story drives home the reality that these efforts were as much the work of women as of men, and they also give a powerful clue to the role that religious faith played in these efforts. Anne lived to publish the edited version of her adventures in 1824. She died two years later and lies buried in the graveyard of a Presbyterian church at Perry Township, Pennsylvania.[41] Her grave sits far away from the others in that small churchyard along a distant wall, alone and by itself. To the present day, a local legend in that small community still holds that this solitary resting place was Anne's dying wish, to be left alone away from others, and there she remains to this day.[42] Although she has been at rest for almost two centuries, her enduring legacy continues in the thousands of descendants who owe their lives to the children whom she helped survive during their hard voyage down the Mississippi River. Anne's experiences on the frontiers of Spanish Louisiana serve as a stark historical testimony reconfirming, for all those who read her remarkable story, the notion that the greatest reservoirs of courage in the human spirit can sometimes be found in the most seemingly commonplace of individuals.

Notes

1. Light Townsend Cummins, "Oliver Pollock and George Rogers Clark's Service of Supply: A Case Study in Financial Disaster," in *Selected Papers from the 1985 and 1986 George Rogers Clark Trans-Appalachian Frontier History Conferences*, ed. Robert J. Holden (Vincennes, IN.: National Park Service, 1988), 1–13; J. G. Randall, "George Rogers Clark's Service of Supply," *Mississippi Valley Historical Review* 8 (1921): 250–63; James A. James, *Oliver Pollock: The Life and Times of an Unknown Patriot* (New York: Appleton-Century, 1937); Light T. Cummins, "Oliver Pollock's Plantations: An Early Anglo Landowner on the Lower Mississippi, 1769–1824," *Louisiana History* 29 (Winter 1988): 35–48.

2. This essay is based on a manuscript at the Newberry Library in Chicago, Illinois, that has not been previously cited by scholars. This document came into the

possession of the Newberry Library by purchase from a dealer in 1929. It is located in the Ayer Collection as Manuscript 691. The manuscript is a narrative memoir written later in life by Anne McMeans, in which she recounts her journey down the Mississippi River in 1780. No scholar has previously identified it as Anne McMeans's full narrative because this manuscript has been erroneously catalogued. Initially, the bibliographer attributed this manuscript to a person named Sarah Peairs, based on a misreading of a name written on the first page. Later, a recataloging of the manuscript determined the name to be Sarah Beavis. The cataloger apparently listed Sarah Beavis as the author in the Newberry cataloging system because the first page of the manuscript carries the handwritten notation, "Sarah Beavis Her Pamphlet." Examination of the manuscript, however, definitively substantiates that it is indeed a handwritten manuscript of the narrative of Anne McMeans. It is the opinion of the author that the miscataloging occurred because Sarah Beavis was its owner at some date in the provenance of the manuscript before it became part of the Ayer Collection. Sarah Beavis's name on the first page of the manuscript should hence be taken as a statement of possession rather than authorship, especially since her name is written in an observably different style of handwriting from the contents of the narrative. Substantiation of authorship is not difficult because the text of the narrative has not been completely unknown to scholarship. The 1824 published edition of the narrative, with significant editing, along with several other little-noticed extant versions that are based on it, can be found in various archival repositories. The "Beavis" manuscript at the Newberry Library, however, provides much additional, very rich, and more detailed information beyond the 1824 edited version and those that later flowed from it, all of which have failed to attract much historical attention as primary sources.

3. Anne Jamison, *An Interesting Narrative*, ed. Joseph Patterson (Pittsburgh: J. Patterson, 1824). This edition has been reprinted as part of The Garland Library of Narratives of North American Indian Captives Series, number 37 (New York: Garland, 1977).

4. My research has identified a number of different versions of the Anne McMeans narrative, most of which are obscure and/or inconveniently accessible to modern readers. Each of these have differences one from the other, and none of them are as complete as the one at the Newberry Library. Since Anne McMeans subsequently had a second marriage after her return to Pennsylvania, the 1824 published edition appeared under the author name of Anne Jamison. See Jamison, *An Interesting Narrative*. Additional versions include a handwritten copy located in the Draper Manuscript Collection of the Wisconsin Historical Society. See Carl R. Baldwin, *Captain of the Wilderness* (Belleville, IL: Tiger Rose, 1986), 180. In 1919, one of Anne's descendants donated a typescript copy of her narrative to the Filson Club of Louisville, Kentucky, where it remains today. H. H. Glenn to the Filson Club, April 12, 1919, St. Paul, MN, Manuscript Department, Filson Historical Society, Louisville, KY. The Filson Historical Society typescript has been edited, annotated, and published by Kenneth C. Carstens and Sara Jean Rivers as "Life on the

Eighteenth Century Frontier: The Narrative of Anne McMeans Jamison," *Filson Club Historical Quarterly* 74 (2000): 31–44. In 1932, an attorney from St. Paul, Minnesota, furnished a copy of the H. H. Glenn version to the local newspaper in Wickliffe, Kentucky, which published an abbreviated and edited version. See "Indians Drove Old Settlers away from Fort Jefferson," *Ballard Yeoman* (Wickliffe, KY), November 4, 1938, 6. A McMeans descendant, Robert Aiken, included yet another version of the narrative in a small pamphlet that he published in 1904. This was reprinted for distribution at a family reunion in the 1960s. *Annals of the Robert Aiken Family* (Cleveland: privately printed, 1964). The Historical Society of Pennsylvania in Philadelphia holds a copy of this pamphlet, along with a typescript index to it. See "Index to the Annals of the Robert Aiken Family," typescript, Family History Room. Another McMeans descendant has posted a hypertext copy of the narrative on the internet. See "Re: Andrew McMeans (B. 1740 in Marylan [*sic*]," February 27, 2002, https://www.genealogy.com/forum/surnames/topics/mcmains/229/ (accessed April 27, 2005).

5. A McMeans descendant has written a novel in the romance genre that is based on Anne's narrative. This novelization is mostly fiction but does recount as part of its storyline most of the events described in the 1824 narrative, albeit with a good measure of literary embellishment. See Martha Barron Barrett, *God's Country* (New York: Bantam Books, 1987).

6. The couple had eight children.

7. "Willson Pedigree," posted by Annette Holms, January 26, 2003, www.ancestry.comicgi-bin.cgi?op+AHN&db=.2367159&id4511641919 (subscription required, accessed August 24, 2004). See also Richard E. Willson, *The Willson Family, 1672–1959* (Ottawa, IL, 1979); and Willson, *Willson Family Supplement, 1959–1979* (Ottawa, IL, 1979); Martha Emma Hutcheson Wilson, *The Willson Family Tree* (Wampello, IA: Louisa Publishing, 1956); and John H. Wilson, *The Willson (Wilson) Family* (Fort Worth: J. H. Wilson, 1970).

8. This dispute was eventually resolved by splitting the area. The location where the McMeans lived is now part of Pennsylvania. Alfred Creigh, *History of Washington County: From Its First Settlement to the Present Time. . . .* (1871; repr., Apollo, PA: B. Singerly Printer, 1987).

9. Deed Book C, Washington County, PA, September 24, 1778, www.uh.edu/-jbuler/geankuthapplegate.html (accessed September 10, 2004; URL no longer valid).

10. This information comes from the McMeans family Bible, which at this writing is in the personal possession of Wayne McMeins, a descendent. Wayne McMeins to the author, August 30, 2004, letter in possession of the author. See also "Re: Andrew McMeans (1780)," April 28, 2000, https://www. genealogy.com/forum/surnames/topics/mcmains/136/ (accessed July 10, 2004).

11. Light Townsend Cummins, *Spanish Observers and the American Revolution, 1775–1783* (Baton Rouge: Louisiana State University Press, 1991), 85; John W. Caughey, *Bernardo de Gálvez in Louisiana, 1776–1783* (Berkeley: University of California Press, 1934), 56.

12. Robert V. Haynes, *The Natchez District and the American Revolution* (Jackson: University Press of Mississippi, 1976), 58–72; John W. Caughey, "Willing's Expedition down the Mississippi in 1778," *Louisiana Historical Quarterly* 15 (January 1932): 5–36.

13. James A. James, *The Life of George Rogers Clark* (Chicago: University of Chicago Press, 1928; repr., New York: Greenwood, 1969): 114–15; Lowell Harrison, "George Rogers Clark: The Early Years," in *The Life of George Rogers Clark, 1752–1818*, ed. Kenneth C. Carstens and Nancy Son Carstens (Westport, CT: Greenwood, 2004), 7–17.

14. George H. Yater, *Two Hundred Years at the Falls of the Ohio: A History of Louisville and Jefferson County* (Louisville, KY: Heritage, 1979), 17–18.

15. Kathleen Jennings, *Louisville's First Families: A Series of Genealogical Sketches* (Louisville, KY: Standard Printing, 1920), 166.

16. The junction of Floyd's Fork and the Salt River is located a few miles east of present-day Shepherdsville, Kentucky, in Jefferson County, approximately twenty miles south of Louisville. *Rand-McNally Commercial Atlas and Marketing Guide* (New York: Rand-McNally, 2000), 171.

17. Robert E. McDowell, "Bullitt's Lick: The Related Salt Works and Settlements," *Filson Club Quarterly* 30 (1936): 240–69.

18. Yater, *Two Hundred Years at the Falls*, 18.

19. This quotation comes from the "Beavis" version of the Anne McMeans narrative, which is located at the Newberry Library. All subsequent quotations in this article are taken directly from this manuscript, with some modernization of spelling and punctuation.

20. The discussion of the history of Fort Jefferson in the following paragraphs is based on the work of Kenneth C. Carstens, who has published numerous studies examining the fort as part of a longstanding, comprehensive documentary-research and historical-archeological project dealing with its site near modern Wycliffe, Kentucky, which he has supervised for over a quarter century. See Carstens, *George Rogers Clark's Fort Jefferson, 1780–1781: Kentucky's Outpost on the Western Frontier* (Berwyn Heights, MD: Heritage Books, 2005); Carstens, comp. and ed., *The Calendar and Quartermaster Books of General George Rogers Clark's Fort Jefferson, Kentucky, 1780–1781* (Bowie, MD: Heritage Books, 2000); Carstens, "George Rogers Clark's Fort Jefferson, 1780–1781," *Filson Club Historical Quarterly* 71 (1997): 259–84; Carstens, "The Role of Women in Kentucky's Western Colonial Frontier," in *Historical Archaeology in Kentucky*, ed. Kim A. McBride et al. (Frankfort: Kentucky Heritage Council, 1995), 157–67; Carstens, "The 1780 William Clark Map of Fort Jefferson," *Filson Club Historical Quarterly* 67 (1993): 23–43; Carstens, "Fort Jefferson, 1780–1781: A Summary of Its History," in *Selected Papers from the 1991 and 1992 George Rogers Clark Trans-Appalachian History Conference*, ed. Robert J. Holden (Vincennes, IN: National Park Service, 1994), 43–58; Carstens, "Praise the Lord and Pass the Ammunition: Munition Supplies at George Rogers Clark's Fort Jefferson, 1780–1781," in *Selected Papers from the 1989 and 1990 George Rogers*

Clark Trans-Appalachian History Conference, ed. Robert J. Holden (Vincennes, IN: National Park Service, 1991), 21–32.

21. James H. O'Donnell III, *Southern Indians in the American Revolution* (Knoxville: University of Tennessee Press, 1973), 92; Guy Braden, "The Colberts and the Chickasaw Nation," *Tennessee Historical Quarterly* 17 (1958): 222–23.

22. Piggott was a native of Connecticut who served in the Eighth Pennsylvania Regiment during the early years of the American Revolution. He had lived in Westmoreland County, Pennsylvania, near the McMeanses, most likely knowing them as neighbors. Piggott became associated with George Rogers Clark in recruiting the first families who settled Corn Island in 1778. Later, after the failure of Fort Jefferson, Piggott moved to the St. Louis area, where he eventually became a territorial judge. He spent his final years living at Cahokia, where he operated a ferryboat service on the Mississippi River. For Piggott's biography, see Baldwin, *Captain of the Wilderness*, esp. 178–85.

23. Kenneth C. Carstens notes that the document referred to by Anne was probably not a settlement agreement for the civilians going to Clarksville. "No records indicating that the Fort Jefferson civilians signed with a land company have been discovered," he has observed. Instead, he believes that the document was probably the muster-roll agreement since Andrew McMeans did serve in the militia unit commanded by James Piggott at Fort Jefferson and Clarksville. Carstens and Rivers, "Life on the Eighteenth Century Frontier," 34. There is a high likelihood of this having been the case regarding that document. Indeed, it should be noted that the Filson Historical Society typescript of the narrative, edited by Professor Carstens and Sara Jean Rivers, refers to the document as having been an "agreement with the company," while the orthographic "Beavis" manuscript instead says only that "he had added his name to [the] paper."

24. Based on the location of artifacts, Kenneth Carstens had concluded that "the site of Fort Jefferson was not located on top of 'Fort Jefferson Hill,' where a roadside historical marker is located, but rather about a half-mile south of the hill, 200 feet west of Kentucky highway 51, and approximately a half-mile east of the present Mississippi." Carstens, "Fort Jefferson: A Summary," 45. An infrared aerial photograph and map of the area appears in Carstens, *George Rogers Clark's Fort Jefferson*, 207–9. Fort Jefferson Hill, which affords a breathtaking western panorama of the Mississippi River, is today the location of a ninety-five-foot-high metal cross, which constitutes one of the major landmarks along that section of the river. Mark R. Chellgren, "Non-Denominational Cross: A Contradiction in Terms," *Kentucky Post* (Covington), April 27, 2000.

25. Gregory F. Holm, "Supply Issues of the Illinois Regiment under George Rogers Clark," in Carstens and Carstens, *Life of George Rogers Clark*, 148–75.

26. Pollock had great difficulty securing supplies for the fort due to the state of Virginia's poor credit. He complained to Captain Robert George about this in several of his letters to the commander of Fort Jefferson. "Notwithstanding I have done everything that can be done for that intent," he wrote Captain George, "and have

reason to believe that something favorable must turn up, but in the meantime you must have a little more patience and be as frugal as possible." James, *Oliver Pollock,* 226.

27. Thomas E. Chavez, *Spain and the Independence of the United States: An Intrinsic Gift* (Albuquerque: University of New Mexico Press, 2002): 169–72.

28. J. Barton Starr, *Tories, Dons, and Rebels: The American Revolution in British West Florida* (Gainesville: University Press of Florida, 1976), 156–57.

29. At the author's request, a group of faculty members from the medical staff at the University of Texas Health Science Center at San Antonio reviewed the symptoms noted in the "Beavis" version of Anne's narrative. They concluded that the symptoms experienced early in the voyage, before starvation complicated their conditions, were consistent with the progression of malaria. Dr. Ronald Philo, UTHSC-San Antonio, to the author, December 12, 2004, letter in possession of the author. The incubation period for malaria is from ten to thirty-five days, after which there occurs "irregular low-grade fever, malaise, headache, myalgia, and chilly sensations." This would indicate that the McMeanses had already contracted the disease before their departure. The symptoms of malaria follow a cyclical course since, after a time, they lessen and the patient feels better, only to experience thereafter recurring episodes, each one more severe. Robert Berow, *Merck Manual of Diagnosis and Therapy* (Rahway, NJ: Merck, 1982), 239–40.

30. Carstens and Rivers also agree that those in the McMeans boat suffered from malaria. Carstens and Rivers, "Life on the Eighteenth Century Frontier," 36. During the eighteenth and nineteenth centuries, the mid-Mississippi valley was considered to be particularly endemic for malaria contagion. Indeed, it may have been so common that many reported historical cases of "fever" and "ague" might have been cases of malaria. As one epidemiological study of this region notes: "Textbooks of medical geography, memoirs, travel reports, army statistics, and medical journals of the period all agree that malaria was the American disease and, while the older states had emerged from its worst vexation, its hotbed was what was up to the 1850s still called 'the west,' the valley of the Mississippi and its tributaries." Erwin H. Ackerkenecht, *Malaria in the Upper Mississippi Valley, 1760–1900* (Baltimore: Ayer, 1945), 16.

31. After reviewing the physical symptoms presented by the McMeans children who died, Dr. Ronald Philo of the University of Texas Health Science at San Antonio suggests that ingestion of a toxic substance, instead of malaria, caused the death of the youngest children. The progression of symptoms suffered by Isaac and the other children who later died does not indicate malaria as the cause of death. Instead, Dr. Philo notes, regarding the smaller children, that "it is more likely they ate or drank possibly something different between the adults and children." Dr. Ronald Philo to the author, December 12, 2004, letter in possession of the author.

32. In humans, ingestion of Moonseed fruit causes abdominal pain, lethargy, confused thinking, and convulsions. The symptoms suffered by the children in the McMeans boat are consistent with this course of illness. Additionally, it may be

that James Young and Anne ate Moonseed since they also manifested symptoms consistent with this toxin in addition to their malarial condition, especially Young, who clearly suffered from obtunded thinking and mental confusion. The toxins in Moonseed grapes cause rapid and profound liver damage that manifests as signs of liver failure, which may include weight loss, depression, and other abnormal behavior, jaundice, and anemia. See R. J. Huxtable, "The Toxicity of Alkaloids in Foods and Herbs," in *Food Poisoning Handbook of Natural Toxins*, ed. Anthony T. Tu (New York: CRC, 1992), 237–62. These are typical symptoms of acute viral hepatitis, which is today usually caused by substance ingestion. Berkow, *Merck Manual of Diagnosis and Therapy*, 839.

33. Fox grapes are a species of edible grape that appears wild throughout the eastern United States.

34. "This wood-twining vine grows to twelve feet. The large, broad leaves are eight inches long and slightly lobed, resembling grape leaves but with smoother edges. The grape-like fruit forms in clusters and is bluish black with a crescent-shaped pit. The plant may be confused with wild grape." Kenneth F. Lampe and Mary Ann McCann, *AMA Handbook of Poisonous and Injurious Plants* (Chicago: American Medical Association, 1985), 117. See also Walter Conrad Muenscher, *Poisonous Plants of the United States* (New York; Macmillan, 1951), 94.

35. George M. Diggs Jr., et al., *Shinners and Mahler's Illustrated Flora of North Central Texas* (Fort Worth: Botanical Research Institute of Texas, 1999), 824.

36. For the natural range of Moonseed in the Mississippi valley, see George E. Burrows and Ronald J. Tyrl, *Toxic Plants of North America* (Ames: Iowa State University Press, 2001), 1233.

37. As one authority notes, "the fruit, however, look like small purple grapes, and may easily be mistaken for the latter by children. Loss of life in children has been reported." John M. Kingsbury, *Poisonous Plants of the United States and Canada* (Englewood Cliffs, NJ: Prentice-Hall, 1964), 147. See also Carol Lerner, *Moonseed and Mistletoe: A Book of Poisonous Wild Plants* (New York: William Morrow, 1988).

38. Barbour was bringing goods to the Illinois country, which Pollock was sending as supplies to the fort. Pollock wrote to George Rogers Clark: "This will be handed you by Capt. Philip Barbour whom I beg leave to recommend to your protection. . . . He carries some cloathing [*sic*] and other Articles with him for Sale, which I hope you'll find useful for your Troops." Barbour's shipment also included sugar, tafia, soap, coffee, tobacco, writing paper, saws, carpenter's tools, rum, swords, gunflints, and powder. This would prove to be the last shipment that Pollock ever sent to Fort Jefferson. James, *Oliver Pollock*, 216–17; Carstens, *George Rogers Clark's Fort Jefferson*, 211.

39. Jamison, *An Interesting Narrative*, 1.

40. Various historical documents note that Barbour brought a large shipment of goods from New Orleans to Fort Jefferson on an upriver voyage during November and December. For a full discussion of this trip, see Holm, "Supply Issues of the Illinois Regiment," 158–60. Discussion of this trip also appears in the papers of

Robert Morris, chair of the Secret Committee of Correspondence at the Continental Congress. E. James Ferguson et al., "Morris Diary, September 27, 1782, Philadelphia," in *The Papers of Robert Morris, 1781–1784*, 9 vols. (Pittsburgh: University of Pittsburg Press, 1973), 6:441.

41. Dwight Edward Cooper, *Cemeteries of Lawrence County Pennsylvania, Book 8, Perry Township, Washington Township* (Apollo, PA: Closson, 1990), 8.

42. Reverend Donald Hurray, pastor of the Mountville Presbyterian Church, Perry Township, PA, to the author, September 10, 2004, letter in possession of the author.

CHAPTER 6

Oliver Pollock's Plantations

An Early Anglo Landowner on the Lower Mississippi, 1769–1824

As noted several other places in this volume, British West Florida attracted thousands of English-speaking settlers to the lower Mississippi valley during the 1760s in the decade before the American Revolution, after which it became Spanish territory, and many of them remained as residents under the rule of Spain. They rebelled, however, in 1810 and declared the Republic of West Florida, that area that later became part of the state of Louisiana and is known today as the "Florida Parishes." The English-speaking residents in that part of Spanish Louisiana were by 1803 the southern edge of an arch of Anglo-American settlements running from the upper Ohio valley, down through the great confluence of the Ohio and the Mississippi, and south to New Orleans and its environs. By the end of the eighteenth century, at the time of the Louisiana Purchase, these settlers had established the towns of Louisville, Potosi, Herculaneum, and New Madrid. Older cities from the Spanish era, including St. Louis, Natchez, and Baton Rouge, along with settlements on the Amite River north of Lake Pontchartrain, also gained large English-speaking populations prior to the Louisiana Purchase. These towns and their hinterlands created a continuous line of settlements down the Mississippi River that would become jumping-off places for further movements into Texas, the Spanish Southwest, and beyond to California. The nineteenth-century beginnings of what would become known in US history as Manifest Destiny began along the Mississippi River in Spanish Louisiana during the late eighteenth century.

Archival land records relating to these Mississippi valley settlements are mostly extant today. Such historical documents, often including titles and survey records, have survived because land is an economic asset passed from generation to generation. These land transactions trace the pathways followed by many individual settlers as they moved into Spanish territory and beyond, sometimes several times during one person's lifetime. It is thus possible for historians to make aggregate statements about these demographic movements while they can also speak to specific people across time. Some of these landholdings remained in the same families for many decades. This proved to be the case for Oliver Pollock, who counted himself a member of the commercial elite in the lower Mississippi valley from the 1760s to the 1820s. One of the first properties he secured became one of his most profitable and enduring enterprises, purchasing plantation land at Tunica Bend, on the river north of Baton Rouge, in partnership with James Willing. This landholding remained in his family down to the Civil War. It constitutes for the historian a meaningful case study in one individual's landownership along the Mississippi as a representative example of the Anglo-Americanization of Spanish Louisiana. The early chapters of Samuel A. Hyde's *A Fierce and Fractious Frontier: The Curious Development of Louisiana's Florida Parishes, 1699–2000* (2004) provides much context for the settlement of Tunica Bend.

Light Townsend Cummins, "Oliver Pollock's Plantations: An Early Anglo Landowner on the Lower Mississippi, 1769–1824," *Louisiana History* 29 (Winter 1988): 35–48.

OLIVER POLLOCK provided timely assistance to the rebel cause as the congressional commercial agent at New Orleans during the American Revolution, thereby earning the historical reputation as the "Financier of the Revolution in the West."[1] In 1776 and 1777, he shipped gunpowder from Spain and Cuba via the Mississippi River to George

Washington's army. He also superintended the supply efforts that provisioned the expeditions of James Willing and George Rogers Clark. Although studies of his patriot efforts during the Revolution abound, no historian has heretofore examined in detail Pollock's personal business transactions in the Mississippi valley. This essay will survey the landholding career of Oliver Pollock as an Anglo merchant and planter who came to the region prior to the Revolution, who owned extensive lands in British and Spanish territory, and who retained these holdings under the subsequent rule of the United States. His experiences and activities in this regard were typical of a larger group of Anglo settlers who came to the lower Mississippi as landowners in the years prior to the Revolution. They were the vanguard of Anglo-American settlement in Spanish colonial Louisiana.[2]

An analysis of Pollock's personal business transactions is complicated by the fact that all of his personal papers and records were destroyed during the Civil War when a Federal gunboat shelled the home of a descendant at Bayou Sara, Louisiana. There is, however, a wealth of information about his private transactions, which exists in the public records of the various governments under which Pollock lived in the lower Mississippi valley. These historical sources are widely dispersed in the various archives of England, Spain, and the United States due to the shifting territorial sovereignty and fortunes of war in the region during the late 1770s and early 1780s. In many cases, records about Pollock do not exist in their entirety, and many that are extant offer vague or conflicting evidence. Such is not true for an important and little-used source available to any historian who wishes to study Anglo settlers who came to the Mississippi valley prior to the American Revolution: land records. The British-era land documents and grant maps are intact at the Public Record Office in London.[3] The Spanish land grants and sale transactions can be found either as part of the conveyances in various Louisiana parishes or scattered among archival collections in the United States.[4] Many of these documents (either in the original or by certified copy) are easily consulted today because they came into the possession of the governments of Louisiana or the United States after 1803, when landowners pressed for American reconfirmation of British and Spanish land titles.

These land records permit the historian to learn much in general about the individual careers of Anglo settlers along the lower Mississippi and about Oliver Pollock in particular.

Given this, it must be understood that when Oliver Pollock arrived in the lower Mississippi valley during 1769, he carried with him citizenship as a subject of King George III and took full advantage of this status in West Florida. British West Florida and Spanish Louisiana shared a common boundary in the years between the Peace of Paris (1763) and the American Revolution, when the holdings of Great Britain thereafter became Spanish territory. Prior to the military conquests of Bernardo de Gálvez in 1779, the east bank of the Mississippi north of the Iberville River (located between Baton Rouge and New Orleans) was part of British West Florida. The entire west bank of the Mississippi and the Isle of Orleans, which included the city of New Orleans, along with land on the east bank south of the Iberville, belonged to Spain. To the British authorities in the West Florida capital of Pensacola, Pollock was, prior to the Revolution, only one of many Anglo merchant-planters trading along the Mississippi and Gulf coast, except, unlike some of the others, he had been more fortunate in cultivating support and acceptance from the Spanish government at New Orleans.[5]

During his business career in the region prior to the Revolution, Pollock received land grants from the West Florida authorities, operated plantations in English territory, later had some of his British titles confirmed by the Spanish after the revolt, and maintained these plantations until his death in 1824. In addition, various members of his family moved into the area and secured additional land. The Pollock family's landholding history in lower Louisiana seems to have been illustrative of other British-era proprietors who stayed in the region to live under the Spanish and then the American government. Indeed, Pollock's descendants continued to live on their holdings along the Mississippi River for generations.

Oliver Pollock came to the Mississippi valley in 1769 on the heels of the military expedition led by Spanish general Alejandro O'Reilly, who was sent to reassert Spain's control over Louisiana after the abortive governorship of Antonio de Ulloa. Pollock, representing the Philadelphia firm of Willing and Morris, for whom he had been a correspondent for six years at Havana, clearly sought to curry favor with O'Reilly, an individual he had first met years before in Cuba. Pollock visited with O'Reilly on the Spanish flagship while it lay at anchor below New Orleans. Based on these discussions, O'Reilly, even before arriving in New Orleans, awarded Pollock a contract to supply the city with flour. This arrangement provided Pollock with the firm base upon which he established, over the next few years, a successful merchant house that operated both in Spanish Louisiana and British West Florida.[6]

The Spanish government (especially under the regime of Luis de Unzaga) tolerated Anglo merchants like Pollock, along with John Fitzpatrick, Charles Strachan, David Ross, and many others, because it had no alternative if the colony's economy were to continue functioning. These persons traveled freely between Spanish Louisiana and British West Florida. They imported needed commodities into Louisiana and ensured capital migration into the Spanish province. Like others in this group, Pollock speedily opened a lucrative trade between the Mississippi valley and Philadelphia via the Gulf of Mexico and the Atlantic Ocean. In addition, he frequently traveled throughout West Florida and maintained a residence there as well, although he made his primary home in New Orleans, where he operated a merchant house.

Between 1769 and 1775, Pollock received several major grants of land in British West Florida under the terms for awarding such to subjects of King George III.[7] As well, he bought land from other British grantees who wished to sell.[8] In all, he owned four large tracts of land in West Florida in addition to lots in several of the English towns. One of his earliest grants from the British government was made in 1769 for four hundred acres on the Tangipahoa River some thirteen miles north of Pass Manchac.[9] Other than this grant, however, Pollock favored land on the Mississippi River because of its obvious financial value and geographic convenience to New Orleans. He secured two tracts from the British in this district: acreage immediately south of Baton Rouge, upon which today stands part of the campus of Louisiana State University, and a second holding on the east bank of the river across from Pointe Coupee. Both of these properties had improvements on them, including houses, and Pollock operated them as plantations during the British period.[10]

During the early 1770s, Pollock also interested several of his business colleagues in securing lands in British West Florida. Robert Morris and Thomas Willing, the Philadelphia merchants for whom he served as corresponding agent, secured two grants on the Mississippi from authorities in Pensacola. Pollock organized these tracts as working plantations and hired a resident manager, Alexander Henderson, who operated them for the firm of Willing and Morris. Henderson had thirty-four slaves on these two tracts and successfully grew rice prior to the Revolution.[11]

These plantations, located immediately adjacent to the river, were well suited to the method of rice cultivation employed on the lower Mississippi during this era. Their fields could be conveniently flooded by constructing a small system of levees. Rice was sown as bedding plants in time for the spring floods, the high water from which flowed into the paddies through diversion canals. After the water had stood for approximately two weeks, it was drained from the young plants into neighboring swampland by means of secondary ditches. Once the rice matured, a second flooding from the river covered the crop until shortly before harvest time. Slaves then cut the rice with sickles, bound it into bundles, and thrashed it by hand. Although rice production satisfied the local market, it never became a significant crop because of the need for intensive labor and the limited amount of land suitable for growing it. In addition, many colonists considered it an inferior food reserved for slaves and the poorer classes. Nevertheless, the growers of rice found a steady market for it in New Orleans.[12] Pollock served as financial manager for the Willing and Morris rice plantations, kept their accounts, and operated as their factor in New Orleans. By the mid-1770s, however, he fell into controversy with Henderson, the overseer. Both men accused the other of mismanagement, and with falling rice prices, Thomas Willing attempted unsuccessfully to remove Pollock from active management in this venture.[13]

Pollock found greater favor with members of the Willing family other than Thomas. James Willing, a younger brother of Morris's partner, became Pollock's most significant associate in the Mississippi River plantations. Young Willing came to the region at Oliver Pollock's invitation. The New Orleans merchant had become convinced that the most important and potentially valuable land on the Mississippi between Baton Rouge and Natchez could be found at Tunica Bend. Here the river made a sharp turn where two bayous, Tunica and Spring, entered the Mississippi on the east bank. Moreover, the two small streams joined at the foot of a hill that was high enough to be safe from flooding. Land at Tunica Bend had early attracted the interest of various individuals who had passed through the region. Rufus Putnam visited the bayous in 1772 while on a trip through West Florida. He was most impressed with the site, which he noted in his journal would be the perfect location for a settlement. A later traveler described the area as "a rich and hospitable country."[14] British grants made in the late 1760s deeded this area in two separate tracts to Henry Fairchild and General Frederick Haldimand.[15]

Pollock proposed to James Willing in 1772 that they create a partnership to purchase and develop this land. Willing secured the hilly area along Spring Bayou from General Haldimand and, by late 1772, was engaged in the growing of rice and corn. He built a magazine on the high ground and opened a small trading post on the bank of the river.[16] Pollock purchased the tract to the north along Tunica Bayou from Henry Fairchild.[17] Both partners built houses for themselves on the property, which was managed as one plantation. For a time during the late eighteenth century, Spring Bayou temporarily became known as Willing's Bayou, thereafter taking the name of Pollock's Bayou, a designation by which it is still known today. Pollock purchased Willing's land shortly before the outbreak of the Revolution and combined the tracts into one holding, which eventually became known as the "Old Tunica Plantation." Here Pollock planted indigo and regularly made crops of rice, tobacco, and vegetables. Vessels passing on the Mississippi routinely stopped to purchase supplies and foodstuffs at the small trading post. A cousin from Pennsylvania, Hamilton Pollock, arrived in the mid-1770s to live at Tunica Bend and oversee the operation of the plantation. This arrangement would continue until his death in 1814, with the exception of a period during the 1780s when wartime debts removed the Pollock family from control of Old Tunica Plantation.[18]

The plantation became locally known for its indigo crop. During the 1770s, in fact, the entire area along the river north of Baton Rouge became an important area for indigo production. The planters at Pointe Coupee, for example, made a total of 50,000 pounds of dyestuff in 1775, while most producers on both banks of the river had plantings that yielded at least 75 pounds of refined indigo per acre. Since indigo dye usually sold for a dollar per pound, this represented an attractive crop for most planters. In addition to Pollock and his plantations, the holdings of Isaac Monsanto, Maurice Conway, Benjamin Farrar, John McCarty, and Patrick MacNamara all produced large crops of the blue dye. Many Englishmen of the era, including the author Captain Philip Pittman, considered Mississippi valley indigo to be superior in quality to that grown in the Carolinas and the West Indies. Old Tunica Plantation continued to prosper with this crop to the close of the Spanish period, although demand for the dyestuff outside Louisiana lessened by the end of the century because of Spain's restrictive trade laws.[19]

By 1776, Oliver Pollock had thus emerged as one of the most prosperous merchants and landowners in the lower Mississippi valley. He invested in lucrative ventures and had ample capital for various business transactions. From his base at New Orleans, he operated an extensive mercantile network and also bought real estate in Spanish territory. He purchased a house on present-day Royal Street in New Orleans at public auction in December 1777, reselling it to James Harris less than three months later.[20] He also secured land during 1769 to the north of New Orleans in Spanish territory, including a tract that would, in a later era, become part of Elmwood Plantation.[21] The American Revolution changed for all time Pollock's economic position when he became the most prominent supporter of the rebel cause in the Mississippi valley. He used the safe residence extended to him in Spanish territory by a succession of governors to support the Americans. In so doing, Pollock lost his own personal fortune in the process.[22]

His landholdings in West Florida, however, remained intact. In spite of the rebel activities of some West Floridians, the British apparently made no move to expropriate lands from pro-American partisans. The 1779 campaigns of Bernardo de Gálvez, at any rate, removed the British from the Mississippi and ended this risk. The Mississippi River district of British West Florida fell to Spanish control. Although Governor Gálvez did nothing to legitimize British land titles in Spanish law, all Anglo landowners who remained in the region retained at least de facto control of their properties until the policies of Governor Esteban Miró, formulated between 1785 and 1787, permitted legal reconfirmation.[23]

Financial losses caused by his support of the Americans, however, forced Oliver Pollock to return to the Atlantic coast at the close of the Revolution, and in the process, he lost many of his landholdings to creditors. By 1781, his personal debts in Louisiana had become considerable: he owed the Spanish government 74,087 pesos, which had been borrowed in the name of the Continental Congress, while he found himself in debt for an additional 29,440 pesos to various New Orleans residents. Pollock declared bankruptcy in early 1782 and liquidated many of his assets and personal possessions in an effort to satisfy his debts.[24] By February of that year, he had assigned to individual creditors his slaveholdings, his residential property in New Orleans, and the Mississippi River lands near Baton Rouge and Pointe Coupee, while Old Tunica Plantation became the property of Carlos Trudeau.[25] In late April 1782, he left Louisiana and returned to the United States.[26] He saw this trip as the only way by which he could personally lobby Congress to repay the loans he had negotiated in New Orleans on its behalf. His absence from Louisiana would last six years, take him to a Cuban prison, and have both Congress and the state of Virginia question his claims for reimbursement.

The period of Oliver Pollock's absence from the lower Mississippi valley, however, did not mean that he was completely forgotten. Thomas Patterson had Pollock's general power of attorney in New Orleans and continued to negotiate disputes with the creditors. In addition, the elder Daniel Clark acted as correspondent for Pollock in various business dealings directed from Cuba and the Atlantic coast. Pollock maintained a credit account with Clark, whom he already owed money stemming from Revolutionary War debts.[27] Having secured a partial repayment from Congress and Virginia, Pollock returned to Louisiana in 1788. He arrived in New Orleans shortly after the disastrous fire of that year.

Taking advantage of increased demand for supplies needed for the rebuilding effort, Pollock sold building materials to local residents. He also convinced the Cabildo to make belated purchase of a pump fire engine that he had imported from Philadelphia.[28] As well, Pollock engaged in trading slaves all along the river in order to generate additional capital. By May 1790, he had settled all of his overdue accounts with the individual creditors at New Orleans, although he still owed money to the Spanish government.[29]

The profits from these transactions permitted Pollock to begin buying land along the Mississippi once again. In the wake of the fire, he purchased several town lots in New Orleans and constructed houses on them, which he sold at a profit. He also regained legal ownership of the Old Tunica Plantation in 1789, when he repurchased it from Trudeau. The cousin, Hamilton Pollock, returned to the plantation, immediately began a series of improvements, assembled a slave crew, and resumed agricultural production at Old Tunica.[30] Oliver Pollock also purchased other plantation lands in the Feliciana district. He bought one thousand acres along Bayou Sara. As well, he sought reconfirmation of his earlier British title to the Tangipahoa River property under the terms of the 1785 decree.[31] Other members of the Pollock family also secured property during the 1790s in the area as part of an Anglo-American influx into the region. Hamilton Pollock was granted one thousand acres on the southern part of Bayou Sara, while Thomas Pollock, a nephew, secured a nearby tract. George Pollock, a distant cousin, received a large grant on the Amite River.[32]

Although various family members remained in the area, Oliver Pollock returned to the United States in 1791, and there he lived for the next twenty-eight years. He first resided in Carlisle, Pennsylvania, and, after the death of his first wife, he moved to Baltimore, where he remarried. Old Tunica Plantation, however, continued as an important family asset, along with the lands owned by Hamilton, Thomas, and George Pollock. As well, shortly after the Louisiana Purchase, Pollock's eldest daughter Mary, her husband, Dr. Samuel S. Robinson, and their children moved to present-day Wilkinson County, Mississippi, a few miles north of Tunica Bend at a location then in the United States. They made frequent visits to the Old Tunica Plantation in Spanish Territory from their home in nearby Pinckneyville, and with the passing of Hamilton Pollock in 1814, they undertook management of the plantation. By this time, the Florida Parishes region of southeastern Louisiana had become heavily populated with Anglos and was in the process of breaking away from Spanish control. Cotton as well had become the major crop at Tunica Bend. The increasing volume of steamboat traffic on the river also provided the opportunity for additional profit. The Pollocks and Robinsons built a levee at the foot of Tunica Bayou and opened a woodyard.

Old Tunica Plantation eventually encompassed considerable improvements. A cluster of buildings stood along the north bank of Tunica Bayou on the eastern edge of the plantation, well away from the Mississippi River. Here could be found a modest home with ample open porches on both the front and back sides, a washhouse, a kitchen building, a log smokehouse, and related structures. The house at this location, still standing and today known as the Trudeau House, was built as a raised Creole cottage, although it mixed freely the architectural features of Spanish, French, and Anglo styles. Set on a large hill, it had a view of vessels passing on the river, while it was situated to take advantage of summer breezes on its wide galleries.[33] The Robinson family, which included Pollock's daughter and grandchildren, resided temporarily in this home before establishing permanent resident in Pinckneyville. In 1813, the Pollock family sold the parcel of land upon which this complex stood to a neighbor, Phillip Alston, and concentrated their operations nearer to the river at the mouth of Tunica and Pollock Bayous.

Along Pollock Bayou just east of the river could be found the overseer's quarters, which were occupied by Hamilton Pollock from the 1790s until his death in 1814. This home, less opulent than the Trudeau House, had been constructed by Oliver Pollock prior to the American Revolution as his personal residence on the property. This building served as the plantation headquarters during Hamilton's lifetime and was surrounded by various slave cabins, cotton barns, and corncribs. A small group of buildings also existed at the site where the two bayous flowed into the Mississippi. A few lots at this location had been sold over the years to various individuals by the Pollocks, thereby creating a small, rude settlement known as "Viejo Tunica." This consisted of the general store and woodyard owned by the family, along with several private residences and related outbuildings. The Pollock family, in addition to engaging in planting directly, also rented parts of the plantation to various persons. In 1817, for example, Washington White, a local farmer, cultivated approximately eighteen acres of corn, while Oliver Ratliff, another tenant, farmed a fifty-acre tract on the south side of the plantation. The Pollock family usually rented land for six dollars an acre in the late 1810s.[34] The Tunica Bend district, of which the plantation was a part along with the holdings of other planters in the area, had become by this time one of the most populated stretches on the river between Baton Rouge and Natchez. As a traveler noted, the area was "a handsome settlement, extending about twelve miles along the east side of the river."[35]

Oliver Pollock returned to the lower Mississippi in 1819 upon the death of his second wife, and there he lived out the remaining years of his life. He maintained his legal residence at the Pinckneyville, Mississippi, home of his daughter. This town apparently had little to offer him. "Pinckneyville," as one observer of the period recorded, "is a straggling village of ten houses, mostly in decay, and some of them uninhabited. It has a little church, a tavern, a store, and a post office."[36] Pollock therefore preferred to stay on the Old Tunica Plantation whenever possible. He also owned a home in nearby St. Francisville, where he occasionally resided. Although a man in his eighties by the early 1820s, it seems that Pollock still had the inclinations of an entrepreneur. He and some of his children laid elaborate plans for the development of a major townsite on the plantation where Bayou Tunica entered the Mississippi. His heirs continued these efforts after Pollock's death in December 1824. They eventually filed town plans with the state of Louisiana and, in 1829, offered lots for public sale at Tunicaville, the main thoroughfare of which bore the name Pollock Street.[37] Although the settlement eventually received a post office, it never prospered, and the Pollock family realized little profit from the venture. They also became involved in a title dispute regarding the plantation that stemmed from Pollock's wartime debts to

Patrick Conway and Alexander Baudin. A final resolution in this matter did not come until the late 1820s, when they gained a clear title. In financial need, they sold parcels of the plantation to other planters, although they kept some of the original holding for themselves. A grandson, Oliver Pollock Robinson, lived on part of the property until the Civil War. Other Pollock descendants also maintained homes in St. Francisville and at the nearby hamlet of Bayou Sara.

As well, in the mid-1830s, the Pollock family initiated a series of complicated legal claims that sought to regain titles to the British-era land grants that Oliver Pollock had assigned to creditors as part of his 1782 bankruptcy and that he had been unable to resecure during his lifetime. Dr. Robinson, Pollock's son-in-law, argued before the commissioners of the General Land Office that his father-in-law's Revolutionary War debts had been incurred in the name of the United States government and that the use of the plantation lands as collateral in the 1780s had been illegal. Nothing resulted from these efforts, however, since they were obscured and eventually dismissed among the thousands of Louisiana land claim cases that came before the United States General Land Office and its commissioners in the antebellum era.[38] Nevertheless, Oliver Pollock's descendants continue to the present day as residents along the Mississippi River, although they sold their remaining interest in the Old Tunica Plantation and moved to the Natchez area after the Civil War.

The story of Oliver Pollock's land tenure in the Mississippi valley seems to have been fairly typical of a larger group of Anglo settlers who came into the region prior to the American Revolution. Like Pollock, others of them and their families developed traditions of land tenure in the lower Mississippi valley that endured across the shifting eras of domination by Great Britain, Spain, and the United States. Future research by historians in the land records of British West Florida, Spanish Louisiana, and the United States may well provide both the individual stories and a demographic portrait of these Anglo settlers who came to the Mississippi valley as British subjects prior to the American Revolution and who remained, no matter whether they had been patriots, loyalists, or neutrals. As a group, they have been largely forgotten by history.

They were the opening wedge of the Anglo-American influx into the lower Mississippi valley in the decades prior to the Louisiana Purchase.

Notes

1. The standard studies of Pollock and the Revolution are James A. James, *Oliver Pollock: The Life and Times of an Unknown Patriot* (New York: Appleton-Century, 1937); John W. Caughey, *Bernardo de Gálvez in Louisiana, 1776–1783* (Berkeley: University of California Press, 1934); William F. Mullaney, "Oliver Pollock: Catholic Patriot and Financier of the American Revolution," *Historical Records and Studios of the US Catholic Historical Society* 28 (1937), 164–236; Horace E. Hayden, *A Biographical Sketch of Oliver Pollock* (Harrisburg, PA: Lanes, Hart Printers and Binders, 1883); and Egle, *Notes and Queries, Historical and Genealogical, Chiefly Relating to Interior Pennsylvania*, vol. 1 (Harrisburg, PA: Harrisburg Publishing, 1894), 475–81.

2. Studies of Anglo immigration into the lower Mississippi valley generally ignore this pre-Revolutionary immigration, instead stressing the events of the 1780s and 1790s. Pollock, along with others, including the families of Urquhart, Ross, Barrow, Comyns, and others, came to the region first, secured the most desirable land, and helped influence the later Anglo-American migration in the final decades of the century. For the standard studies of the later Anglo migration into the lower Mississippi region, see Mattie Austin Hatcher, *The Opening of Texas to Foreign Settlement, 1801–1821* (Austin: University of Texas Press, 1927); Hatcher, "The Louisiana Background of the Colonization of Texas, 1763–1803," *Southwestern Historical Quarterly* (hereinafter cited as *SHQ*) 24 (1921): 169–95; C. Richard Arena, "Landholding and Political Power in Spanish Louisiana," *Louisiana Historical Quarterly* 38 (1955): 23–39; Gilbert C. Din, "Colonización en la Luisiana espanola; proyectos de emigración en la Luisiana del siglo XVIII" (Ph.D. diss., University of Madrid, 1960); Din, "The Immigration Policy of Governor Esteban Miró in Spanish Louisiana," *SHQ* 73 (October 1969): 155–75; Din, "Spain's Immigration Policy in Louisiana and the American Penetration, 1792–1803," *SHQ* 76 (January 1973): 255–76; William S. Coker, "The Bruins and the Formulation of Spanish Immigration Policy in the Old Southwest, 1787–88," in *The Spanish in the Mississippi Valley,1762–1804*, ed. John Francis McDermott (Urbana: University of Illinois Press, 1974), 61–71; and C. Richard Arena, "Land Settlement Policies and Practices in Spanish Louisiana," ibid., 51–60.

3. The British land-grant ledgers and conveyances are contained in the Public Record Office, Kew Gardens, London, CO 5/601–17. There are also detailed grantee maps in the PRO. The Library of Congress has copies of most of them in its Geography and Map Division. The State Land Office of Louisiana in Baton Rouge also has a random selection of copies made in the early nineteenth century.

4. Although there is no one guide to these diverse Spanish-era land records, the following provide an introduction to the locations of significant collections: Glenn R. Conrad and Carl A. Brasseaux, *A Selected Bibliography of Scholarly Literature on Colonial Louisiana and New France* (Lafayette: Center for Louisiana Studies, 1982), 6–7; Winston De Ville, *Louisiana and Mississippi Lands: A Guide to Spanish Land Grants at the University of Michigan: Properties at Ascension, Attakapas, Baton Rouge. . . .* (Ville Platte, LA: Polyanthos, 1985); and Paul Hoffman, "La documentation colonial en la Luisiana," *Archivo Hispalense*, nos. 207–8 (1985): 335–44. A set of Louisiana land records, popularly known as the Trudeau Survey Papers, has been the recent object of a replevin controversy, during which various archival repositories disputed the present-day ownership of these documents, which include numerous Spanish-era land surveys and related manuscripts. These papers are currently in the possession of the Historic New Orleans Collection in New Orleans. For both sides of the ownership controversy and a description of the documents, see Patricia A. Schmit, "Spanish Land Documents at the Historic New Orleans Collection," *Manuscripts* 37 (Fall 1985): 275–82; and Edward F. Haas, "Odyssey of a Manuscript Collection: Records of the Surveyor General of Antebellum Louisiana," *Louisiana History* 27 (Winter 1986): 5–26.

5. The best treatment of early Anglo merchants in Spanish Louisiana, a heretofore badly neglected subject, is Robin F. A. Fabel, "Anglo-Spanish Commerce in New Orleans during the American Revolutionary Era," in *Anglo-Spanish Confrontation on the Gulf Coast during the American Revolution*, ed. William S. Coker and Robert R. Rea (Pensacola: Gulf Coast History and Humanities Conference, 1982), 25–51. As Fabel notes of these individuals, the term "Anglo" merely describes one who was of British heritage, even though some might have preferred to have been called American. Many of them were capitalists who sometimes placed the opportunity for profit before national loyalty. "In general," Fabel asserts, "they were less interested in flags than in Spanish milled dollars, livres, and golden guineas."

6. Oliver Pollock to the Captain General of Cuba, June 22, 1796, Archive General de Indias, Seville, Spain (hereafter cited as AGI), Papeles de Cuba, Legajo 1469; Pollock to Luis de las Casas, July 14, 1796, ibid. For the Cabildo deliberations on the scarcity of flour in New Orleans during this period, see Actas del Cabildo, New Orleans, October 5, 1770, August 2, 16, 1771, 1:20, 32, 33, WPA Transcripts in Spanish on Microfilm, New Orleans Public Library, New Orleans.

7. For a discussion of the method and procedures by which the British government in West Florida administered land grants, see Cecil Johnson, "The Distribution of Land in British West Florida," *Louisiana Historical Quarterly* 16 (October 1933): 539–53. The only published information on a Pollock West Florida grant concerns the Tangipahoa property as noted in Gordon M. Wells, "British Land Grants: The William Wilton Map of 1774," *Journal of Mississippi History* 28 (1956): 152–59.

8. For descriptions of these land purchases, see State Land Office, Baton Rouge, *Greensburg Land Claims*, Book 2, pt. 2:69, 94, 109–10; *American State*

Papers: Public Lands (Washington, DC: Duff Green, 1834), 3:46, 4:313; Acts de Andres Almonester y Rojas, vol. 9, March 5, 1778, f. 176, Orleans Parish Notary Archives, Civil District Courts Building, New Orleans (hereafter referred to as Orleans Notary Archives). The Geography and Map Division of the Library of Congress contains copies of several maps by British cartographers that note the locations of these properties, including *Map of the Mississippi River from the Mouth of the Yazoo River to the Southern Part of Louisiana, 1774* and *Plan of the Rivers Mississippi, Iberville, Mobile, and Bay of Pensacola in the Province of West Florida, September 1772*. See also the conveyance, Philip Comyns to Oliver Pollock, January 21, 1774, Peter Force Collection, Division of Manuscripts, Library of Congress.

9. *Louisiana, Mississippi, and West Florida*, [1770], Uncatalogued Vault, Geography and Map Division, Library of Congress.

10. The locations and improvements on these properties have been extrapolated by examining maps made of Mississippi River plantations prior to the American Revolution. *A Plan of the Coast of Part of West Florida and Louisiana including the River Mississippi from its entrances as high as the River Yazous* [*sic*], 1778, [popularly known as Gauld's Map], Map Library, Louisiana State University School of Geoscience, Baton Rouge; *Map of the Mississippi River from the Mouth of the Yazoo River to the Southern Part of Louisiana, 1774*, Geography and Map Division, Library of Congress.

11. "Proceedings Instituted by Don Olivero Pollock for the Purpose of Settling Certain Accounts with His Principals through an Arbitration Board," April 27, 1782, Spanish Judicial Records of Louisiana, Louisiana Historical Center, Louisiana State Museum, New Orleans. For a synopsis of this case, see *Louisiana Historical Quarterly* 11 (1935): 230.

12. For a discussion of rice culture on the lower Mississippi in the Spanish period, see Lewis C. Gray, *History of Agriculture in the Southern United States to 1860*, vol. 1 (Washington, DC: Carnegie Institution, 1932), 65–66.

13. From Philadelphia, Thomas William wrote: "I dislike Mr. Pollock's Conduct altogether I dont [*sic*] wish to be involved further with him." Thomas Willing to Robert Morris, November 3, 1777, in *Willing Letters and Papers*, ed. Thomas Balch Willing (Philadelphia: Allen, Lane, and Scott, 1922), 58. Morris instead convinced his partner to retain Pollock's services, an arrangement that continued until the early 1780s.

14. Albert C. Bates, ed., *The Two Putnams, Israel and Rufus, in the Havana Expedition, 1762, and in the Mississippi River Exploration, 1772–1773, with an Account of Their Military Adventures* (Hartford, CT: Connecticut Historical Society, 1931), 134; Fortesque Cuming, *Selections of a Tour to the Western Country . . . Commenced at Philadelphia in the Winter of 1807* (Pittsburgh: Cramer, Spear, and Eichbaum, 1810), 304.

15. The William Vousdan resurvey of the Fairchild plat, dated April 28, 1783, Undocketed Materials—Natchez, Louisiana Survey Materials, Historic

New Orleans Collection, New Orleans (formerly in the collection of the Western Reserve Historical Society, Cleveland).

16. James Willing to Frederick Haldimand, January 3, 1773, Haldimand Papers, pt. 4, mss. 21729, Division of Manuscripts, Library of Congress.

17. Probate of Oliver Pollock, File 81, Probate Proceedings, Clerk of the Court Records, West Feliciana Parish Courthouse, St. Francisville, LA; *Baudin v. Roliff* et al. *Robinson* (1823), Case Files, Docket 1282, West Feliciana Parish Courthouse, St. Francisville, LA.

18. *Baudin v. Roliff* et al. *Robinson* (1823), Case Files, Docket 1282, ff. 15–17.

19. James A. Robertson, ed., *Louisiana under the Rule of Spain, France, and the United States*, 2 vols. (Cleveland: Arthur H. Clark, 1911), 1:154. For a full discussion of indigo production in colonial Louisiana, see Jack D. L. Holmes, "Indigo in Colonial Louisiana," *Louisiana History* 8 (1967): 329–49.

20. Acts of Andres Almonester y Rojas, vol. 23, March 4, 1773, f. 45, vol. 4, March 7, 1774, f. 68, vol. 8, February 15, 1777, f. 130, Orleans Notary Archives; Acts of Juan Bautista Garic, vol. 5, July 30, 1774, f. 143, vol. 8, July 8, 1777, f. 280, ibid.

21. William D. Reeves, *De La Barre: The Life of a Louisiana Creole Family* (New Orleans: Polyanthos, 1980), 45.

22. James, *Oliver Pollock*, 61–104; "Memorial of Oliver Pollock to the President of the Congress," September 18, 1782, vol. 50, Papers of the Continental Congress, National Archives, Washington, DC.

23. Din, "Immigration Policy of Esteban Miró," 156–58.

24. "Resolution Setting Forth the Value of Oliver Pollock's Services as US Commercial Agent at New Orleans during the Revolution and Urging a Settlement of His Accounts," October 22, 1782, E. A. Parsons Collection, Humanities Research Center, University of Texas at Austin; Thomas Jefferson to Bernardo de Gálvez, November 8, 1779, Archivo General de Indias, Seville, Spain (hereafter referred to as AGI), Papeles de Cuba, Legajo 2370; Acts of Rafael Perdomo, vol. 13, January 16, 1789, f. 19, Orleans Notary Archives; Acts of Leonardo Mazange, vol. 3, February, 1781, f. 66, ibid.; *Santiago Monon v. Oliver Pollock*, April 20, 1782, Spanish Judicial Records of Louisiana, Louisiana Historical Center.

25. For representative liquidations, see Acts of Andres Almonester y Rojas, vol. 13, February 5, 1782, f. 99, Orleans Notary Archives; Acts of Leonardo Mazange, vol. 2, August 7, 1780, f. 621, vol. 3, March 3, April 11, 1781, ff. 171, 248, vol. 4, November 6, 1781, f. 495, vol. 5, January 28, February 4, 1782, ff. 102, 136, ibid.

26. Oliver Pollock to Esteban Miró, April 27, 1782, AGI, Papeles de Cuba, Legajo 2370.

27. Acts of Leonardo Mazange, vol. 5, April 29, 1782, f. 443, Orleans Notary Archives; Acts of Rafael Perdomo, vol. 13, May 5, 1789, f. 230, ibid.

28. For a description of the destruction during the 1788 fire, see "Report of the Demands of the Citizens of New Orleans after the Fire, March 21, 1788," Parsons Collection. Pollock set forth his intentions to sell goods for the rebuilding of the city in a letter to the Spanish governor. See "Instancia de Olivero Pollock," February 10, 1789, AGI, Audiencia de Santo Domingo, Legajo 2553, f. 628.

29. Acts of Rafael Perdomo, vol. 12, December 19, 1788, f. 548, Orleans Notary Archives; vol. 15, May 3, 1790, f. 232, ibid.

30. "Pollock Mortgages," Book A, 89, Recorder of Mortgages, Civil Clerk of Court, Orleans Parish Courthouse; Acts of Rafael Perdomo, vol. 15, March 20, 1790, f. 124, Orleans Notary Archives; Oliver Pollock to Baron Carondolet, May 3, 1792, AGI, Papeles de Cuba, Legajo 184-A.

31. State Land Office, Baton Rouge, *Greensburg Land Claims*, Book A, 48–51.

32. All of these transactions are recorded in a series of survey records popularly known as the "Pintado Papers." The originals are in the Division of Archives and Manuscripts of the Louisiana State University, Baton Rouge. They are also available at various other repositories in Louisiana as translated typescripts compiled in the 1930s by the Works Progress Administration. The citations for the above transactions are noted in the following WPA Books, which have been checked against the originals: Hamilton Pollock, 9:5; Thomas Pollock, 7:131–35; George Pollock, 4:172.

33. Mark Baum et al., "The Trudeau House: A Report Prepared May 10, 1982," Division of Historic Preservation, State of Louisiana, Baton Rouge.

34. *Baudin* v. *Roliff* et al. *Robinson*, (1823), Case Files, Docket 778, ff. 15–17.

35. Jervis Cutler, *A Topographical Description of the State of Ohio, Indiana Territory, and Louisiana* (Boston: Charles Williams by J. Belcher, Printer, 1812), 90.

36. Cuming, *Selections of a Tour to the Western Country*, 303.

37. "Plan of the First Square of Tunicaville," May 30, 1829, Notary Book C, 187, Clerk of the Court Records, West Feliciana Parish Courthouse, St. Francisville, LA.

38. For the history of this category of land claim, see Harry L. Coles Jr., "The Confirmation of Foreign Land Titles in Louisiana," *Louisiana Historical Quarterly* 38 (October 1955): 1–22.

CHAPTER 7

"In Territories So Extensive and Fertile"

Spanish- and English-Speaking Peoples in Louisiana before the Purchase

Spain's decision to encourage English-speaking settlement rested on the need to maintain control of Louisiana and, thereafter, Texas. The province of Louisiana, which fell to Spain's sovereignty with the Peace of Paris in 1763, constituted a borderlands colony unlike any other that European power had ever administered. The region had been settled by the French starting in the last decade of the 1600s. Relations between Europeans and Native Americans had been set for over seventy-five years before the Spanish took possession. French-speaking settlers had fanned out across the lower Mississippi for three generations. New Orleans enjoyed established commercial ties that made it a viable port city, with stabilized parameters for its trade products. French land-acquisition policies, the activities of the church, and the founding of interior towns such as St. Louis and Natchitoches had long been stabilized. The Gallic population presented Spain with new challenges because the Spanish king had gained a functioning colonial holding that had to be administered in ways far different from what had been the norm for his other New World possessions. Both the governing policies and the assumptions upon which they were based had to be revaluated and recast for Spanish Louisiana.

Spain's need to administer Louisiana had one particular consideration never experienced before in the history of its colonization in the Americas: few Spaniards ever went as civilian settlers to live in the new colony. Unlike all of its other colonial possessions, which had a European majority of Spanish settlers, Louisiana represented a polyglot population of different nationalities but with a predominate French presence. The cooperation of these residents proved difficult to achieve. Disenchanted former subjects of the French king rose in open rebellion against Antonio de Ulloa, the first of Spain's Louisiana governors. These considerations eventually motivated a new policy regarding immigration and land policy. Creating a diverse population in Louisiana, one in which no one group became a majority, had the benefits of a "divide and conquer" approach, enabling the Spanish colonial government to attempt a calculated measure of social control. This meant encouraging a diverse immigration into Louisiana. In particular, liberalization of landownership policies would provide a mechanism for Spain to incorporate the English-speakers of West Florida while perhaps also offering a means to control migrants coming from the United States into Spanish territory.

Accordingly, authorities in Louisiana accepted non-Spanish immigrants into the colony for much of the late eighteenth century, except during a few short periods that witnessed the temporary suspension of these measures for a variety of reasons. Displaced Acadians began to arrive in the province with the start of Spanish rule. Additionally, German migrants continued to find their way to the Mississippi valley, where that group had been settled since the French colonial era. Irish merchants received a ready welcome at New Orleans and grew in number throughout the Spanish period, especially those who espoused Roman Catholicism. The 1790s saw the arrival of Gallic planters and their slaves from Saint Domingue. The largest and most visible influx of new settlers, however, came from the United States. Spain not only welcomed them but also put in place land policies that encouraged these English-speakers to settle in Louisiana, attracted by relatively liberal provisions centered on free land. In the mid-1780s, Louisiana governor Esteban Miró caused English-speaking settlement to expand noticeably by establishing a quick and almost effortless method whereby new Anglo-American arrivals could gain citizenship and receive land grants. They would take a loyalty oath to the king of Spain, adopt the Roman Catholic faith (which could be nominally accomplished), and agree to live by the Spanish legal system. Fulfilling these requirements resulted in grants of free land. For the rest of the eighteenth century, thousands of people from the United States appeared in Spanish Louisiana to avail themselves of securing land under Miró's edicts. One of them was a future president of the United States, Andrew Jackson, who arrived as a young man in 1789 at Spanish Natchez, where he swore the loyalty oath to Spain in order to get land. The essay below explores the social-control policies implemented by Spain in Louisiana that encouraged this migration into the Mississippi valley. Governor Miró established a policy of "defensive colonization," whereby Spain hoped the loyalty of English-speaking settlers could be purchased by land grants. This would later serve as the underpinning of the "empresario era" in Spanish Texas. F. Todd Smith, in his 2014 book *The Louisiana Frontier and the Gulf South Frontier, 1500–1821*, provides a full survey of the groups who immigrated into Louisiana during the Spanish period while presenting a detailed analysis of their relationships with Native Americans in the region.

Light Townsend Cummins, "'In Territories So Extensive and Fertile': Spanish and English-Speaking Peoples in Louisiana before the Purchase," in *The Louisiana Purchase and Its People: Proceedings from the New Orleans Conference*, ed. Paul Hoffman (Lafayette: Louisiana Historical Association and the Center for Louisiana Studies, 2004), 117–25.

LOUISIANA'S Spanish period witnessed vibrant growth, remarkable expansion, and a conspicuous progress that have left indelible influences on the modern state. This was especially the case regarding the creation of a distinctive ethnic diversity; that is, a historically identifiable colonial complex that clearly rivaled in durability and sophistication those elsewhere in North America. Although a complete analysis of the lower Mississippi valley as such a region is beyond the limited scope of this essay, it can be noted that one means whereby the Spaniards helped to forge this area into a well-defined colonial complex was social control.

Spain had no choice upon receiving Louisiana after the Seven Years' War (1756–63) but to implement and maintain a determined social control over the colony. Social control, as used in this context, is—as sociologist Joseph S. Roucek has noted in his seminal work on the subject - "the collective term for those processes . . . where one group determines the behavior of another group" in order "to stabilize society and to provide a means for orderly and continuous adaptation and change."[1] In Louisiana, Spain used two methods to achieve this social control.

Spain's efforts to maintain social control involved, first, the firm establishment of Spanish political, economic, and social institutions along the lower Mississippi in an effort to bring order and structure to an increasingly varied population and, second, the expansion of that population with persons of various ethnicities, making it even more diverse. Spaniards found and added to a unique blend of Euro-African norms in Louisiana in areas such as colonial government, art, architecture, economic development, society, culture, and religion. The ethnic parameters of this Louisiana colonial complex expanded during the three decades of Spanish sovereignty to include Acadians, Canary Islanders, French refugees from the Haitian Revolt, a considerable number of African slaves, and, notably, the welcoming of English-speaking settlers in larger numbers. Spain encouraged the inclusion of this English-speaking population as an additional means of maintaining social control in Louisiana. This defensive colonization became a tool whereby Spain could hopefully hold the province in the face of threatening international encroachments. In short, the immigration that Spain fostered in Louisiana became a means of social control because it diffused social, cultural, economic, and political power among different groups of settlers. The result was the creation of a unique colonial complex that was neither French, Spanish, Anglo-American, nor African, but a combination of all of them.

Spanish colonial administrators in Louisiana faced, from the very moment that Spain received the colony at the Peace of Paris in 1763, the difficult and daunting task of governing a colony whose population was predominately non-Hispanic, whose governmental institutions were not those of Spain, and whose geopolitical situation guaranteed that Louisiana would be a crossroads of many conflicting interests. Governing the colony was an almost overwhelming task because relatively few Spaniards ever came to the colony, and many of those who did were sojourners in the category of governmental officials, military officers and soldiers, or other public servants.

The efforts of the Spanish government to maintain social control in this colonial atmosphere can be seen, by way of example, in the actions of several royal governors who served in the colony. Antonio de Ulloa, Spain's first governor in Louisiana, was a renowned naturalist and scientist, a founder of the Natural History Museum in Madrid, a member of the British Royal Society, and the first scientific researcher to identify platinum as a distinct metal. It is somewhat ironic, therefore, that Ulloa's tenure as governor of Louisiana ended in disaster and disgrace when an unruly mob of protestors drove him from the colony. The collapse of his administration, however, had an unforeseen result: social control became the centerpiece for Spain's governmental emphasis in Louisiana. It would be accomplished both by coercion and cooption.

General Alexander O'Reilly was the first of Spain's administrators who left a lasting mark on the history of Louisiana. He used coercion when he arrested the leaders who had revolted against his predecessor, Antonio de Ulloa. Several of them received the death penalty, while others paid with long prison sentences. O'Reilly, however, also used cooption in creating a workable system of social controls for Spanish Louisiana. Students of law and jurisprudence know that he promulgated the famous Code O'Reilly, which blended the influences of Spanish law with French procedure to create the lasting singularity of Louisiana law. He also addressed an additional series of political and legal matters that dealt with such diverse concerns as landowning and slavery in Louisiana. His land regulations of 1770 changed the basic structure of property acquisition in Louisiana. This decree outlined the process whereby land grants were to be made, set procedures for landowning. and institutionalized a system permitting provincial administrators to begin making a substantial and increasing number of land grants. As one historian has noted of this decree: "Its provisions represented a liberality of land grants that would not be seen in the United States until the Homestead Act of the 1860s."[2] The Code O'Reilly also outlined the basic provisions of slaveholding that would give a distinctive character to that institution in Louisiana. O'Reilly abolished the previous French Code Noir, substituting in its place the Spanish laws on slavery that harked back to Las Siete Partidas that were promulgated in the 1260s. These laws were more humane than those of France, and later of the United States. "Overall," as historian Gilbert C. Din has noted, "Spanish law came down strongly on the side of slaves who sought freedom and against their masters who tried to prevent it."[3] O'Reilly also turned his attention to governmental structures. It was he, for example, who created the singular Louisiana local political units of the parishes, a uniqueness that remains until the present day. He also dissolved the French Superior Council and instituted the Cabildo as New Orleans's municipal governing body.

Although he governed in Spanish Louisiana for only a scant seven months, General O'Reilly engaged in numerous other activities that left their mark on the colony. He ordered the taking of the first accurate and impartial census in 1769. He improved relations with Native Americans while he also attempted to stop British smuggling along the lower Mississippi River. He was also the first administrator, but most certainly not the last, who attempted to bring order to New Orleans's teeming and colorful urban life when he issued decrees to regulate taverns, bars, inns, billiard parlors, and public houses. O'Reilly also organized the Louisiana militia. And not least, he undertook a series of public improvements that included levee and road construction.

O'Reilly's successor, Luis de Unzaga y Amezaga, began to exercise administrative power as Louisiana governor at the time of O'Reilly's departure in March 1770. "He exhibited many characteristics of a pacifier," one historian has written of Unzaga, "having skills as an organizer, a calm temperament in decision making evenhandedness, and a methodical nature that sometimes frustrated subordinates who sought quick and expedient action."[4] He proved to be the perfect sort of governor to bring tranquility to Louisiana while he continued to implement policies of social control. During his tenure, Unzaga strengthened the Spanish judicial system instituted by O'Reilly. He opened a public school at New Orleans. Unzaga had a commitment, as well, to increasing the colony's trade connections. The commerce of Louisiana, for that reason, greatly expanded during the period of his leadership, although an upswing in smuggling—especially with British merchants in nearby West Florida—was an unintended result of his liberal commercial policies. Governor Unzaga also had to deal with the opening phases of the American Revolution and the impact that this conflict had on the lower Mississippi. As Louisiana governor, he permitted rebel expeditions to take refuge in the city while he unofficially sanctioned at New Orleans the pro-American activity of Oliver Pollock, who would eventually receive a formal appointment as the agent of the Continental Congress in the Crescent City.

It was Unzaga's successor as governor, Bernardo de Gálvez, who dealt with the military pressures in Spanish Louisiana that the British colonial revolt created. Gálvez, as a member of a powerful and well-connected family at court in Spain, put Louisiana on a sound military footing starting in 1777, when he took office. The governor also showed overt sympathy for the American rebels while he treated the British as traditional enemies, which they had always been to the Spaniards. Once Spain entered the war as a belligerent in 1779, Bernardo de Gálvez won a series of military victories over the next three years that conquered all of British West Florida. Gálvez's contributions, however, were not limited to his exploits during the American Revolution. He paid particular attention to maintaining social control over Louisiana's increasingly diverse population. His administration witnessed the settlement of New Iberia and the strengthening of Louisiana's fugitive-slave laws.

Gálvez's successor as governor of Louisiana, Esteban Rodriguez Miró, assumed office at New Orleans on an interim basis during the American Revolution while Gálvez, still holding the appointment as governor, was absent from the colony conducting his military campaigns. Miró officially became governor in 1785 and remained on the job until 1791. It was during these years that the demographic pressure of an expanding United States began to be felt in Spanish Louisiana. Like his predecessors who faced a Francophone majority, Miró also adopted social-control policies clearly favoring cooption rather than coercion. He promulgated land-distribution policies that sought to control the influx of English-speaking settlers into lower Spanish Louisiana, especially in the Natchez District, as a "counter-colonizing" measure. He welcomed all Anglo-American settlers who would pledge loyalty to Spain in exchange for ownership of land. It is impossible to overestimate the historical importance of this action on Miró's part. It was Miró's idea in 1785 and 1786 that the potential rivalry between Spanish colonial authority and Anglo-American frontier folk could be resolved by trading land for national loyalty. Miró's policy set in motion an ever-increasing immigration of Anglo-Americans into the lower Mississippi valley. All of these English-speaking settlers signed loyalty oaths to the king of Spain in exchange for land and the promise of a new life on it. Beyond this rather momentous impact on the development of Louisiana history, Miró also shaped the colony further by negotiating treaties with the Native Americans of the area, holding a series of congresses at Pensacola and Mobile. He also became involved in the frontier intrigues of General James Wilkinson, that roguish frontier rascal who schemed to make the western part of the United States independent and ally it with Spain. Miró put the American general on the Spanish payroll as a spy and informant. Miró saw his arrangements with Wilkinson as part of the larger scheme to settle English-speaking immigrants on the lower Mississippi in Spanish territory.

Miró's successor, Francois-Louis Hector, the Baron de Carondelet, replaced Miró as Louisiana governor in 1791, continuing in effect all of his predecessors' policies and programs of social control. This was especially the case regarding immigration of English-speaking settlers into the colony. Like Miró, Carondelet sought to attract new migrants from both Europe and the United States, hoping to convert them into loyal Spanish subjects in exchange for land. But unlike his predecessors, he had to deal full force with the social-control issues that the French Revolution of 1789 created in Louisiana. In the face of this revolution, the Francophone European majority in Louisiana manifested varying degrees of sympathy or revulsion for events in France. Carondelet, a monarchist by inclination, worked to defend Louisiana against what he saw as revolutionary sedition. This became a very real problem for the Louisiana governor when a group of New Orleans residents sent representatives to France to express support for the revolutionary cause. Carondelet took stern measures to stamp out what he styled "Jacobinism" by augmenting the number of royal troops stationed in the colony and by requiring loyalty oaths from residents. He also engaged in a series of arrests and banishments. He worked to place in positions of local government and militia command only those residents who rejected the French Revolution and supported Spanish hegemony. Carondolet's problems with revolutionary fever did not come only from the problems in Louisiana relating to the French Revolution. The difficulties associated with the Haitian slave revolt on the island of Saint Domingue also threatened the social control of Spanish Louisiana throughout his period as governor.

Carondelet believed that the cruelty of the Saint Domingue planters toward their slaves had been a key cause of the 1791 revolt eventually led by Toussaint L'Ouverture. He thus decided to regulate slave affairs in Louisiana to the end of preventing abuses along the Mississippi that he felt had been endemic in the French West Indies. He also sought to improve the lot of free blacks in the colony as part of this process. Although a laudatory policy by modern standards, Carondelet's attempt to liberalize slave conditions had the opposite effect because slaves in some areas of Louisiana began to challenge their masters' authority and engage in other obstreperous behaviors. This caused the governor to retreat from his previously proclaimed policy and issue stern proclamations. Such actions on his part were no doubt a contributing factor to unrest among the slaves of the Point Coupee District north of Baton Rouge in the mid-1790s. Although historians have subsequently debated about how real the Point Coupee Slave Conspiracy was, Governor Carondelet and the Louisiana planters had no such doubts in 1795. They were convinced that the Point Coupee District harbored disloyal slaves who threatened the safety and security of the colony as they supposedly organized for revolt. The governor swiftly sprang into action as Spanish officials arrested sixty supposed slave conspirators. Twenty-three of them were executed and their heads hung on poles along the river as a warning to future conspirators, while the remaining slave prisoners received forced-labor sentences under the most harsh of conditions. This was social control at its most coercive. Carondelet's fears about the influences of the French Revolution, coupled to his concerns about organized slave insurrection, resulted in his issuing a comprehensive set of policy codes and slave regulations in 1795. "The new code established," one historian has noted of Carondelet's edict, "a draconian slave regime under which all Blacks were subject to the complete authority of any and all whites, regardless of which whites owned them."[5]

These slave regulations made the lower Mississippi a more attractive destination for French West Indian planters, who brought their slave gangs to Louisiana in order to escape unrest in the Caribbean. This refugee population brought a distinct brand of French Creole culture to Louisiana that permeated the entire province by the time of the Louisiana Purchase. As one scholar has noted, "many of the strong French cultural influences so visible to Anglo-American residents during the early statehood period existed due to the influx of recent immigrants from Saint-Domingue, who were still in the process of becoming acculturated to Louisiana, especially at New Orleans."[6] In addition, this immigration gave the institution of slavery in Spanish Louisiana at the close of the eighteenth century a distinctly West Indian flavor that it had not previously had and that would endure well into the American period.

By the time Carondelet departed from Louisiana, the role that the province played in the Spanish colonial system had begun to change. The mid-1790s witnessed the rise of Napoleon in France and the entrance of an independent United States onto the stage of European diplomacy. These changes came in the face of a decline in the internal stability of the Spanish government following the death of King Charles III in 1787. The new Spanish king, Charles IV, presided over a court in Spain at which corruption and debility became the order of the day. Louisiana, as a Spanish possession, increasingly became a pawn in the diplomacy of the 1790s even as it suffered disastrously from a decline in governmental vitality. Partly for that reason, the final years of Spanish Louisiana after Carondelet lacked the strong and decisive leadership that characterized much of the early era of Spanish social control along the lower Mississippi.

By the closing years of the 1790s, the enduring impact of Spanish rule had become apparent; namely, there existed a population of pronounced ethnic diversity in the colony. This was the great legacy of Spanish attempts at social control in Louisiana. The government of

Spain, from the time of Ulloa to the closing of the eighteenth century, encouraged immigration into Louisiana, and the total population increased fivefold. Few of these persons, however, were Spanish speaking. Instead, new groups came to the Mississippi valley, including Canary Islanders (who spoke Spanish), Acadians, French West Indians, and—most importantly—English-speaking settlers. As well, a significant number of new arrivals were African or African American slaves who came with no choice in the matter. Since the influx of slaves was tied directly to the expansion of agriculture, it is not surprising that the increase in the size of the slave population accounted for approximately one-half of the total demographic growth in Louisiana during the Spanish period. All of this immigration made Louisiana increasingly diverse in its society and culture, with a provincial population in 1803 of about 50,000 people. New Orleans had about 10,000 of them. This immigration also fragmented and isolated the social, political, economic, and cultural power of the Francophone population.

The increasing number of these migrants changed forever the nature of the lower Mississippi valley. This was most certainly the case for the English-speaking population. In effect, these English-speaking settlers fostered a demographic movement that preordained the Louisiana Purchase. This Anglo-American population, which constituted a significant segment of the colony's inhabitants by 1803, came mainly from three sources. First, a number of them arrived on the lower Mississippi early in the period of Spanish domination as merchants and traders who secured permission to reside in Louisiana, especially at New Orleans. Many of these English-speaking inhabitants, including persons such as Oliver Pollock and Daniel Clark the elder, were Irish or Scotch Irish Roman Catholics, hence the Spaniards accepted them. Second, a considerable number of English-speaking people were residents of conquered British West Florida and subsequently became Spanish citizens of Louisiana. Third, the largest number of English speakers in the colony resulted because of immigration into Louisiana from the United States. They were frontier folk and planters who appeared in the Mississippi valley in ever-increasing numbers as the eighteenth century moved toward its end.

The Spanish policy of welcoming English-speaking settlers into Louisiana if they declared their loyalty seemed a prescient solution to problems of social control. Spain found in these people a source of, at the least theoretically, loyal colonists who could further Louisiana's stability while they served as a possible counterweight to the Francophone majority. With Miró's policies, starting in the mid-1780s, various entrepreneurs and potential land agents began appearing at New Orleans with proposals to sponsor the migration of Anglo-Americans into Louisiana. One of the most ambitious, the Frenchman Pierre Wouves d'Arges, actually traveled to Spain, where he appeared at court in order to seek permission to bring 1,500 English-speaking United States citizens into Louisiana, where they were to become Spanish subjects. This French entrepreneur argued that these settlers would constitute a defensive bulwark that could hold the colony under Spanish control in the face of potential United States territorial expansion. They might also provide a needed economic boom to the colonial economy. The court approved d'Arges's ambitious plans, although circumstances eventually determined that he would never implement his scheme. Nonetheless, others took advantage of such opportunities. By the mid-1790s, Carondelet had worked with various land agents in order to encourage American immigration into Louisiana. The Marquis of Mason Rouge, for example. received a large grant of land for such purposes. Others, including Joseph Piemas, Louis de Vilemont, William Murray, the Baron de Bastrop, George Morgan, and Moses Austin, received grants of land for the settling of English-speaking immigrants all along the river from the Baton Rouge area northward to St. Louis. All of this caused Thomas Jefferson to observe that he wished "a hundred thousand of our inhabitants" would take advantage of these opportunities.[7]

Many of these English-speaking settlers in Spanish Louisiana quickly began to play significant roles in the life of the colony. Indeed the governmental records of the province contain numerous examples of the considerable commercial and agricultural activities of these people, many of whom amassed financial fortunes and established family dynasties that lasted well into the nineteenth century and, in some cases, beyond. This was especially so in the Natchez District and in the Felicianas, where

Spanish colonial documents make numerous mention of such families, including the Percys, the Williamsons, the Russes, the Lovels, the Pollocks, and the Joneses. Evan Jones, by way of example, can be mentioned as an individual success story in this regard. He first came to the lower Mississippi valley in 1765 as a West Florida merchant. He took an active role in the life of the British colony, serving in the Provincial Assembly, which met at Pensacola. He, like hundreds of others, remained in Louisiana after the American Revolution, becoming a Spanish subject. In the mid-1780s, Jones moved his residence to New Orleans, where he lived in a home on present-day Bienville Street. Governor Miró, as he did for all of these English-speakers in Jones's circumstances, reconfirmed all British landholdings with new, valid Spanish titles, thereby ensuring that Jones remained a wealthy man. He served during the 1790s in the colonial militia of Spanish Louisiana while he represented the United States along the lower Mississippi as the American vice consul at New Orleans. With the Louisiana Purchase of 1803, Jones was elected to the New Orleans City Council and served as a director of the Bank of the United States.

Many other English-speaking Louisianans during the Spanish period had life stories similar to Evan Jones's. These included, among many others, Daniel Clark, James Mather, James Jordan, Oliver Pollock, and Thomas Pollock. Of these, Daniel Clark the younger had become perhaps the richest person in Spanish Louisiana by the time of the Purchase in 1803. Young Clark came to the Mississippi valley in 1786 to join his uncle, Daniel Clark the elder. The older Clark was already a successful merchant at New Orleans. Young Clark, once in the colony in the late 1780s, proved to be very successful in the export of Louisiana trade goods while he invested heavily in land along the Mississippi from New Orleans to Natchez. He also profited greatly in the slave trade. Daniel Clark's landholdings eventually numbered in the hundreds of thousands of acres, with one tract along the Ouachita River alone comprising over 200,000 acres. The Clark fortune eventually produced one of Louisiana's most prolonged and complicated legal disputes, which involved the unsuccessful efforts of Myra Clark Gaines across much of the nineteenth century to gain clear title to many of these holdings.

The point to be drawn from the foregoing discussion of English-speaking migration into Spanish Louisiana is a simple and valid one for the historian. The Anglo-Americanization of Louisiana began several decades before the Louisiana Purchase of 1803. Indeed, by 1803, the process was a demographic reality that had only to be translated into a political one by the Louisiana Purchase. These Anglo-American, English-speaking Louisiana citizens were more than an opening vanguard of settlement, they were the settlement itself, and they made Spanish Louisiana the first frontier of expansion of national territory legitimized by the Purchase of 1803. The net result of these considerations regarding Spanish- and English-speaking peoples leads to the conclusion that the colonial rule of Spain in Louisiana had a profound impact that can still be seen today in the modern state, especially in its economic, social, cultural, and racial diversity. Even today, the vast and beautiful land that is Louisiana still resonates to historical rhythms that began during its relatively brief existence as a Spanish colony. Jefferson himself acknowledged this when he reported the Louisiana Purchase to the Congress in 1803. He said: "On this important acquisition, so favorable to the immediate interests of our Western citizens, so auspicious to the peace and security of the nation in general which adds to our country territories so extensive and fertile and to our citizens new brethren to partake of the blessings of freedom and self-government, I offer to Congress and our country my sincere congratulations." In reality, however, Jefferson misplaced his congratulations here. They were instead owed to the Spanish colonial administrators whose efforts during the previous thirty-five years to maintain social control created a distinct and enduring late-eighteenth-century colonial complex that blended different peoples into a single territorial province of striking ethnic diversity. It was that diversity, as much as the additional territory acquired by the United States, that made the Louisiana Purchase so remarkable as a seminal event in this nation's history.

Notes

1. J. S. Roucek, ed. *Social Control*, 2nd ed. (New York: Greenwood, 1956), 3.

2. Light T. Cummins, "Spanish Louisiana Land Policy: Antecedents to the Anglo-American Colonization of East Texas," *East Texas Historical Journal* 33 (1995): 21.

3. Gilbert C. Din, *Spaniards, Planters, and Slaves: The Spanish Regulation of Slavery in Louisiana, 1763–1803* (College Station: Texas A&M University Press, 1999), 43.

4. Light T. Cummins, "Luis de Unzaga," in *The Louisiana Governors: From Iberville to Edwards*, ed. Joseph G. Dawson III (Baton Rouge: Louisiana State University Press, 1990), 54.

5. Carl A. Brasseaux, "The Baron de Carondelet," ibid., 69.

6. Bennett H. Wall et al., *Louisiana: A History*, 4th ed. (Arlington Heights, IL: Harlan-Davidson, 1997), 78.

7. Quoted in Jeremy Adelman and Stephen Aron, "From Borderlands to Border: Empires, Nation-States, and the Peoples in Between in North American History," *American Historical Review* 104 (1999): 828.

CHAPTER 8

Oliver Pollock and the Creation of an American Identity in Spanish Colonial Louisiana

Historians over recent decades have turned to the concept of identity as an analytical tool for examining the past. For example, a book I edited in 2016 is entitled *Texan Identities: Moving Beyond Myth, Memory, and Fallacy in Texas History*, the introduction of which traces the development of identity studies in US historiography. The increasing attention historians have given to identity as a historical parameter is due to the influence of research methodologies used in other disciplines, especially the social sciences. This has been the case regarding the field of sociology, whose practitioners, concerned with how people organize themselves and construct social groupings, have long employed group identity as an important denominator of academic analysis.

In US history, scholars have embraced analytical models based on determining historical identity to examine the regional, ethnic, religious, economic, political, and social groups that are integral components of development over time. How do people in groups come to conceptualize common boundaries of membership? Why do people develop particular group identities? Historians of the American Revolution very early on led the way in employing these techniques in the evolution of the scholarly literature about the United States. They used this concept to examine why some colonists joined the rebel cause, while others remained loyal to Great Britain, establishing models and research techniques subsequently adopted by other historians studying different topics and time periods. The identity of being an American played a role both in causing the American Revolution and, as the conflict progressed, in forming new social distinctions. Recent studies have postulated the creation of an American identity proved to be one of the most significant occurrences of the Revolution. Blossoming in 1770s, this identity had evolved throughout the eighteenth century and became pronounced with the outbreak of the revolt.

An American identity also affected English speakers in Spanish Louisiana and, later by extension, in Texas during both the Spanish and Mexican periods. This proved a somewhat unusual development, given that many English speakers who moved into Spanish Louisiana never lived in an independent United States. Even those migrants who left the new nation to settle along the lower Mississippi River did not arrive with a longstanding, fully established American identity. Their national loyalty and self-conceptualization as Americans (as opposed to being British, Irish, or linked to a former English-speaking colony) thus rested on other factors than prolonged residence in the United States, if any at all. Sometimes an American identity formation might have been related to one's point of origin, such as Pennsylvania, New Jersey, New York, or other places that later became part of the United States. Sometimes being Irish or Scottish may have played a role in gravitating to an American identity. Against the odds, conceptualizing oneself as part of the United States did take root among English-speaking residents of Spanish Louisiana well before the Purchase of 1803. Individuals such as Oliver Pollock, whose life is considered in several essays in this volume, proved to be a solid example of this because he embraced the rebel cause at its beginning and manifested himself as being an American from the start of the colonial revolt. Similar identity formation took place all across the English-speaking population in the lower Mississippi valley, especially among the merchants at New Orleans, likely reflecting the fact that a considerable number of them came from the former British colonies of the Atlantic coast. They remained in touch with these eastern localities through their continuing trade relations, which probably influenced their identity formation. The increasing arrival of migrants from the United States after the mid-1780s sped up these developments. So, in terms of an existing American identity, the Louisiana Purchase only legitimized a process that had been underway for several decades. David Narrett has written a comprehensive survey of Anglo-Americans in Spanish Louisiana and the Gulf borderlands during the late eighteenth and early nineteenth centuries. Published in 2015, his *Adventurism and Empire: The Struggles for Mastery in the Louisiana-Florida Borderlands, 1762–1803*, greatly expands on themes discussed in this essay.

Light Townsend Cummins, "Oliver Pollock and the Creation of an American Identity in Spanish Colonial Louisiana," in *Nexus of Empire: Negotiating Loyalty and Identity in the Revolutionary Borderlands, 1760s–1820s*, ed. Gene Allen Smith and Sylvia L. Hilton (Gainesville: University Press of Florida, 2011), 198–218.

THE ECONOMY of Spanish Louisiana experienced a transformation during the last four decades of the eighteenth century. English-speaking merchants played a large part in these profound changes. One of the most successful of these merchants, and also one of the best known to history, was Oliver Pollock, who has long been recognized in the scholarship of the American Revolution. He was a significant source of supply at New Orleans for the rebel cause. Pollock shipped from New Orleans the gunpowder used by the Continental Army at the Battle of Saratoga. He also served as George Rogers Clark's service of supply in the American conquest of the British Illinois country.[1] Important as these accomplishments proved to the course of history, Oliver Pollock also played a larger, more pivotal role in a subtle process that had an equally large historical impact on the region. Pollock, along with other English-speaking merchants in Spanish Louisiana, participated in shifting the fundamental structures of Louisiana's private economy from what has sometimes been called a "frontier exchange" system, based on barter and localized trade, to a more complex one that involved the colony's meaningful participation in the sophisticated Atlantic market system during the late eighteenth century.[2] "The swift ascent of sugar and cotton," as Ira Berlin has noted of this process, "moved the lower

Mississippi valley from the periphery of the plantation world into its center."[3] A sophisticated market economy had already linked together earlier in the century much of the north Atlantic world into an intricate network that moved staple crops, consumer goods, and slaves through an expanding international commerce that relied upon capital migration and centralized credit as its motive force.[4] Louisiana was a late arrival when it joined this trade network during the Spanish period. It was Oliver Pollock, and other merchants of his ilk, who brought Louisiana into this system. By that time, the Atlantic market economy had already been crafted and dominated by Great Britain early in the eighteenth century; but after the American Revolution, the appearance of the infant United States threw the whole system into open rivalry as Atlantic coast merchants in the newly independent nation quickly became competitors to their British counterparts, especially in the Western Hemisphere.[5]

Oliver Pollock was the first English-speaking merchant to understand the role that Spanish Louisiana would come to play in the late eighteenth-century Atlantic market economy. Pollock, and others of Louisiana's English-speaking merchants who came after him, provided the mechanism for this trade. This process began when Oliver Pollock arrived in Louisiana early in the Spanish period. His merchant career lasted over fifty years until he died at Pinckneyville, Mississippi, in 1823. His descendants continued to operate plantations in the Felicianas for several generations thereafter.[6] Pollock was born in Northern Ireland, most probably in 1737. His family lived in the linen-drying areas to the south of Derry City, then known by the English name of Londonderry. The Pollock family traced its lineage to the Scottish settlers who came to Northern Ireland during the early waves of immigration from Scotland in the early 1600s. Many of his ancestors settled along the Burn Dennett, a small tributary of the River Foyle north of Strabane. The small village of Pollockstown became their ancestral seat, and some of Oliver's ancestors prospered in the rich farming and linen-drying economy of the district. His father, Jaret, did not find economic success, however, most likely because of the mid-eighteenth-century financial crisis in Ulster resulted in higher land rents and depression in the linen markets. Moving first to the town of Coleraine with several of his children after the death of his wife, the father and several of his sons, including Oliver, eventually departed for America in 1760.[7] At this time, Oliver Pollock was clearly by background a person who solidly viewed himself as a Presbyterian and as being very much Scotch Irish.

Once in British North America, Oliver Pollock became an active part of the Scotch Irish merchant network in Pennsylvania. He, his father, and his brothers initially settled in the Ulster-dominated backcountry near Carlisle. After a year there, Oliver moved to Philadelphia and began to work for major mercantile houses in that city. He became associated with the firm of Willing and Morris, one of the largest commercial houses on the eastern coast of British America. Pollock traveled to Havana in 1762 as the corresponding agent of Willing and Morris in order to sell supplies to the British army that had occupied the Cuban port during the Seven Years' War (1756–63). Once resident in Cuba, Pollock's background enabled him to manipulate his identity in order to become Celtic Irish and Roman Catholic. This gave him better commercial advantages. In so doing, he befriended an Irish priest in the city. He also became part of the circle of loyal acquaintances that evolved around Alejandro O'Reilly, a Spanish general of Irish lineage who was stationed at Havana. The two men socialized together and eventually enjoyed a warm friendship. Pollock married an Irish woman, Margaret O'Brien, who was then living with her merchant father at Havana.[8]

This marriage resulted in Pollock deciding to move his mercantile operations to New Orleans in order to increase his growing fortune. He thus followed Alejandro O'Reilly to New Orleans in 1769 when the general led an expedition there to restore Spanish control in the wake of a local revolt against Governor Antonio de Ulloa two years earlier. Oliver Pollock therefore became the first English-speaking merchant allowed in the Spanish-controlled city by his friend General O'Reilly. The general awarded Pollock a contract to supply New Orleans with flour since Louisiana was then experiencing a lack of that badly needed commodity. The price for flour had risen to the equivalent of $30.00 a barrel, and partly because of that high price, it was in short supply. Pollock had arrived on his ship, the *Royal Charlotte*, which carried a cargo of flour that he had bought specially in Baltimore for the New Orleans market. He met with

O'Reilly and offered him the cargo of flour at a greatly reduced price. This won the Spanish general to his cause. O'Reilly granted Pollock free-trade rights in the city as a result of this. "And I did," Pollock wrote later, "enjoy that privilege so long as I staid in the country."[9]

This flour contract provided Pollock with the economic foundation upon which he established a successful merchant house in Louisiana. Pollock prospered quickly and thereafter served as corresponding agent at New Orleans for Willing and Morris in Louisiana and the lower Mississippi valley. He also became an agent for other Atlantic-coast merchant firms. He accordingly reaped great profits, especially as Louisiana and the lower reaches of the river became increasingly a center of trade.[10] He noted: "I was supplied dry goods from London, Negroes from Africa, and flour from Philadelphia to the River Mississippi (for all of which I had no bills protested); and by the correspondence I had with the principal commercial houses in Philadelphia, I became known to the United States."[11] In that regard, Pollock cooperated with other English-speaking merchants, including those in the Illinois region and British West Florida, including George Morgan of the Philadelphia firm Baynton, Wharton, and Morgan. This firm established stores at Kaskaskia, Cahokia, and Vincennes. Starting in 1766, this company began sending flat boats down the Ohio from Fort Pitt. Pollock also served as the agent at New Orleans for David Franks and Company of Philadelphia, a firm represented by William Murray. Pollock and Murray, who eventually settled in the Feliciana District of Spanish Louisiana after the American Revolution, would remain lifelong friends. George Morgan eventually gave up his merchant activities in the Ohio valley and returned to Philadelphia. He left his unpaid accounts and his unsold stock to Murray. Morgan told his clients to settle their accounts by shipping pelts to Pollock in New Orleans. Pollock, acting as agent for Baynton, Wharton, and Morgan, shipped the pelts to Philadelphia.[12]

Although Spanish imperial trade laws, in theory, restricted at various times such commerce, in actual practice the province's participation in the larger Atlantic market economy proceeded unabated during the entire Spanish period. This was because, over the final decades of the eighteenth century, Spain progressively relaxed her mercantile-trade restrictions in order to profit from this commerce. As Arthur P. Whitaker has noted: "Spain was then at the height of its 'Bourbon renaissance' and the court seemed to be making considerable progress in its efforts to adjust its regulations to the needs of colonial commerce."[13] This proved especially the case for Louisiana. As early as 1768, the Spanish permitted Louisiana merchants to have a larger circle of foreign trading partners than those in the other of Spain's colonies. The Reglamento de Comerico Libre of 1778 expanded these privileges, while additional trade regulations in 1782 further increased the commercial flexibility of merchants in the province. As well, smuggling was often tolerated unofficially as New Orleans merchants openly conducted a routine trade with Philadelphia and other ports in the United States through French colonies in the Caribbean as waystations, a legal commerce permitted by Spanish mercantile regulations.[14] Boom times for English-speaking merchants and planters of Louisiana arrived definitively in 1788 when a royal order from the Spanish court permitted the shipment of goods from the Ohio and upper Mississippi valleys down the rivers to New Orleans for export, a beneficial situation.[15] Pollock and other merchants tied to the burgeoning Atlantic trade network amassed great fortunes in various aspects of the trade and commerce available to them in Spanish territory.

This certainly proved the case regarding the commerce in staples between New Orleans and ports such as Philadelphia and Baltimore. From 1769 onward, Pollock annually contracted with the Philadelphia firm of Willing and Morris to supply cargoes of badly needed flour, and for the rest of the century, a continuing series of Atlantic-coast merchants, including Robert Dorsey at Baltimore, Robert Smith from Philadelphia, and others shipped cargoes of this foodstuff to their corresponding agents at New Orleans and Natchez.[16] In turn, shipments of indigo and tobacco flowed from the lower Mississippi to the Atlantic coast starting in the 1770s. Then, with the growing preponderance of cotton in the late 1780s, a number of Anglo-American merchants turned to specializing in this staple. One recent study of the New Orleans export trade indicates that, between 1793 and 1796, over 50 percent of all commerce in Louisiana cotton occurred with ports in the United States.[17] The significance of this mercantile activity went far beyond the profits of the trade itself. It also created an important byproduct: a lively movement of bills of exchange between Spanish Louisiana and Atlantic-coast merchant houses in the United States. This activity provided rudimentary banking and credit services for Spanish Louisiana that, by the 1790s, had irrevocably tied the lower Mississippi valley to the United States, while also moving the province further away from participation in Spanish and French trading networks.[18]

Hence, the profits of English-speaking merchants expanded throughout the period of Spanish rule in Louisiana.[19] Much of Pollock's personal fortune rested on slave trading. He actively began selling slaves in Spanish New Orleans soon after his arrival in the colony. In 1769, for example, he sold two house servants to a local resident for 265 pesos fuertes. Although these sales might have been in technical violation of Spanish law since Pollock was not a Louisiana citizen at that time, government complicity for such commerce could be assumed since one of the other eager purchasers was none other than General Alejandro O'Reilly, who bought several slaves.[20] Pollock took full advantage of this situation. He imported an entire boatload of over eighty African slaves to the lower Mississippi valley in 1773. He had apparently purchased them in the West Indies, although all of them were native Africans who had come by way of the middle passage to the New World. Pollock's bill of sale described them as "brutish males, females, and children who were not baptized."[21] The following year, Pollock sailed to the Atlantic coast, where he purchased another shipment of slaves that he brought back to the lower Mississippi valley, also selling them at a great profit.

The importation of consumer goods into Louisiana constituted a second category of economic activity for Oliver Pollock, coequal to that of the slave trade, additionally linking Spanish Louisiana to the Atlantic market economy. English-speaking residents all along the river wanted manufactured items and various consumer products, both for domestic and agrarian use, in order to maintain their accustomed lifestyle of daily existence. In large measure, these items served as "cultural markers" around which an America identity formed.[22] Like the slave trade, the networks for furnishing these consumer goods shifted from French to British sources, starting in the late 1760s, and after the American

Revolution, this commerce linked the lower Mississippi valley to supply centers controlled by merchants in the United States. Oliver Pollock imported large amounts of consumer goods from Atlantic ports during the Spanish period. He regularly sold items such as farm implements, clothing, shoes, coffee, tea, nails, and other manufactured goods to the English speakers who frequented his store at New Orleans. Pollock also opened a store at Tunica Bayou, north of Baton Rouge, during the early 1770s. He operated this store in partnership with James Willing, the brother of the Philadelphia owner of the merchant house for whom he served as correspondent at New Orleans. The store at Tunica Bayou stocked goods such as premade clothing of the latest American fashion, bridles, saddles, cut saw files, readymade shoes, and a wide variety of similar dry goods. Pollock and Willing even made concerted efforts to sell supplies to the British for use in the Native American trade. In 1773, James Willing wrote to General Frederick Haldimand, commandant at Pensacola: "I have taken the Liberty of addressing you to acquaint you of my arrival here with a cargo of goods suitable to the Indian Illinois trade. I propose setting off tomorrow with my goods to Manchac and there to stay with my goods until further hearing from you."[23]

The importing of consumer goods into Spanish Louisiana followed an established hierarchy of commerce. The larger firms on the Atlantic coast shipped consumer items to the major merchant houses of New Orleans. From there, they went to an increasing number of local stores that rapidly sprung up all across Louisiana during the late Spanish period. The trading post or small general store came to exist as a fixture of almost every settlement in the region, and after the early 1780s, such establishments became equated with English-speaking merchants in every quarter of Spanish territory. These local stores also became social gathering places for the English-speaking settlers in their neighborhoods, thus adding to the growth of a community spirit that had an impact on identity formation. A variety of social interactions that revolved around the English-speaking trading posts and general stores furthered the creation of a new group identity. Drinking, gambling, and the work of entrepreneurial mechanics who plied their trades at such locations proved to be motivations for group cohesion. As one historian of the

Thompson Creek area, north of Baton Rouge, wrote in the 1780s about the settlement that grew up around the Cochran and Rhea Store: "The men loved to visit and frequently met at one another's house to discuss the business of pirating and smuggling that took place on the river. They would remain for several days, drinking, playing cards, and catching up on the news of the world."[24]

The proliferation of smaller, rural stores reflected the expanding commercial grasp of the larger New Orleans firms into the lower Mississippi hinterlands. The significance of these stores increased in the 1780s, when the new and expanding English-speaking populations served by this network of stores developed a tendency to remain separate from the Gallic and Hispanophone populations in areas where these groups already resided. That was so because the English-speaking planters who came to Louisiana in the 1780s and 1790s tended to found new communities in areas proximate to the already existing communities. Many of these new, relatively small, and—at least initially—very rural communities were located short distances from the established, older settlements such as St. Louis, Ste. Genevieve, and Natchez, where there had traditionally resided large numbers of non-English speakers.[25] Moreover, the rural store became the social community center for these new settlements. Such places included New Madrid, Bayou Sara, Carondelet, and Nueva Bourbon.

Acquisition of land and the ownership of plantations also became an additional road to wealth for Oliver Pollock as he aggressively pursued the acquisition of land and plantations once he arrived in the lower Mississippi valley.[26] During the early 1770s, he found himself in the enviable position of holding British citizenship while he enjoyed all of the rights that came with approved residence in Spanish Louisiana. This unique status permitted him to receive land grants and purchase property in both Louisiana and British West Florida. By 1775, Pollock had received several large land grants from the British government in West Florida. His first such acquisition consisted of some 400 acres along the Tangipahoa River near Pass Manchac. He also received grants of land on the east bank of the Mississippi near Pointe Coupee and at Baton Rouge, the latter being of property upon which today partially sits the campus of Louisiana State University.[27] Pollock secured his largest land holding in 1772, when he purchased a large tract at Tunica Bayou from Henry Fairchild, a British settler in West Florida. This plantation, locally known as "Old Tunica," grew indigo, rice, tobacco, and vegetables. Pollock built a house on the property, while he constructed a small boat landing at the point where the bayou enters the Mississippi River. A nephew from Pennsylvania, Hamilton Pollock, arrived at Tunica Bend in the mid-1770s in order to superintend the operation of this plantation.[28] A description of this property noted that "the land in cultivation was of excellent quality" and that there were several good fields for the planting of crops near the river. Improvements eventually consisted of a large farmhouse, a warehouse, a log smokehouse, corncrib, and various cabins.[29] Pollock also purchased town lots at St. Francisville and at New Orleans. He as well secured property in Spanish Louisiana, including several plantation tracts north of New Orleans, all on the east bank of the Mississippi River.[30] Hence, by the mid-1770s, Oliver Pollock owned over a dozen tracts of land in both Louisiana and West Florida, some of which he held for investment and others of which he actively farmed using slave labor.

All of these commercial interests increasingly moved Oliver Pollock toward political, economic, and cultural solidarity with an American identity. The American Revolution served as a catalyst for this significant change in the manner by which Oliver Pollock conceptualized his own identity. To that time in his life, he had variously presented himself as an Ulsterman, a Scotch Irishman, or Celtic Irish, while at times he cast himself as a Presbyterian and at other times a Roman Catholic. The American colonial revolt served as the motivation that helped him form a permanent identity. Clearly, his being of Irish stock disinclined him to support the British; in overwhelming fashion, however, it was Pollock's career as a Spanish Louisiana merchant that brought him to an American identity. Although he had apparently never before professed an American colonial viewpoint and had lived in the British North American colonies for less than two years, the events that began at Lexington and Concord marked a significant change in the way he defined his own personal identity. This had become very apparent by the spring of 1776, when a Virginia military officer named George Gibson arrived at Spanish New Orleans. It was Gibson's mission to purchase goods and supplies at New Orleans for use by colonial troops. The Virginia officer quickly made contact with Oliver Pollock, who enthusiastically agreed to intercede with the governor of Louisiana on his behalf. Pollock arranged for a large shipment of gunpowder to be sent by Gibson up the Mississippi and Ohio Rivers to Fort Pitt. Captain Gibson also carried with him on his return trip a letter that Pollock wrote to Robert Morris, who, in addition to having been a partner in the firm of Willing and Morris, then served in Congress as chair of the Secret Committee of Correspondence. Pollock declared unequivocally and absolutely his American identity in this letter to Morris, the man who had been his merchant contact in Philadelphia for almost twenty years. He wrote: "Permit me therefore to make tender my hearty services and to assure you that my conduct shall ever be as to merit confidence and approbation of the country to whom I owe everything but my birth."[31]

Oliver Pollock had become an American and had largely done so because of his mercantile connections. Over the next four years, he engaged in a wide variety of activities in support of the rebel cause. The year following Gibson's visit to New Orleans, Pollock materially assisted in supporting the expedition that Pennsylvania captain James Willing led to the lower Mississippi valley. This was, of course, the same James Willing who had lived in British West Florida and who had operated during the early 1770s the store at Tunica Bend in partnership with Pollock. Young Willing had returned to the United States, received an officer's commission, and led an expedition down the Mississippi in the spring of 1778 for the purpose of capturing British West Florida. Willing's expedition caused a tremendous amount of upset in British territory along the Mississippi during the spring of 1778. He and his men raided British plantations, took valuable prizes, and arrived at New Orleans, where the members of the expedition sought to sell their plunder. During April 1778, Pollock superintended the sale of this property and the slaves that had also been taken during the Willing raid. Later in that same year, Pollock began assisting George Rogers Clark, who was involved in conquering British territory in the Illinois country. Pollock became the chief source of supplying for George Rogers Clark's troops while they conquered the British territory along the lower Ohio and upper Mississippi Rivers. Hence, by the end of the American Revolution, Oliver Pollock had become an American. So too had many of the other English-speaking merchants in the region who had cooperated with him, including Daniel Clark, Thomas Patterson, Alexander Graydon, and several others who were also engaged in the Philadelphia trade from the lower Mississippi valley.

Many of these English-speaking merchants who had become Americanized, including Pollock, had never lived for substantial amounts of time in the infant United States or in the British colonies from which the new nation had been born.[32] They nonetheless saw themselves as part of a new, emerging identity in the region: that of being an "American."[33] Peter J. Kastor has noted for the late Spanish period regarding English speakers in the lower Mississippi valley and those in the United States: "Americans and Louisianans conceived of citizenship and nation hood in very similar ways." For that reason, "by 1800," he observes, "both groups saw advantages in equality among white male citizens and benefits from broad networks of interest."[34] Although writing about Boston merchants during the late eighteenth century, the views of historian Phillis Whitman Hunter have some measure of applicability to the creation of this American identity in Spanish Louisiana. "The privileged status of the mercantile elite was distinctly white," she writes of Boston, and "whites defined their privileged position by objectifying others."[35] This same process can be seen in the lower Mississippi valley in the patterns of American identity formation that took place there. This was a compelling development in Spanish Louisiana because many, if not most, of these English speakers failed to conceptualize themselves as advance agents of United States imperium. Pollock certainly did not when he arrived. Instead, the majority of them lived in the lower Mississippi valley during the period of Spanish dominion largely for personal reasons, mostly because they wanted the success that mercantile pursuits could bring them and their families. They did not come for reasons of national expansion or geopolitical aggrandizement. Once these people had arrived Louisiana, they nonetheless engaged in economic practices that fostered group identity formation that made them disposed to a new identity. This American identity should not be confused with nationalism because it was significantly more subtle and operated independently from any individual relationship to the concept of nation. It was instead cultural and social in nature. As Stuart Hall has written of such identity, it was "a sort of collective 'one time self,' hiding inside the many other, superficial and artificially imposed 'selves,' which people with a shared ancestry hold in common." Indeed, it may be that the forging of a perceived cultural identity predates the formation of a national identity historically, as was the case in Spanish Louisiana. "Within the terms of this definition," Hall notes, "our cultural identities reflect the common historical experiences and shared cultural codes which provide us as 'one people' with stable, unchanging and continuous frames of reference and meaning beneath the shifting divisions and vicissitudes of our actual history."[36]

The market economy did provide English-speaking merchants in Spanish Louisiana with such a common experience based on tangible manifestations of "shared cultural codes," especially in areas of material culture and lifestyles, upon which an explicit cultural identity formed. This was significant because Pollock and most of the other English-speaking residents who came to live in Spanish territory before the Louisiana Purchase arrived with a wide variety of preexisting and related identities, none of which could initially be styled "American." Some called themselves English, others were Ulster folk, and still others saw themselves as Celtic Irish. Some were Protestant, while some were Roman Catholic. Others saw themselves as British, while others styled themselves as being Scottish. They were from Georgia, South Carolina, Pennsylvania, or New Jersey. A few even called themselves Jamaicans or Bahamians. During the American Revolution, some of these settlers were staunchly tory; others were committed rebels. They lived during the late eighteenth century in all parts of Spanish Louisiana but especially in the Natchez District and the Felicianas, as the former British colony of West Florida became known in the Spanish era after the American Revolution.[37]

Indeed, Pollock and these English-speaking merchants had come to represent the colony's most efficient link with the outside world by the late 1780s. On two occasions after disastrous fires at New Orleans in

1788 and 1794, English-speaking merchants played the key role in reprovisioning and rebuilding the city, thus enabling its material recovery and the restoration of its infrastructure. After the 1788 conflagration, Oliver Pollock chartered a special vessel at Philadelphia, loaded it to capacity with needed domestic goods lost in the fire, and sailed it to New Orleans on what turned out to be a particularly profitable voyage. That cargo included, a bit belatedly, a used pump fire engine sold to the Spanish Cabildo that Pollock had purchased from Benjamin Franklin's Philadelphia Fire Company. Presumably, this first fire engine in Louisiana later saw service in the second major New Orleans fire of 1794, an event that Pollock did not witness.[38]

Oliver Pollock had returned to the United States to live in 1791, and there he remained for the next twenty-eight years. He moved to Pennsylvania, where he operated a tavern and small store at the village of Silver Spring near Carlisle. After the death of his wife, Margaret, he married a woman from Baltimore and became a merchant in that city. In partnership with his son, Procopio, who had been born years earlier in Spanish New Orleans, Pollock engaged in maritime trade between Philadelphia, Baltimore, Havana, and New Orleans. Members of his family, however, continued to reside in Spanish Louisiana on the Tunica Bend Plantation, which continued under his ownership as an important asset. His nephew Hamilton looked after Oliver's affairs from his own plantation near Bayou Sara. Pollock's eldest daughter, Mary, and her husband, Dr. Samuel S. Robinson, had settled in present-day Wilkinson County, Mississippi, a few miles north of Tunica Bend, an area that became part of the United States in 1797. The Robinsons made frequent visits to the Tunica Bend Plantation from their home in nearby Pinckneyville, and with the passing of Hamilton Pollock in 1814, they began the active management of the plantation.

By the 1790s, cotton dominated this area as the most important staple and, as a result, had become the major crop grown at Tunica Bend. The Pollock family continued to prosper with the arrival of cotton to the area. In so doing, they reflected the common patterns of landholding and agriculture that had become prevalent among all of these English speakers in Spanish Louisiana. The rise of cotton caused subsistence farming to be replaced all across the lower Mississippi valley by a reliance on staples during the closing decades of the century. As historian Roger G. Kennedy has noted of the Mississippi valley and Gulf coast for the early decades of the nineteenth century: "The economy of the borderlands was in transition from subsistence agriculture of white and Indian yeoman, growing their own crops and supplementing their diets with meat secured by hunting, to a plantation system, growing cotton and rice for sale to international markets."[39] A recent study of land records from the 1760 to the 1800s clearly establishes that many planters engaged in staple-crop production migrated into what would become the Louisiana Purchase territory, bringing their slaves with them.[40] As historian John Hebron Moore has noted, most of these English-speaking settlers who came "to the lower Mississippi valley were agriculturalists lured away from worn-out farms or plantations in the South Atlantic states by the attraction of easily obtained fertile virgin lands," and because of them, New Orleans had become one of the world's leading cotton-exporting cities by the time of the Louisiana Purchase.[41] "The province of Louisiana yields very rich produce," John Bonfeld reported to Thomas Jefferson in 1785 from Bordeaux, France, noting that "the two cargoes arrived here will amount to two Million Livres in furs and Indigo."[42] In 1794, the Natchez District produced about 36,000 pounds of cotton. Four years later, in 1798, estimates for the annual amount of cotton production rose to 1.2 million pounds. "We continue to cultivate cotton with very great success," William Dunbar noted of the 1790s, "it is by far the most profitable crop we have ever undertaken in this country."[43] The slave population of the Natchez District grew accordingly, increasing from approximately 500 bondmen in 1784 to over 2,000 by 1796.[44] Many of the vessels that sailed with cargoes of cotton from Louisiana to Atlantic ports returned to the lower Mississippi with new settlers as passengers. "There is a vessel now laying at Philadelphia," Thomas Jefferson wrote a correspondent in 1791, "advertising to receive immigrants to Louisiana gratis, on account of the Spanish Government."[45]

Susan Garrett Davis has noted of this phase of English-speaking migration: "Coming overland or down the Mississippi on flatboats, these Upland South settlers migrated from the Southern Appalachian and

Southern Piedmont areas of eastern Tennessee, Kentucky, West Virginia, and Carolina [*sic*], northern Georgia, and Alabama."[46] In 1810, one of the English-speakers at Bayou Sara wrote to a New Orleans newspaper in order to report that many of these recent settlers were "generally Americans, and many of them purchased lands and settled in Florida since the cession of Louisiana to the United States; fully impressed with the belief that they would soon find themselves under their former laws and government."[47] Not all of these immigrants, however, represented the more upstanding elements of society. As historian Samuel C. Hyde Jr. has observed about some of them, "the region served as a haven for Tories, army deserters, and desperados, all of whom exploited the prevailing instability and absence of American control."[48]

Oliver Pollock returned to the lower Mississippi valley in 1819 upon the death of his wife, and there lived out the remaining years of his life. He maintained his legal residence at the Pinckneyville, Mississippi, home of his daughter but often stayed at Tunica Bend, by that time a part of the Florida Parishes of the state of Louisiana. Although a man in his eighties, it seems that Pollock still had the inclinations of an entrepreneur. The increasing volume of steamboat traffic on the river provided him the opportunity for profit. The Pollocks and Robinsons built a levee at the foot of Tunica Bayou and opened a woodyard.[49] This became a popular reprovisioning stop for boats traveling on the river between New Orleans and St. Louis. The success of the woodyard motivated yet other changes. Pollock and some of his children laid elaborate plans for the development of a town on the plantation at the boat landing, where Tunica Bayou enters the Mississippi. He laid off street lines, began to sell property, and hoped for the prosperity of this town, which he named Tunicaville. Pollock, however, died on December 17, 1823, before the town could be developed fully. Some of the Pollock children tried to carry forward with promoting Tunicaville. It did eventually receive a post office, but it never grew, and the Pollock family realized little profit from the venture. They eventually sold parcels of their plantation itself to other planters, although they kept approximately one-half of the original holding for themselves. One grandson, Oliver Pollock Robinson, lived on the Tunica Bend Plantation until the Civil War. Others maintained homes in St. Francisville and at the hamlet of Bayou Sara. As well, in the mid-1830s, the family initiated a series of unsuccessful legal claims that sought to regain titles to some of Pollock's Spanish-era land grants, which had never been reconfirmed by the United States government.[50]

The life story of Oliver Pollock in Spanish Louisiana, and of the family dynasty that he established in the lower Mississippi valley, may be seen as an example of a process of American identity formation in the region. Indeed, by the 1790s, the existence of an American identity could be clearly seen in the life histories and writings of various merchants whose primary point of contact with the United States had been because of their participation in the Atlantic market economy. Oliver Pollock was chief among them. These merchants and planters, including Daniel Clark, the Jones brothers, James Mather, and many others from the entire English-speaking community of Spanish Louisiana, shared similar life histories that moved them to form an American identity without any prior explicit identification with the United States.

This Americanized identity based on an amalgamation of English-speaking groups in the region thus appeared in tandem with the economic development of Louisiana and its hinterland in the late eighteenth and early nineteenth centuries. This identity had an impact greater that the actual number of English-speaking residents in the colony prior to the Louisiana Purchase. Historical estimates, given the lack of accurate or extant census information, hold that approximately 50,000 persons (exclusive of Native Americans) lived in the Purchase territory when it became part of the United States, of whom perhaps as many as one-half were African slaves or free persons of color. These figures exclude the five to seven thousand individuals in the Natchez District who became United States citizens in 1797, when that area passed from Spanish control, along with the some 1,600 persons who continued to live in Spanish West Florida until after the Revolt of 1810.[51] The net result is that the English-speaking population of Spanish Louisiana constituted no more than several thousand persons, but all of them were individuals who had profitable mercantile businesses. They formed an emerging elite that eventually became a foundation for the subsequent hegemonic Americanization of Louisiana in areas such as culture, economics, and politics. Hence, in some measure, the Louisiana Purchase of 1803 can be seen as the legitimization by territorial acquisition of a preexisting link to the United States created by the presence of an American identity that had been fashioned by joining Spanish Louisiana to the Atlantic market economy and that, in so doing, firmly connected the lower Mississippi valley to major East Coast ports such as Philadelphia and Baltimore. Although the social commentator Hector St. John de Crevecoeur did not visit Louisiana during his residence in British North America in early1780s, his famous essay "Letters from an American Farmer" does have pertinence to the process of identity formation that occurred in the Spanish province. He asked, "what is an American," and from "whence came all these people?" Crevecoer's answer: "They are a mixture of English, Scotch, Irish, French, Dutch, Germans, and Swedes." "From this promiscuous breed," he observed, "that race now called Americans have arisen."[52] The Americanization of Louisiana was therefore not entirely initiated by the diplomatic events that occurred in 1803 with the Louisiana Purchase. The formation of an American identity in Louisiana was caused in large part by Spanish Louisiana's entrance into the late eighteenth-century Atlantic market economy, a process set in motion by Oliver Pollock's arrival at New Orleans in 1769.

Notes

1. Light Townsend Cummins, "Oliver Pollock and George Rogers Clark's Service of Supply: A Case Study in Financial Disaster," in *Selected Papers from the 1985 and 1986 George Rogers Clark Trans-Appalachian Frontier History Conferences*, ed. Robert J. Holden (Vincennes, IN: National Park Service, 1988), 1–17.

2. For a full discussion of the frontier exchange economy, see Daniel H. Usner, *Indians, Settlers, and Slaves in a Frontier Exchange Economy: The Lower Mississippi Valley before 1783* (Chapel Hill: University of North Carolina Press, 1992).

3. Ira Berlin, *Many Thousands Gone: The First Two Centuries of Slavery in North America* (Cambridge, MA: Harvard University Press, 1998), 325.

4. Spanish Louisiana must be considered by the historian as an emerging part of the late eighteenth-century Atlantic World in terms of identity formation regarding the various groups that lived along the lower Mississippi River. As Michael J. Braddick has written: "The movement of goods and people around the Atlantic world created a shared material culture which reflected common assumptions about status distinctions. . . . By the eighteenth century these forces had fostered

a marked convergence of elite sensibilities across all the territories of the nascent British Empire." Braddick, "Civility and Authority," in *The British Atlantic World, 1500–1800*, ed. David Armitage and Braddick (New York: Palgrave Macmillan, 2001), 93. In addition, many historians view the commercial development involved in the creation of the Atlantic World within the context of metropolitan centers and colonial peripheries. "By the time the colonists were numerous enough and wealthy enough to interest the metropole," note Amy Turner Bushnell and Jack P. Greene, "they were also strong enough to resist it and to seize control over their own backcountry." Bushnell and Greene, "Peripheries, Centers, and the Construction of Early Modern American Empires," in *Negotiated Empires: Centers and Peripheries in the Americas, 1500–1820*, ed. Christine Daniels and Michael V. Kennedy (New York: Routledge, 2002), 11. In analogous fashion, such a generic relationship eventually developed in the region between English speakers and the Spanish governments of Louisiana and West Florida, although the Louisiana Purchase obviated conflict in much of the region, except in the Felicianas, where a revolt in 1810 did occur. For a full analysis of Louisiana as part of the Atlantic World complex, see D. W. Meinig, *Atlantic America, 1492–1880*, vol. 1 of his *The Shaping of America: A Geographical Perspective of 500 Years of History* (New Haven, CT: Yale University Press, 1986), 193–202, 416–17, and 424–25; and Alan Taylor, *American Colonies: The Settling of North America* (New York: Penguin Books, 2002), 363–95. See also Ian K. Steele, "Exploding Colonial American History: Amerindian, Atlantic, and Global Perspectives," *Reviews in American History* 26 (1998): 70–95.

5. The best introduction to the Atlantic market economy of the eighteenth century is John J. McCusker and Kenneth Morgan, eds., *The Early Modern Atlantic Economy* (Cambridge: Cambridge University Press, 2000); and William M. Reddy, *The Rise of Market Culture* (Cambridge: Cambridge University Press, 1987).

6. James A. James, *Oliver Pollock: The Life and Times of an Unknown Patriot* (New York: Appleton-Century, 1937). Light T. Cummins, "Oliver Pollock's Plantations: An Early Anglo Landowner on the Lower Mississippi, 1769–1824," *Louisiana History* 29 (Winter 1988): 35–48.

7. Extensive genealogical information about the Scottish branch of the Pollock family may be found in boxes 40, 68, and 69 of the MacLeod Collection and in box 4 of the Graham Collection, Royal Society of Genealogists, Charterhouse Buildings, London, England.

8. James, *Oliver Pollock*, 4–7.

9. Oliver Pollock to the Captain General of Cuba, June 22, 1796, Archivo General de Indias, Seville, Spain, Papeles de Cuba, Legajo 1469; Pollock to Lu de las Casas, July 14, 1796, ibid. Pollock's contract was for the supply of flour. For the Cabildo deliberations on the scarcity of this commodity, see Actas del Cabildo, New Orleans, October 5, 1770, August 2, 16, 1771, 1:20, 32, 33, WPA Transcripts in Spanish on Microfilm, New Orleans Public Library, New Orleans.

10. The standard book-length studies of Oliver Pollock in the Revolution are James A. James, *Oliver Pollock*; and John A. Caughey, *Bernardo de Gálvez in Louisiana, 1776–1783* (Berkeley: University of California Press, 1934). See also Light

Townsend Cummins, *Spanish Observers and the American Revolution* (Baton Rouge: Louisiana State University Press, 1991).

11. James, *Oliver Pollock*, 54; Pollock to Governor Beverly Randolph of Virginia, January 22, 1791, *Calendar of Virginia State Papers* (Richmond: J. H. O'Bannon, 1888), 6:251.

12. James, *Oliver Pollock*, 4950; Saville, *George Morgan, Colony Builder*, 5275.

13. Arthur P. Whitaker, "Reed and Forde: Merchant Adventurers of Philadelphia: Their Trade with Spanish New Orleans." in *The Spanish Province of Louisiana, 1763–1803*, ed. Gilbert C. Din (1937; repr., Lafayette: Center for Louisiana Studies, 1996), 246.

14. Arthur P. Whitaker, "The Commerce of Louisiana and Florida at the End of the Eighteenth Century," *Hispanic American Historical Review* 8 (May 1928): 219–20.

15. Whitaker, "Reed and Forde," 249–50.

16. Firms in the United States and Great Britain included Baynton, Wharton, and Company at Philadelphia; Bridgen and Walker at London; Dennis and Smith at New Haven; Hindley and Needham at London; Walker and Dawson at London; Hugh and Alexander at Philadelphia; and Willing and Morris at Philadelphia.

17. Jesus Lorente Miguel, "Commercial Relations between New Orleans and the United States, 1783–1803," in *The North American Role in the Spanish Imperial Economy, 1760–1819*, ed. Jacques Barbier and Allen Kuethe (Manchester, UK: University of Manchester Press, 1984), 180.

18. Light T. Cummins, "Anglo Merchants and Capital Migration in Spanish Colonial New Orleans, 1763–1803," *Gulf Coast Historical Review* 4 (Fall 1988): 22.

19. Jack D. L. Holmes, "Some Economic Problems of Spanish Governors in Louisiana," *Hispanic American Historical Review* 42 (November 1962): 521–41; John W. Caughey, "Bernardo de Gálvez and the English Smugglers on the Mississippi, 1777," *Hispanic American Historical Review* 7 (1932): 46–58. Most of the periodic attempts to stop contraband trade were usually symbolic actions designed to give the appearance that Spanish governors were vigorously enforcing Spain's mercantile policies. In reality, a succession of Louisiana governors from the 1770s to the 1790s often looked the other way in order to permit the dealings of the Anglo-American merchants, whose mercantile activities were deemed essential to the functioning of the colony. See Caughey, *Bernardo de Gálvez in Louisiana*, and the various biographies of Louisiana governors in Joseph G. Dawson III, ed., *The Louisiana Governors: From Iberville to Edwards* (Baton Rouge: Louisiana State University Press, 1990).

20. Actos de Andres Almonaster y Rojas, vol. 1, February 9, 1770, f. 9, New Orleans Notary Archives, Civil Courts Building, New Orleans.

21. Acts of Juan Bautista Garic, vol. 4, March 10, 1773, New Orleans Notary Archives.

22. Sociologists postulate that objects of material culture constitute a matrix on which cultural identity forms. In modern times, items such as athletic shoes and CD players serve as "cultural markers" of perceived group identities. One leading

sociologist has noted, "Identities are produced, consumed, and regulated within culture—creating meaning through symbolic systems of representation about the identity positions which we might adopt." Kathryn Woodward, ed., *Identity and Difference* (London: Sage, 1997), 2, 12.

23. Account Book of William Dunbar, Records of Antebellum Plantations, ed. Kenneth M. Stampp, Microform Collection, ser. J, reel 1; James Willing to James Haldimand, Manchack, January 3, 1772, Haldimand Add. Mss. 21, 729, f. 280, British Museum, London.

24. Virginia Lobdell Jennings, "Narrative of the Settlement at Thompson Creek, 1716–1832," *Louisiana Genealogical Register* 42 (June 1995): 209.

25. Antonio Acosta Rodríguez, *La población de Luisiana española, 1763–1803* (Madrid: Ministerio de Asuntos Exteriores, 1979), 234.

26. Cummins, "Oliver Pollock's Plantations," 42–45.

27. *A Plan of the Coast of Part of West Florida and Louisiana including the River Mississippi from its Entrances as High as the River Yazous*, Map Library, School of Geosciences, Louisiana State University, Baton Rouge.

28. The survey of the Old Tunica Plantation is located in Undocketed Materials—Natchez, Louisiana Survey Materials, Historic New Orleans Collection, New Orleans. A description to the plantation is located in Probate of Oliver Pollock, File 81, Clerk of the Court Records, West Feliciana Parish Courthouse, St. Francisville, LA.

29. *Alexander Baudin v. G. Davy, Washington White, Widow of W. Roliff and Samuel Robinson*, April 13, 1821, Case 2048, box 778, Records of the Supreme Court of Louisiana, Earl K. Long Memorial Library, University of New Orleans.

30. Cummins, "Oliver Pollock's Plantations," 38–40.

31. James A. James, "Oliver Pollock, Financier of the Revolution in the West," *Mississippi Valley Historical Review* 16 (1929): 71.

32. Peter Dobson Hall has postulated a clear connection between economic activity and formation of group culture. As he has written of this generic process during the twentieth century: "American culture in the twentieth century is characterized by masses of individuals who produce goods and services that they do not consume and consume goods and services that they do not produce—and by institutional mechanisms that coordinate the flow of goods and services as well as the recruitment and training of managers of those institutions on a national basis." Hall, *The Organization of American Culture, 1700–1900: Private Institutions, Elites, and the Origins of American Nationalism* (New York: New York University Press, 1982), 2. In protonascent form, the foundations of this twentieth-century characterization of culture can be seen in the formation of an American elite identity in Spanish Louisiana.

33. I employ the term "American" in the strict sentiment of the Spanish term *estadosunidense*. It is an imprecision of our vernacular English that those persons who are from the United States have no exact and singular popular term by which they are denominated in order to distinguish them with accuracy from other residents of this hemisphere.

34. Kastor further develops this theme by writing: "For settlers of European birth and ancestry in the United States and in Louisiana, the creation of national communities was in large part contingent on white supremacy." Peter J. Kastor, *The Nation's Crucible: The Louisiana Purchase and the Creation of America.* (New Haven, CT: Yale University Press, 2004), 29.

35. Phillis Whitman Hunter, *Purchasing Identity in the Atlantic Words: Massachusetts Merchants, 1670–1780* (Ithaca, NY: Cornell University Press, 2001), 89.

36. Stuart Hall, "Cultural Identity and Diaspora," in Woodward, *Identity and Difference*, 51.

37. The areas known as the Old Natchez District and the Felicianas constitute historically the regions of the lower Mississippi valley where English-speaking residents dominated territorial space for the longest continuous period of time, from the 1770s until the early antebellum period and beyond. The Natchez District and the Felicianas composed a common physiographic area along the east bank of the Mississippi Rover, starting in the south at the Iberville River and running north past Baton Rouge, Bayou Sara, and Natchez to the Big Black River near present-day Grand Gulf. Oriented toward the Mississippi itself, the settled areas sometimes extended only a few files inland, although settlement eventually went far eastward to Mobile and beyond. Over time, this area experienced complicated territorial shifts of national sovereignty, as various part of it existed under the shifting domination of Spain, Great Britain, and the United States.

38. For a description of destruction during the 1788 fire, see "Report of the Demands of the Citizens of New Orleans after the Fire, March 21, 1788," E. A. Parsons Collection, Humanities Resource Center, University of Texas at Austin. Pollock sets forth his intentions to sell goods for the rebuilding of the city in a letter to the Spanish governor. See "Instancia de Olivero Pollock," February 10, 1789, Archivo General de Indias, Seville, Spain, Audiencia de Santo Domingo, Legajo 2553, f. 628.

39. Roger G. Kennedy, *Mr. Jefferson's Lost Cause: Land, Farmers, Slavery, and the Louisiana Purchase* (New York: Oxford University Press, 2003), 144.

40. Cummins, "Merchants and Capital Migration," 7–27.

41. John Hebron Moore, *The Emergence of the Cotton Kingdom in the Old Southwest: Mississippi, 1770–1860* (Baton Rouge: Louisiana State University Press, 1988), 5.

42. John Bondfeld to Thomas Jefferson, Bordeaux, August 20, 1785, in *The Papers of Thomas Jefferson*, ed. Julian P. Boyd, 43 vols. (Princeton, NJ: Princeton University Press, 1953–2017), 8:412.

43. Moore, *Emergence of the Cotton Kingdom*, 5.

44. Berlin, *Many Thousands Gone*, 341.

45. Thomas Jefferson to William Short, Philadelphia, August 29, 1781, in Boyd, *Papers of Thomas Jefferson*, 22:96.

46. Susan Garrett Davis, "The Felicianas," in Louisiana Folklife Program, *Folklife in the Florida Parishes*, http://www.louisianafolklife.org/LT/Virtual_Books/Fla_Parishes/book_florida_feliciana.html (accessed September 24, 2006).

47. Letter signed by "Common Sense," *Louisiana Gazette* (New Orleans), July

2, 1810, quoted in Stanley C. Arthur, *The Story of the West Florida Rebellion* (St. Francisville, LA: St. Francisville Democrat, 1935), 39.

48. Samuel C. Hyde Jr., *Pistols and Politics: The Dilemma of Democracy in Louisiana's Florida Parishes, 1810–1899* (Baton Rouge: Louisiana State University Press, 1996), 2. See also Andrew F. McMichael, "'May God Damn My Soul if I Don't Split Your Brains Out': Cross-Border Crime and Regional Instability in West Florida, 1800–1810" (paper presented to the Omohundro Institute of Early American History and Culture, Glasgow, Scotland, July 2001); and Samuel C. Hyde Jr., ed., *A Fierce and Fractious Frontier: The Curious Development of Louisiana's Florida Parishes, 1699–2000* (Baton Rouge: Louisiana State University, 2004), esp. Robin F. A. Fabel, "Boom in the Bayous: Land Speculation and Town Planning in the Florida Parishes under British Rule," 44–59.

49. *Baudin v. Roliff* et al. *Robinson* (1823), Case Files, Docket 1282, Records of the Supreme Court of Louisiana.

50. For records of these claims, see State Land Office, Baton Rouge, *Greensburg Land Claims*, Book 2, pt. 2:910.

51. The best population study of Spanish Louisiana remains Rodríguez, *La población de Luisiana española*. For other population estimates, see Gilbert C. Din, "Slavery in Louisiana's Florida Parishes under the Spanish Regime, 1779–1803," in Hyde *Fierce and Fractious Frontier*, 63–64.

52. J. Hector St. John de Crevecoeur, *Letters from an American Farmer and Sketches of Eighteenth-Century America*, ed. Albert E. Stone (1782; repr., New York: Penguin Books, 1981), 68.

CHAPTER 9

Spanish Louisiana Land Policy: Antecedent to the Anglo-American Colonization of East Texas, 1769–1821

The Anglo-American settlement of Texas in the 1820s and 1830s constitutes a significant chapter in demographic expansion of English speakers into Spanish and Mexican territory. As such, it was an era of historical development that attracted the attention of historians from the very beginnings of scholarship in Texas history. Henderson Yoakum wrote in his 1855 book about the influx of English speakers into Texas. Seventy years later, Eugene C. Barker presented the activities of Stephen F. Austin as a prototypical frontiersman. Most Texas history textbooks follow this historiographical tradition. For the most part, however, such interpretive treatments of this crucial time in Texas history consider the important demographic movement across the Sabine River in isolation from the more complex, longer-running, and complicated story of English-speaking migration as an almost *de novo* occurrence. In reality, the empresario era in Texas history descended directly from Spanish land policies that began in Louisiana during the early 1770s. As such, the Anglo-American settlement of Texas did not spring full bloom with Moses Austin at the start of the 1820s.

The arrival of English speakers was actually the final chapter in the ongoing story of settlement interaction between Spain, Mexico, and English-speaking North America that began when the first Anglo-Americans arrived in the Mississippi valley during the era of the American Revolution. Texas empresario activities therefore had their roots deep in the historical institutions of the Spanish frontier. What we today in Texas call the empresario era can be seen as the meeting of two different streams of historical development: first, the evolving nature of Spanish and Mexican institutions of frontier settlement across several centuries of movement into the Spanish borderlands; and second, the geographical expansion of the US frontier into the Mississippi valley and Gulf coast during the fifty years before Moses Austin's arrival at San Antonio de Bexar. The Spanish/Mexican legal traditions of land settlement merged with the expansion of English-speaking North America, first in Spanish Louisiana, then later in Texas.

The empresario era, in net sum, represents the endpoint of a long process that occurred across several generations of Anglo-American settlement that began in Spanish Louisiana. That expansion centered first on the lower Mississippi valley, moved northwestward to Spanish Missouri and territorial Arkansas, and then turned to Spanish Texas. Although identified by some historians as having been a product of policies promulgated by Antonio Martinez, the last governor of Spanish Texas, the empresario system was part and parcel of Spain's historical experience on its northeastern frontier in North America. Land policies during the empresario era combined the centralized and corporate characteristics of Spanish New World expansion with the late eighteenth- and early nineteenth-century need for Spain to manage the expansion of English speakers, their movement into Texas constituting a final chapter in this process. Anglo-Americans quickly became accustomed to the empresario system, eventually adopting its structure during the Republic of Texas in the 1840s to manage continuing immigration from the United States. In the final analysis, it was this system that set Texas on the pathway of land disposition it has followed since the 1820s. John Martin Davis has complied a comprehensive and annotated document-based history of land grants in Texas, for which I wrote the introduction. Entitled *Texas Land Grants, 1750–1900: A Documentary History* (2016), this volume provides a context for the development of Spanish land disposition in the state as embodied during the empresario era.

Light Townsend Cummins, "Spanish Louisiana Land Policy: Antecedent to the Anglo-American Colonization of East Texas, 1769–1821," *East Texas Historical Journal* 33 (1995): 18–26.

LAND HUNGER played an important, if not unique role in the expansion of the United States from the era of the American Revolution to the closing of the frontier late in the nineteenth century. Historians of the United States from the time of Frederick Jackson Turner in the 1890s to the present have understood the overwhelming influence that the desire for land has worked on the nation's development. Much of the historical literature regarding this phenomenon, however, suffers from a historiographical deficiency because it is written from the national perspective of the United States. There is a tendency on the part of some frontier historians to approach the expansion of the United States as if the Anglo-American pioneers moved westward into a territorial vacuum.[1]

Such was not the case historically, and especially so in considering the Anglo-American settlement of Texas in the 1820s. The westward movement of Anglo-Americans into East Texas was a continuation of an earlier migration into Spanish Louisiana and the Mississippi valley.[2] Historians of colonial New Spain and the Hispanic frontier of North America, of course, always realized this historical truism, and much of their work reflects this relatively more sophisticated understanding of the process.[3] History written from the perspective of the Spanish frontier in North America clearly shows that Spain manifested consistent land policies throughout her vast colonial region that, late in the eighteenth century, ran from Florida westward to California.[4]

This fact gives rise to an essential question largely ignored by historians of Texas: namely, was Spanish colonial land policy in Louisiana itself a major contributing factor to the westward movement of the United

States into Texas during the 1820s? Surprisingly, no historian has systematically examined the land policies implemented by the Spanish governors of Louisiana as motivations for the later decrees that permitted Anglo-American settlement in Texas. This essay compares the land policies of three pivotal Spanish administrators: Alejandro O'Reilly, who implemented the basic land policies in Louisiana that Spain thereafter would follow in Texas; Esteban Miró, the governor of Louisiana whose land decrees set in motion the first large influx of Anglo-Americans into the lower Mississippi valley and Gulf coast during the 1780s and 1790s; and Manuel Gayoso de Lemos, whose Louisiana Land Decree of 1797 became a model for Texas governor Antonio María Martinez, whose dealings with Moses and Stephen F. Austin began the empresario era in Texas.[5] This essay will show that all three Louisiana administrators followed similar policies that brought similar results. These policies were first implemented in Spanish Louisiana, starting with a decree of General O'Reilly in 1770. Further refinements provided by Louisiana governors Miró and Gayoso set into common practice the procedures later followed in Spanish Texas. In a larger sense, Spanish Louisiana land law and the legal methods by which ownership of landholdings served as a direct contributing factor to encouraging the westward movement of Anglo-American settlers. Hence, Spanish colonial land policy as first implemented in Louisiana had a direct impact on the Anglo-American settlement of East Texas.

Alejandro O'Reilly began the process. He is best remembered to history as the stalwart Spanish general who firmly established Spanish control in New Orleans in 1769, just over a year after the revolt that drove Antonio de Ulloa from power after Louisiana's transfer from French to Spanish sovereignty following the Seven Years' War (1756–63).[6] Born in County Meath, Ireland, in 1723, O'Reilly had immigrated to Spain as a small child with his Roman Catholic family. He enlisted in military service, served in the Hibernian Regiment, and earned many distinctions during his military career, including the undying admiration of his monarch, King Charles III, whose life he had saved during a riot in Madrid in 1766. O'Reilly embarked upon a career of service in the Indies early in the 1760s, when he helped restore Spanish control at Havana after the British occupation.[7] The general was chosen to reestablish Spanish government in New Orleans in 1769. He arrived there on July 24 in command of over 2,000 troops. Although never the governor of Louisiana by appointment, O'Reilly spent almost two years in the province while he successfully planted the flag of Spain firmly in the lower Mississippi River valley.[8] "He reorganized the governmental structure of the colony along Spanish lines," as one historian has noted, "created a Cabildo for New Orleans, instituted the Spanish legal system, extended Louisiana's trade to Cuba and certain Iberian ports, established a militia, organized military defenses, set guidelines for relations with the Indians of the area, and promulgated regulations for awarding land grants."[9]

It was in this latter activity that O'Reilly might have had the greatest lasting impact on the Hispanic frontier in North America. His land regulations of 1770 changed the nature of Spanish landholding in the northeastern provinces of New Spain. Previously, land policy in New Spain had rested on historic Castilian influences, which were based on the granting of land by the king for certain traditional reasons, none of which assumed the purpose of such grants was to devolve public land to private ownership for economic reasons. Instead, based on the provisions of *Siete Partidas* and the *Leves de Toro,* Spanish monarchs for almost three centuries had awarded grants of lands to royal subjects in the concept that land was a reward for royal service or for merit.[10] The *adelantado* and *encomienda* grants of sixteenth-century New Spain rested on such assumptions. By the seventeenth century, the legal classification of the various categories of land in New Spain also reflected the assumption that private ownership of land was tied to the personal beneficence of the monarch for actual or potential merits and services rendered by the grantee.[11]

By the mid-eighteenth century, the need to settle the northern frontier of New Spain made for a radical change in policy. Starting with the frontier settlement of Canary Islanders in Texas during the 1730s, land policy began to reflect a new motivation: attracting individual inhabitants by the promise of household-based grants made to family units.

The formal agreement of a potential settler to inhabit the land granted by the monarch was itself deemed a sufficient-enough service for the Crown to warrant the grant. This became policy in 1754, when royal instructions to the viceroy of New Spain implemented new regulations that had greater similarity to methods employed in British America than to earlier practices in the Spanish Indies.[12] Basic decisions regarding land law were transferred from Spain to regional commanders in the Indies. In particular, the power to make and confirm grants of land was settled directly on Spanish governors, who now had the power to set policy in keeping with the needs of their districts.[13] In many cases, the ultimate purpose of the grant became the giving of land as an inducement for settlement by individual holders.

General O'Reilly used the regulations of 1754 as the basis for a policy of land granting that would be repeated at important junctures during the remaining decades of Spanish colonial control in Louisiana and Texas. On February 18, 1770, General O'Reilly issued a formal proclamation outlining the procedures and regulations to be followed in granting land to settlers in Louisiana.[14] This proclamation did something no previous Spanish land decree had done. It attempted to blend the Spanish legal system into that of another nation: France. This was a necessity because grants of land already had been made by the French in Louisiana. As the general himself noted, the decree came as a result of "diverse complaints and petitions, which have been addressed to us by the inhabitants of Opelousas, Attacapas, Natchitoches, and other places of this province joined to the knowledge we have acquired of the local concerns, culture, and means of the inhabitants." For such reasons, the expressed purpose of O'Reilly's decree was "new regulation which should fix the extent of the grants which should hereafter be made."[15]

The twelve provisions of O'Reilly's decree became a model for all subsequent decrees issued by Spanish administrators along the Hispanic frontier of North America, eventually including Texas. Among its important and new features was the fact that grants of land would be made to heads of households based on the size of the family unit. As well, O'Reilly provided for a relatively easy method of survey and grant registration and required that grantees make improvements on their land to obtain permanent title. The general even anticipated the role that livestock raising would play. "All cattle shall be branded by the proprietors," the decree noted, "and those who shall not have branded them at the age of eighteenth months cannot thereafter claim a property therein."[16] Taken as a whole, O'Reilly's decrees put Spanish administrators at the provincial level in the land-office business for the first time, a role they would continue for decades thereafter. Although O'Reilly did not have Anglo-American settlers in mind when he wrote his decree, its provisions represented a liberality of land granting that would not be seen in the United States until the Homestead Act of the 1860s. It is little wonder, then, that the Louisiana Land Decree of 1770 would eventually attract the attention of Anglo-American settlers as they pushed into the Mississippi valley. This was so because grants of land in Spanish Louisiana, under the provisions of this decree, would be free of cost financially, while public lands in the United States in the decades after the American Revolution had to be purchased.

If Alejandro O'Reilly was the author of Spain's land-granting policy for the final decades of the northern frontier in New Spain, Louisiana governor Esteban Miró became the first administrator to use it for attracting large numbers of Anglo-Americans into the region. Miró, who had a long career in the Indies, had a basic understanding of land as an inducement to settlement.[17] Born in Catalonia in 1744, he had served in the Zamora Regiment early in the 1760s, then came to New Spain in 1762, where he saw service in the Corona Regiment until his transfer to O'Reilly's Algerian command in 1775. He came to Louisiana in 1778 as the commander of the Fixed Louisiana Regiment, serving as aide-de-camp to Governor Bernardo de Gálvez. Miró became governor of Louisiana on January 20, 1782, and served in that position until 1791, when he was replaced by the Baron de Carondelet.[18]

Starting in the mid-1780s, Miró faced the problem of integrating into Spanish Louisiana large numbers of Anglo-Americans who had resided prior to the American Revolution in the former British province of West Florida, captured by General Bernardo de Gálvez. Now a part of

Spanish Louisiana, Miró turned to the O'Reilly land regulations as a mechanism for including these residents in his province. In so doing, he embarked on a plan that would make possible the continued residence of Anglo-American landowners on their British-era holdings and, at the same time, provided a foundation upon which later Anglo-American settlement would occur. Spain, anxious to populate the territorially expanded province of Louisiana with colonists, already had experienced difficulty inducing Iberian immigrants to the lower Mississippi valley. This was due to financial problems in underwriting a trans-Atlantic migration of Spanish subjects and the unwillingness on the part of individual Hispanic colonists to relocate in Louisiana, which many of them saw as an isolated, economically backward, and undesirable place of potential residence. Hence, Louisiana needed loyal settlers who might come from any acceptable quarter. Anglo-Americans, under the proper circumstances, would meet this need. Such a realization prompted a proposal from Governor Miró in 1785 that permitted British-era residents to retain their holdings. They could become loyal Spanish subjects by taking an oath of allegiance to the king of Spain and adopting Roman Catholicism as their publicly professed religion. Implementation of this plan began during the spring of 1786. Miró created two parishes that covered the former British Natchez District. Each parish received a priest, a military commandant, and a detachment of troops for the protection of the parish.[19]

The Anglo-American settlement of Louisiana accelerated as this policy was quickly applied to new settlers who wished to enter the province as permanent residents. Such efforts were hurried along by the ambitious schemes of Pierre Wouves d'Arges, a Frenchman who had fought in the American Revolution. D'Arges appeared at the Spanish court in 1787 as the author of a scheme to import approximately 1,500 Anglo-American settlers into Louisiana as a loyal buffer-zone population. Although d'Arges offered his proposals as his own ideas, they were in fact those of Governor Miró, with whom he had discussed the proposal during a visit to New Orleans the previous year. The Frenchman argued that Anglo-American settlers would be a defensive force and an economic boon to Louisiana.[20] As one historian has noted, Spain "reasoned that the colonists, assured of their property and free commerce, would adhere to a government that dispensed such advantages."[21] Hence, a royal order of February 18, 1787, revised O'Reilly's land decree of 1770 to meet the needs of this defensive settlement of Anglo-Americans.[22]

Although d'Arges's plan brought no settlers into Spanish Louisiana, Esteban Miró adopted the royal order of 1787 into a successful land-grant policy that brought hundreds of Anglo-Americans into the province during the following decade. Miró's decree of April 20, 1789, which implemented the royal order, made clear the requirements by which immigrants could receive land grants in Louisiana. "They will not be molested on religious matter," he noted, "although no other public worship will be permitted to be publicly exercised than that of the Roman Catholic Church."[23] Most importantly, he ordered that "land will be granted gratis to them at their arrival in proportion of the hands, or faculties each Family should have." The governor guaranteed that each settler would be able to bring his personal property into Louisiana free of duty or taxation. Finally, grants of land would be made to settlers on "the condition they shall at the same time take the due oath of allegiance & bound themselves only to take up arms in defense of this Province against Whatsoever enemy who could attempt to invade it."[24]

The Baron de Carondelet, Miró's successor as governor of Louisiana, continued this policy. Within a few weeks of becoming governor, the baron recommended to his superiors in Spain that additional Anglo-Americans be encouraged to migrate to the province. He felt that these new settlers should be enticed by liberal commercial policies and a great degree of religious toleration, in addition to being given free lands. In an effort to accelerate this process, Carondelet turned for the first time to empresarios, or land agents, as a way to encourage additional immigration.[25] In the mid-1790s, he supported the unsuccessful colonization project of the Frenchman the Marquis of Mason Rouge, whose grants reflected the policies first implemented by General O'Reilly. Other immigration agents followed, including Joseph Piernas, Luis de Vilemont, William Murray, the Baron de Bastrop, George Morgan, and Moses

Austin. All of this activity caused Thomas Jefferson to remark: "I wish a hundred thousand of our inhabitants would accept the invitation. It may be the means of delivering to us peaceably what may otherwise cost a war."[26]

The closing years of Spanish control in Louisiana therefore witnessed the final codification of the land policy that would, in the next generation, provide for the settlement of Texas in the 1820s. Little difference can be found between the instructions of 1797 for the settling of Anglo-Americans in Louisiana and the provisions for the grants later made to Moses and Stephen F. Austin. The 1797 Louisiana instructions, issued by Governor Manuel Gayoso de Lemos, required that all grantees be Roman Catholic in faith: "Those who do not conform to this rule," the promulgation noted, "are not to be admitted." Grants would be made to family units, while unmarried individuals had to receive special exemptions. Each head of family would receive two hundred arpents of land, while an additional fifty would be added for each dependent. Gayoso's instructions also provided that "immediately on the arrival of a new settler the oath of fidelity shall be required of him." Provision also was made for the importation of slaves, provided they were "lawfully and wholly the property of the emigrant."[27]

The Louisiana Purchase of 1803 averted the need for the potential war feared by Thomas Jefferson, but the Anglo-American migration that started in Spanish Louisiana continued into Texas during the first decades of the nineteenth century. After almost two decades of filibustering from the United States, Martinez, as governor of Texas, moved to permit an orderly Anglo-American migration into the province. In so doing, he adopted the land-granting policies and the legal stipulations that had originated earlier in Spanish Louisiana. A native of Jaen in Spain, Martinez had a distinguished career of military service, which began in 1785. Like Miró a generation before, Martinez also had served in the Zamora Regiment. A highly decorated military hero, Martinez became governor of Spanish Texas in March 1817.[28] By late in the 1810s, the problems of filibustering had worked a subtle change in Spanish Texas. Administrators were willing to look with greater favor upon the potential settlement of any groups who would maintain loyalty to the Spanish king. It was at this time that Moses Austin appeared at San Antonio. The story of his success is well known.

Austin, a former resident of the St. Louis area of Spanish Louisiana, already had received a Spanish land grant in the 1790s from the government at New Orleans.[29] He knew the basic legal system to be employed in such matters. In his initial contact with Martinez, Austin had little success until the intervention of Filipe de Neri, better known by his fabricated noble title as the Baron de Bastrop. Neri, or Bastrop, also had earlier experience with Spanish Louisiana land grants, having received title to a huge grant early in the 1790s.[30] Bastrop interceded with Martinez on Austin's behalf, with the result that the governor made a generous grant to the Anglo-American. On January 17, 1821, Moses Austin received permission to settle 300 families in a 200,000-square-mile area. This grant approved by Joaquin de Arredondo as the political chief of the Provincias Internas at Monterrey, contained specific qualifications that the settler should meet:

> Therefore, if to the first and principal requisite of being Catholics, or agreeing to become so, before entering the Spanish territory, they also add that of accrediting their good character and habits, as is offered in said petition: and taking the necessary oath, to be obedient in all things to the government; to take up arms in its defense against all kinds of enemies; and to be faithful to the King; and to observe the political constitution of the Spanish monarchy; the most flattering hopes may be formed, that the said province will receive an important augmentation, in agriculture, industry, and arts, by the new emigrants; who will introduce them.[31]

The untimely death of Moses Austin on June 10, 1821, saw this grant devolve to his son, Stephen F. Austin. As heir, he went to San Antonio late in the summer of 1821, where he had conferences with Governor Martinez.[32] Young Austin secured renewal of the colonization contract given earlier to his father. Thus began the legal Anglo-American settlement of Spanish Texas.[33] Although the independence of Mexico would bring Martinez's land policy to a quick end late in 1821, the basic outlines continued under the colonization laws of Augustín de Iturbide and later the government instituted by the Constitution of 1824.[34] By their content, these Mexican decrees also showed the Louisiana influence of the O'Reilly decree of 1770, Miró's policies of the late 1780s, and Gayoso's regulation of 1797.

These Spanish land policies favored Anglo-American expansion because of their rather unique accommodations to the needs of the settlers from the United States. The fifty years between the land decrees of Alejandro O'Reilly and the Austin colonization contracts negotiated by Antonio Maria Martinez were ones of overwhelming change all along the northern frontier of colonial New Spain. Governmental reorganization, economic dislocations, revolutionary movements, and the westward press of the Anglo-American frontier became historical hallmarks of great change during this era. One rather remarkable constant, however, remained almost unchanged across the course of these turbulent years: Spanish land-grant policy. A liberal policy of granting two hundred arpents of land to heads of households, only nominal requirement of Roman Catholicism, the requirement for minimum improvements on the land grant, and the taking of a loyalty oath constituted the main requirements for settlements. Contrasted to this was the fact that land in the United States had to be purchased by the holder. These Spanish policies favored Anglo-American expansion because of their rather unique accommodations to the needs of settlers from the United States. Given this observation, the historian may be tempted to note that Spanish Louisiana land policy was a motivating factor, if not an outright cause, of the Anglo-American westward movement, rather than a reaction to it. As such, it resulted in the arrival of Anglo-American settlers in East Texas during the 1820s.

Notes

1. Ray Allen Billington, *Westward Expansion: A History of the American Frontier*, (New York: Macmillan, 1974), 15–23.

2. Light T. Cummins, "The English Frontier," in *Comparative Frontier History*, ed. José Sanchez (Albuquerque: National Park Service, 1992), 134; Cummins, "Texas under Spain and Mexico," in *A Guide to the History of Texas*, ed. Cummins

and Alvin R. Bailey Jr. (New York: Greenwood, 1988), 3–16. For background on the Anglo-American settlement of Spanish Louisiana as a prelude to expansion into Texas, see Mattie Austin Hatcher, *The Opening of Texas to Foreign Settlement, 1810–1821* (Austin: University of Texas Press, 1927); Hatcher, "The Louisiana Background of the Colonization of Texas, 1763–1803," *Southwestern Historical Quarterly* 24 (Spring 1921): 169–95; and William S. Coker, "The Bruins and the Formulation of Spanish Immigration Policy in the Old Southwest, 1787–88," in *The Spanish in the Mississippi Valley, 1762–1804*, ed. John Francis McDermott (Urbana: University of Illinois Press, 1974), 61–71.

3. Donald Worchester, "The Significance of the Spanish Borderlands to the United States," in *New Spain's Far Northern Frontier: Essays on Spain in the American West, 1540–1821*, ed. David J. Weber (Albuquerque: University of New Mexico Press, 1979), 1–16.

4. The best recent example of this viewpoint may be seen in David J. Weber, *The Spanish Frontier in North America* (New Haven, CT: Yale University Press, 1992). Weber discusses a common land policy and notes that "Spanish officials also adopted an innovative immigration policy for its most endangered border provinces." Ibid., 280.

5. Early work noting the similarity of Louisiana and Texas land policy was undertaken by Mattie Austin Hatcher in the 1920s, although little has been done by scholars since. See Hatcher, *Opening of Texas to Foreign Settlement*. More recent work on the Louisiana-Texas connection, although not in the area of analyzing land policy, may be seen in Odie B. Faulk, "The Penetration of Foreigners and Foreign Ideas into Spanish East Texas, 1793–1816," *East Texas Historical Journal* 2 (October 1964): 87–98.

6. Bibanio Torres Ramirez, *Alejandro O'Reilly en las indias*, (Seville, Spain: Escuela de Estudios Hispanoamericanos, 1973); José Montero de Pedro, *Españoles en Nueva Orleans y Luisiana* (Madrid: Ediciones Cultura Hispánica, 1979), 25–30; David Ker Texada, *O'Reilly and the New Orleans Rebels*, (Lafayette: Center for Louisiana Studies, 1970), 35–52.

7. Jack D. L. Holmes, "Alexander O'Reilly, Colonial Governor, 1769–1770," in *The Louisiana Governors: From Iberville to Edwards*, ed. Joseph G. Dawson III (Baton Rouge: Louisiana State University Press, 1990), 49–52.

8. Light Townsend Cummins, *Spanish Observers and the American Revolution* (Baton Rouge: Louisiana State University Press, 1992), 13.

9. Ibid., 14.

10. Guillermo F. Margadant, "Mexican Colonial Land Law," in *Spanish and Mexican Land Grants and the Law*, ed. Malcolm Ebright, (Manhattan, KS: Journal of the West, 1989), 85–95.

11. Ibid., 87.

12. "Royal Regulation of 1754," no. 4, *American State Papers: Public Lands*, (Washington, DC: Gales and Seaton, 1860), 5:655–57.

13. Ibid., 655.

14. "Regulation of O'Reilly," no. 26, *American State Papers: Public Lands*, 5:729–30.

15. Ibid., 729.

16. Ibid., 730.

17. Caroline Burson, *The Stewardship of Don Esteban Miró, 1781–1792* (New Orleans: American Printing, 1940).

18. Montero de Pedro, *Españoles en Nueva Orleans y Luisiana*, 44–50; Gilbert C. Din, "Esteban Rodriguez Miró," in *Louisiana Governors*, 61–64.

19. Gilbert C. Din, "The Immigration Policy of Governor Esteban Miró in Spanish Louisiana," *Southwestern Historical Quarterly* 73 (October 1969): 157–58. Miró's colonization plans are also detailed in Light T. Cummins, "An Enduring Community: Anglo-American Settlers at Colonial Natchez and in the Felicianas, 1764–1810," *Journal of Mississippi History* 55 (May 1993): 133–54.

20. Din, "Immigration Policy of Governor Esteban Miró," 160–61.

21. Ibid., 160.

22. Order, August 23, 1787, Archivo Histórico Nacional, Sección del Estado, Legajo 3889. This legajo contains most of the correspondence dealing with Miró's land policies in the 1780s.

23. "Miró's Offer to the Western Americans, April 20, 1789," in *Spain in the Mississippi Valley, 1765–1794*, ed. Lawrence A. Kinnard, pt. 2, vol. 3 of *Annual Report of the American Historical Association* (1945), 270–71.

24. Gilbert D. Din, "Spain's Immigration Policy in Louisiana and the American Penetration, 1792–1803," *Southwestern Historical Quarterly* 76 (January 1973): 255.

25. Ibid., 257–58.

26. Light T. Cummins, "Colonial Louisiana," in *Louisiana: A History*, ed. Bennet H. Wall et al., 2nd ed. (Arlington Heights, IL: Harlan-Davidson, 1992), 57.

27. "Instructions of Gayoso for the Administration of Posts and the Distribution of Lands," No. 26, *American State Papers: Public Lands*, 5:730–31.

28. Odie B. Faulk, *The Last Years of Spanish Texas, 1778–1821* (London: Mouton, 1964), 36–37.

29. David B. Gracy II, *Moses Austin: His Life* (San Antonio: Trinity University Press, 1987), 93–94.

30. Ibid., 210–12.

31. Antonio Martinez to Moses Austin, February 8, 1821, in *Establishing a Colony*, ed. David B. Gracy II (Austin, TX: Pemberton, 1970), 33–34.

32. Eugene C. Barker, *The Life of Stephen F. Austin: Founder of Texas, 1793–1836: A Chapter in the Westward Movement of the Anglo-American People* (Nashville, TN: Cokesbury, 1925), 43–57.

33. Ibid., 55.

34. Thomas L. Miller, *The Public Lands of Texas, 1519–1970* (Norman: University of Oklahoma Press, 1972), 15–20.

CHAPTER 10

Church Courts, Marriage Breakdown, and Separation in Spanish Louisiana, West Florida, and Texas, 1763–1836

Most of the historical literature dealing with Spanish Louisiana and Texas examines the institutional concerns of government, implementation of policy, military matters, and the activities of the church. In addition, historians have written about the legal system and its structure, matters touching on trade, and relations with Native Americans. This has been the case due to the reality that almost all the extant primary source documents were those generated by the institutions of the government, the church, or the taxing of commercial entities in the local economy. These official documents, today called *pliegos* by Spanish-speaking archivists, deal mostly with matters of imperial concern that chronicle the functioning of government, the work of public officials and priests, and the execution of policy. Commercial records kept by merchants and taxing authorities also provide what might best be called an institutional view of history in Spanish Louisiana and Texas. But it has been very difficult for historians to reconstruct the daily lives of individuals. Little historical notice has been given to topics such as the relationship between men and women, family life, and marital matters.

There are, however, a few historical records dealing with Spanish Louisiana and Texas that touch on these matters, although only where dysfunction brought them to the attention of civil or church authorities. Such sources provide a window into some aspects of personal lives. These records are the Notarial Archives of New Orleans and a Texas collection known in Spanish as the Archivo de Bexár. Both sets of documents contain historical information about the personal lives of residents, especially in matters relating to marital discord, gender relations, and domestic violence. These sources speak to problems stemming from the breakdown of relations between spouses, domestic abuse, or the inability of husbands and wives to live together. These documented marital disputes provide the historian with some ability to observe relations between men and women in ways that are unique, given the paucity of other sources on daily life among the inhabitants of colonial Spanish North America.

These particular sources make poignant testimony to the plight of individual residents caught up in marital difficulties. It is interesting to note that in several cases, the basic thrust of the authorities involved rested on a sincere desire to protect the women involved. The various examples of the adjudicated domestic conflicts in these documents highlight an aspect of daily life not substantiated in the official *pliegos* of Louisiana and Texas: they note the increasing number of male English-speaking migrants who intermarried with Spanish- or French-speaking women. All across the late eighteenth and early nineteenth centuries, male English-speaking settlers were arriving in both Louisiana and Texas. Some of them, at least those noted in these sources, married local women as part of what must have been a desire to establish permanent roots in territories controlled by Spain. The Notary Records of Louisiana and the Archivo de Bexár in Texas contain the names of several hundred Anglo-American men who created family lives for themselves in these two Spanish colonial provinces. There is an additional historiographical consideration embodied in consulting these two sets of records: both Louisiana and Texas experienced the same phenomena regarding marital discord and domestic violence. This underscores the reality that, although separate as distinct governmental entities, both had much in common across a wide spectrum of social, cultural, economic, and institutional activities, although few historians ever link them together. Instead, since the time of historian Herbert Eugene Bolton, Texas has been conceptualized as part of the southwestern area of the Spanish Borderlands, while Louisiana has been considered as belonging to the southeastern region. There is validity to this approach in terms of government administration and church structure. In cases of social matters and family norms, however, there were common values at work in both provinces. The matters noted in this essay confirm that they had many common concerns. The commonality between Spanish Louisiana and Texas is something to which historians should give greater attention in their future research. Working from the same Notary Archives upon which this essay was based, Jennifer M. Spear's *Race, Sex, and Social Order in Early New Orleans*, published in 2009, examines the interactions of sex and gender relations across the entire spectrum of colonial life for all who lived in that city and its surrounding province—European, black, and Native American, whether slave or free. Spear provides a powerful corrective to my observation below that, as of the early 1990s, little had been written about the social order and gender relationships in French and Spanish Louisiana.

Light Townsend Cummins, "Church Courts, Marriage Breakdown, and Separation in Spanish Louisiana, West Florida, and Texas, 1763–1836," *Journal of Texas Catholic History and Culture* 4 (1993): 97–114.

THE PHENOMENON of marital breakdown is clearly reflected in the records of church courts in Spanish colonial Louisiana and Texas from the 1760s through the 1830s.[1] At first glance, the chronological and geographic boundaries of this historiographical focus may appear to be somewhat unorthodox.[2] Historians seldom link these two provinces, except in the broadest definitional sense, as being similar as parts of the Hispanic frontier of North America. Spanish and Mexican Texas are also treated herein as an entity.[3] The restricted geographical orientation of much scholarship on these areas obscures significant points of common reference for the various parts of the North American Hispanic frontier. The conceptualization of social history does not always follow the traditional way in which we view political history. In particular, the day-to-day social and cultural experiences of residents in Spanish Louisiana and Texas in matters of family life, religion, material culture, personal economy, and folkways created a commonality just as remarkable as their dissimilar governmental institutions and administrative structures.

This commonality is certainly the case in considering the family. Louisiana and Texas during the period examined shared the tenets of Hispanic law and the Roman Catholic Church. The study of marriage breakdown, therefore, provides an appealing opportunity to focus on the family for both areas as common parts of a cultural imperium reflecting the same normative social values as embodied in civil and canon law. The records of church-court proceedings regarding marital disputes in Spanish Louisiana (including its post-1783 West Florida district) and Texas contain much information about family values. Such records, however, are anecdotal, limited in number, and therefore statistically unrepresentative.[4] Moreover, as Richard Boyer has observed, divorce records deal with atypical spouses who were "engaged in the politics of marriage in which power and resentment, alliances and isolation, practicality and idealism were jumbled up."[5] Nonetheless, church-court cases do provide a window through which some everyday experiences of family life can be viewed, albeit in a negative sense.

The Roman Catholic Church in Texas and Louisiana, as elsewhere throughout the Spanish Empire, permitted marriage to be terminated by annulment or suspended by separation (*divorcium a mensa et thoro*, or "divorce from bed and board," as it was called). Annulment falls beyond the focus of this essay, but it deserves limited mention. A myth perpetuated from earlier eras of historical writing implies that annulment was a popular and frequent way to end a marriage, especially among the elite classes of Western society. Recent research has called this assumption into question, and now many historians of marriage argue that such was not the case. Evidence from Louisiana and Texas supports the contention that annulment was rarely used as a mechanism to end marriage, and when it did occur, it was not a symptom of marital breakdown. Only two cases in this study involve annulments. Both were related to the special historical circumstances created by Louisiana's proximity to and contact with British areas to the northeast. Annulments could be granted on the "precontract" condition when one of the partners in the union had already been married at an earlier time.

These two cases arose in Louisiana when local residents married immigrants from the Atlantic coast arriving as part of the Anglo-American influx into the province. Both of these actions were brought by men who found that their wives had contracted earlier unions. For example, in 1784, Pedro Boydant brought suit before the ecclesiastical court at New Orleans seeking an annulment of his marriage of six years. He had recently learned that his wife, Susanna, had been married in a Protestant ceremony to an English subject during her earlier residence in New England. Susanna had supposed that her first husband had died, and presumably for that reason, she never informed the trusting Pedro. The first husband, however, had recently surfaced in Jamaica, with the result that Boydant filed suit "to bring into the record" his wife's first marriage under the terms of precontract.

The second case was brought to the church by Antonio Marmillon, who sought an annulment on behalf of his daughter Margarita. The young woman had been married to John Joseph Dorquingny for almost two years, and during that time, Don Antonio reported officially that the marriage had never been consummated. The husband had emigrated from Philadelphia, where he had lived before his residence in Louisiana. News from the Atlantic coast indicated that Dorquingny also had a wife living in the Pennsylvania port city. The husband, however, denied the accusation after being confronted by Margarita and her father. John Joseph's refusal to confess to bigamy forced the ecclesiastical judge, Father Cirilio de Barcelona, to conduct a full-scale inquiry into the matter.

The judge ordered John Joseph to be incarcerated in the public jail until the case was heard by the court, while Margarita was remanded to the protection of the Ursuline Convent for the duration of the proceeding. The judge held formal hearings at which he questioned several Anglo-American ship captains and sailors. All of them reported that it was widely known that John Joseph had two wives, one in Philadelphia and one in New Orleans. Indeed, witnesses reported that the accused even bragged of his sexual exploits with these two women and boasted to compatriots frequenting the New Orleans docks that his "Philadelphia" wife was even more beautiful than his local one. After hearing graphic testimony, the judge speedily annulled the marriage of Margarita Marmillon and remanded the bigamist to the prison at Havana, where he was bound over for criminal trial by the civil authorities.[6]

Apart from annulment, *divortium* (divorce) as a term can mean several things to the historian and therefore must be clarified according to its popular usage during the eighteenth and early nineteenth centuries in the Hispanic world. Today, divorce generally means the total dissolution of a marriage. Both partners are free and unfettered in the negotiation of a new, legal conjugal relationship. Historically, the word "divorce" was popularly used in Spanish Texas and Louisiana to mean something else: separation from bed and board.[7] This legal action, a judicial separation, did not constitute absolute divorce as we know it today. Separation from bed and board merely released couples from the conjugal obligations of the marital bond and permitted them to live apart as legally independent persons. In so doing, civil and ecclesiastical law still recognized the validity of the ruptured marriage as a union of enduring status. Spouses so separated were not free to remarry and, at least in theory, were required to practice sexual abstinence. Significantly, women so divorced did regain control over their dotal property along with their share of community assets. Separation from bed and board constituted the primary legal mechanism by which broken marriages were dealt with in Texas and Louisiana under the regime of Spanish law.[8] It was sanctioned by the Council of Trent and was introduced into Hispanic custom as early as the twelfth century.[9]

A judicial separation could be secured on one of three grounds. First, cruel and violent treatment or abuse of partner by a spouse was grounds for suspending a marriage. In general, this ill treatment was usually by the husband directed against the wife. Such abuse had to threaten "her life, her sanity or her tranquility to such a degree that cohabitation became impossible."[10] Second, adultery was grounds for separation because it threatened the conjugal union at the most fundamental level. Third, separation from bed and board could be granted if the husband refused to provide necessary food, clothing, or shelter for his wife. Individuals seeking a judicial separation "needed a strong case against their consorts."[11] Ecclesiastical authorities granted a separation most sparingly, usually only in those cases that involved the most blatant and irreparable of circumstances. "Neither was it sufficient to prove that the offenses were real," Silvia Arrom has noted for Mexico City during this era, "the plaintiff had to convince the judge both that the danger posed by continued cohabitation was extremely serious and that the delinquent spouse was incapable of reform."[12]

The process that plaintiffs followed in securing a judicial separation from bed and board was simple and direct. Legal jurisdiction for such cases in Texas and Louisiana rested solely with ecclesiastical courts, although the civil courts sometimes meddled in such matters. This jurisdiction was reaffirmed and upheld when the Crown issued a royal order stipulating that all divorce cases in Texas and Louisiana remained exclusively under the church courts and canon law.[13] Such courts usually were composed of one person sitting as judge. The judge of the court (generally the bishop or his designated agent) received the initial complaint filed by the plaintiff, conducted an investigation of the facts, gave the accused spouse the opportunity to file a written rejoinder countering the charges filed, and—if the case was seen as valid—solicited the testimony of at least three independent witnesses before rendering a decision. If the judge decided to grant the judicial separation after considering all of this evidence, he sent his recommendation to the governor, who officially certified the result. At times, the judicial authorities of the civil government in Texas and Louisiana also heard marital disputes, usually when wives brought criminal complaints against their husbands in domestic discords or when property or other economic assets carried into marriages as part of marriage contracts had to be disposed of.[14]

My survey of the ecclesiastical and judicial records for Texas and Louisiana has located almost three dozen cases involving formal legal requests for separation from bed and board from the 1760s to the 1820s.

Approximately one-third of these cases dealt with family violence, another third with adultery, while the final third were grounded in desertion or failure to provide. In about one-third of the total cases, the records were incomplete or the judge terminated the dispute before the full circumstances of the particular action could be read into the record of the proceedings. The picture presented by these cases indicates that the phenomenon of marriage breakdown—especially in the areas of family violence, desertion, and adultery—was generally consistent with such occurrences in other parts of the Western European world for the late eighteenth and early nineteenth centuries.[15]

More than any other circumstance relating to marriage breakdown, family violence and wife abuse were the reasons that brought women before the judge as plaintiffs.[16] Typical of such cases was that of María Antonia Rodríquez, who appeared before the Louisiana ecclesiastical tribunal in 1782 because of the violent nature of her marriage. She asked for a divorce and noted that she had been married to José Molina for five years. During that time, he had been "continually drunk" and given to all manner of excess. He routinely beat her and, on several occasions, forced himself sexually on her when she did not desire it. At various times during their marriage, José had become so violent that María hid in her mother's house, where she sought refuge from his abuses.[17]

Witnesses from María's neighborhood provided the court with stark testimony of José Molina's abusive behavior. Antonio Junque, for example, recounted that Molina treated his wife "no better than a slave" and was known to beat her with regularity. Antonio Delgado told the court that he used to live in the same building as the Molinas, whose fighting often disturbed the neighbors. Molina was "a vagrant without employment" and was "given over to drink." On one occasion, Delgado recalled that Molina came home very drunk, hit his wife repeatedly as they stood in the street, pushed her to the ground, and then roughly dragged her inside, where he forced her to have sex with him against her will. Leon Casteon, another neighbor, recalled an evening when he was in the Molina's kitchen. José, again in a drunken state, attacked his wife. He threw her to the floor, kicked her repeatedly, ripped her clothes, and pushed her crying into the street. María, further adding to the catalog of her husband's misbehavior, told the divorce court that Molina had taken most of her clothing, her other personal possessions, and many of their household items out of their residence, presumably to sell them in order to buy drink. The court immediately granted María separation from bed and board. She also gained control of her antenuptial possessions and the small amount of community property remaining in the Molina home.

Ecclesiastical judges usually had sympathy for wives who were clearly the victims of flagrant physical abuse. In 1784, Margarita Prudome desired a separation from her husband under circumstances similar to those of María Molina. Margarita, who had been married for six years, complained that her husband, Pedro Duranton, led a completely disorganized life. Habitually drunk, he often beat her, tore her clothes, and took whatever property she had of value in order to trade for wine and spirits. Margarita told the judge that she had tried to live with Pedro and be a good wife but that she could no longer stand the violence. Witnesses who appeared on her behalf supported her petition for separation, which the court granted.[18]

Some of the requests for separation from abused women had a plaintive tone, as was the case with Catarina Toupar, who told the court of

> the horrible treatment and deranged conduct of my husband and by which he had spent everything of value which I and my children have, without helping us or providing for us, and because of this I am obliged to live with my children in the most ultimate misery and am thus of the necessity of asking Your Excellency that you be served to divorce us so that we will no longer be married.[19]

Domestic violence and wife abuse were not limited to the unemployed and vagrant classes. At San Antonio de Béxar, María Jiménez requested a divorce from her husband, Bernardo Castillo; she complained that she was the victim of "mal tratos" by her husband, who physically abused her. The ecclesiastical tribunal, upon investigating her claims, was not entirely convinced that she was without fault. In fact, the judge ruled that both María and Bernardo shared equal blame for the fighting and refused to grant a divorce. Instead, the court instructed both parties about proper deportment in a marriage and admonished them to behave in the future.[20] They presumably managed to behave since no record has been found of additional appearances before the court by this couple.

At Baton Rouge, a prominent and wealthy Anglo-American planter, James Mullin, found himself the object of an abuse-based divorce action in 1794 when his wife accused him of having beat her repeatedly. Leonor Miller contended that her husband "abused her badly and tore her clothes off her back, sold her property and deserted her, leaving her penniless."[21] In a similar case, Miguel Eslava (the royal quartermaster and supply officer for the garrison at Mobile) was sued for separation from bed and board by his wife, who also claimed abuse. Miguel had "abused her and thrown her out of the house." She sought both a separation from him and a separate financial settlement for her children. The tribunal granted the separation and oversaw a property settlement that protected her interests.

Abused wives occasionally sought redress from civil authorities even when they did not seek divorce from the church courts. For example, Marie Theresa Leiveille attempted to give away much of her separate property before her death so that her husband would not get it. She had long been the victim of beatings and abuse by her husband, Phillipe Flotte, but had never sought a separation. Suffering in the final stages of a terminal illness, she decided to give friends all of her antenuptial property in an effort to deprive her husband of it. He brought a civil suit attempting to stop her from doing so. The resulting trial offered her the opportunity to make public the family violence that had plagued her marriage. Francois Bertin, a Louisiana surgeon, testified on her behalf that he had treated Marie over the years for "many fractures and injuries as much on the arms as on the head which were very dangerous." He recalled that she had said these injuries "had come from the bad treatment she had received from her husband." The surgeon also informed the court that "Flotte during his wife's [current] illness had maltreated her by injuries and threats so frightful that he was obliged to put him out of the sick room for fear of some injuries to the patient."[22] Governor Luis de Unzaga, sitting as the judge of the court, found for Marie and permitted her to dispose of the property.[23]

The civil authorities also became involved in legal proceedings when divorced spouses failed to execute property settlements resulting from decrees of the ecclesiastical tribunals. For example, Margarita Meilleur sued her husband, Claudio La Coste, from whom she had been judicially separated. She demanded a return from him of her dowry and her share of the common property in addition to seeking protection from his revenge. The two had been married in 1768, and after several years of marriage, Margarita secured a separation based on abuse. In her suit before the civil court, she noted "that for many years her husband has maltreated her, even to the extent of striking her, which gave rise to scandal in the neighborhood." As a result of the previous separation decree, however, she feared that her former husband apparently planned to punish her. As Margarita reported:

> She has now heard that La Coste is prepared to sell all of his property and go to France, and has said that when Father Cirilio will be absent from this city he will take her by violence with him and make a servant of her, and after he gets her in his country he will feed her on bread and water and shut her up in a place where she will never see the sun, in revenge for the grievances he says he has received from her.[24]

Thus, resolution of property disputes was sometimes as great a problem for some women as the securing of the divorce from bed and board itself. Elizabeth Villiers took her separated spouse, Francisco de Volsay, to civil court in an effort to secure restitution of her dowry and her share of their common property. The judge ordered a settlement, to which Francisco agreed. He gave his wife the ownership of a slave, two thousand pounds of deerskins, and 160 pesos in currency. In return, Elizabeth agreed not to make any claims upon his estate after his death.[25] Occasionally, wives also sought legal action against their husbands to resecure control of antenuptial property even when separation was not contemplated. Feliciana Furgangin sought a civil judgement in 1787 against her husband, Joséf Duget, because "he has not only wasted the little means he had, but has squandered a part of her dowry." She requested the civil authorities to issue a decree "so as to enable her to save the property that belongs to her." This the court did.[26]

Adultery, along with physical abuse and family violence, also brought a number of couples before the ecclesiastical tribunals. Spanish law had long addressed the crime of adultery within the patriarchal value system of the Hispanic family. For that reason, adultery was both a civil and religious crime, "which a man commits knowingly by having intercourse with a married woman, or one betrothed to another man."[27] In practice, culpability for adultery, therefore, rested largely with the woman. Few wives accused their husbands of adultery. The majority of actions for separation in Texas and Louisiana grounded in adultery were sought by husbands against their wives.[28]

Judges seemed reluctant to grant separations from bed and board based solely on the grounds of adultery. Instead, the clerics who sat on ecclesiastical tribunals usually attempted to reconcile the erring partners by encouraging them to restore their conjugal fidelity. Texas clerics, to an even greater extent that those in Louisiana, reacted to adultery cases by attempting to effect a reconciliation. At San Antonio de Béxar, María Casimiri Benítez and Juan José Flores reconciled while their case was pending before the tribunal.[29]

The church's reluctance to grant a judicial separation from bed and board solely on the basis of adultery rested in part on the difficulty of documenting indisputably a specific offense since adultery usually occurred secretly. A 1795 Louisiana case at Opelousas stands as testimony to such difficulties. Daniel Callaghan had long suspected his wife of an adulterous affair with Charles Peck, a neighbor. Charles Peck visited the Callaghan home on numerous occasions when Daniel was away on business. Servants and other neighbors reported that Charles and the wife often secluded themselves in the bedchamber of the Callaghan home, but both parties disclaimed any wrongdoing. Daniel Callaghan confronted his neighbor, who vigorously denied the accusations. The irate husband thereupon recruited one of his friends, Thomas Fletcher, to spy on the suspected paramours during one of his regular absences from the district. Thomas Fletcher laid at wait in the night, observed Charles's arrival at the Callaghan home, and peeked through the windows, whereupon he saw the two apparently "in the appearance of enjoyment, one of the other," on the bed. Nonetheless, when Thomas testified before the ecclesiastical tribunal, he was obliged to report honestly that it had been too dark to see if illicit intercourse had actually taken place. In her defense, the wife explained that she was ill and that Charles Peck had been treating her malady. The tribunal therefore took no action on the matter.[30]

Benito Allon had a similar experience when he accused his wife, María Buenaventura, of adultery. Benito complained to the church court that he had contracted a venereal disease from María. He testified that he could not have been exposed to the illness by anyone else since he had been faithful to María. Benito believed that his wife had become diseased from an illicit union with Vicente Cola. The husband told the court that it was a well-known fact that Vicente suffered from the disease. Benito, moreover, produced witnesses who told the tribunal that they had observed María entering Vicente's home and remaining inside the building all night, not leaving until morning. Nonetheless, the court refused the separation and ordered María to live faithfully with her husband and to stop seeing Vicente.[31]

The problem in sorting through adulterous relationships is further illustrated by a long-running case that lasted from the 1760s until the early 1790s. Louis Forneret, the public interpreter for the Spanish government at Mobile, had married Isabel Alexandre in 1767. Shortly thereafter, Louis traveled to France for an extended residence occasioned by the death of his father and the necessity of settling the estate. According to Luis, he found upon his return to the Gulf coast that his wife had moved to Pensacola and had become the mistress of Daniel Ward. Adultery suits and countersuits followed for years in the ecclesiastical courts of Spanish Louisiana. She claimed that she had merely worked for Daniel Ward as a domestic servant and governess and charged Luis with having a sexual relationship with one of his female slaves, by whom he had fathered several children. After several unsuccessful attempts at reconciliation, the court finally ordered in 1793 that the two warring spouses stop bickering and live together without further accusations of adultery.[32]

On some occasions, aggrieved husbands sought a separation from their adulterous wives while they had strong personal feelings of attachment. At Nacogdoches, for example, Francisco López reluctantly filed for separation from his wife, Juana Antonia Ocona, because of her illicit relationship with José Manuel. Francisco wrote his wife a loving and painful letter explaining that he had no other recourse other than to ask that God pardon her marital offenses, for he apparently could not.[33]

As they were with physical abuse, ecclesiastical judges were much more likely to grant separations from bed and board occasioned by desertion (grounded on failure to provide support) than they were for adultery. Desertion was sometimes a reality in Texas and Louisiana because a significant number of residents were military or civil employees of the government whose postings involved assignment to remote or undesirable locations. The demands of frontier life and the hardships that ensued from such an existence also ensured that trailing spouses could not or would not always follow their partners. In 1793, for example, a Spanish soldier at New Orleans sued his wife for separation because she refused to live with him at his new assignment at the Balize fort. Balize, situated in the deep delta of the Mississippi River near its mouth, was a swampy, remote, and unhealthy place, according to the reluctant wife, who flatly refused to leave New Orleans and continue residence with her husband.[34]

At San Antonio de Béxar, Severo Ruiz (an officer in the local garrison and later military commandant at Béxar in 1834) became involved in a complicated series of legal actions that stemmed in part from the alleged desertion of his wife, María del Refugio Sánchez, who resided at Monterrey. She and her family filed numerous complaints against him, charging that he had financially neglected them during his assignment to Texas. He attempted to resolve the matter by returning to Monterrey in order to obtain a separation from his wife and to arrange a property settlement.[35]

Not all desertions, however, involved government servants. The mobility and anonymity of frontier life created an opportunity for spouses to move with relative ease and, in so doing, to subvert their marriages. Church courts sometimes prosecuted such occurrences with vigor. For example, in 1792, Genova Goder, a resident of the Illinois country of Spanish Louisiana, reported to the church tribunal that her husband of eight years, Joseph Lubierre, had moved to the vicinity of Baton Rouge and was living there with a widow. The court acted speedily, ordering the arrest of the husband and decreeing that he henceforth reside with and support his lawful wife.[36]

The circumstances of desertion were not always easy to resolve. Fernando Rodríquez de Meza, a resident of the Canary Islands, had left Santa Cruz in 1772 and moved first to Havana and then to New Orleans, where he eventually established his permanent residence. His wife, Antonia Aguilar, did not emigrate with him but remained at Santa Cruz. Although Rodríquez did not attempt to remarry, he apparently lost contact with his wife. By the 1780s, she had become impoverished and, learning of his location, began to send Fernando requests for money. He refused to support her. She eventually contacted the ecclesiastical court at New Orleans, asking that the judges order Fernando to send her money. He appeared before the tribunal and explained that he had not deserted his spouse. Instead, Antonia had refused to follow him as his wife. He said that she was free to move to New Orleans at any time and resume her residence with him. He also told the court that he had earlier sent her one thousand pesos. This was all she would get unless she reunited with him. In the light of this testimony, the ecclesiastical court refused to be further concerned with the matter.[37]

For the most part, however, church courts exhibited little hesitancy to become involved in petitions for separation from bed and board, especially those grounded in abuse, adultery, or desertion. Although it is impossible to quantify the number of failed marriages out of the total population, the manner in which the authorities in Louisiana, Texas, and West Florida aggressively resolved marriage-breakdown cases, nonetheless, provides a clear picture of family values and social expectations. The church saw protection of the family unit as perhaps the most important assumption underlying separation hearings.

The thoroughness with which these tribunals approached the cases that came before them permits four general conclusions to be drawn. First, separation from bed and board was difficult to obtain because ecclesiastical courts attempted to ensure the viability of marriages rather than legitimating their rupture. These tribunals were, therefore, an important agency in combating marriage breakdown. Separations from bed and board were granted with regularity only in cases of physical violence of husbands against their wives. Except for abuse cases, ecclesiastical judges were reluctant to grant separation, preferring instead to preside over enforced reconciliations. Adultery and, to an extent, desertion were therefore less often accepted as compelling reasons to end a marriage.

Second, separation (reflecting common practice throughout the Hispanic legal world of the eighteenth and nineteenth centuries) was often used by women as a protection against the violent excesses of their husbands. It was the last resort for battered, abused, or deserted women. Hence, in an overwhelmingly patriarchal culture, separation from bed and board represented (albeit in an inherently negative sense) one of the few aspects of social organization weighted in favor of women as victims. At the same time, men who sought divorce from their spouses because of the wife's adultery were often refused relief by the courts. These cases usually resulted in a court decree for reconciliation. This condition lends itself to an interesting speculation that, although supported by the cases examined, is beyond proof because of the limited documentary record: Women who sought separation grounded on abusive treatment actually desired to end cohabitation. On the other hand, men who sought divorce based on the wife's adultery did not seek to end the relationship but were seeking the assistance of church authority in reasserting conjugal control over their spouse.

Third, most divorce cases brought by women as plaintiffs also involved the wife's desire to control her antenuptial possessions or her share of the common property. All the examined cases that were grounded in physical abuse also attempted to substantiate the husband's misuse of property. Courts were careful to make awards of property to wives who successfully secured separation under such circumstances. Separated married women sometimes appeared before civil authorities to compel compliance with orders concerning property. This circumstance raises questions about whether these cases reflect the concerns of the entire society. Did married poor women bother to seek a separation from bed and board when their marriages degenerated into violence? Perhaps they did not. Perhaps poor couples used cheaper, less formal, and more expedient solutions, such as extralegal separation, a simple return to the wife's family, a move to another locality, or other similar strategies in response to solving marital breakdown. Securing a separation from bed and board before the church court might well have been as much an economic phenomenon of social class as a symptom of marital breakdown for abused women on the Hispanic frontier.

Fourth, the study of marital breakdown as reflected in the records of Louisiana, West Florida, and Texas holds a historiographical lesson for the Hispanic frontier of North America. The experience of settlers there, at least in terms of family values, had great similarity in Hispanic law and religion from region to region across differing eras of administration and governmental sovereignty. Like the mission, the presidio, and the villa, the nuclear family was an important and integral institution essential for understanding the sociology of the Hispanic frontier of North America.[38] It too deserves serious and considerate study by historians.

Notes

1. Marital breakdown occurred when physical abuse, domestic violence, adultery, incompatibility, spousal failure to provide the necessities of life, or the failure to consummate or maintain the conjugal union rendered the family unit dysfunctional. Not all marriage breakdowns resulted in suits for separation from bed and board because there were many extralegal ways to end a marriage, especially for the nonelite social classes. Many of these strategies, ranging from mutually agreed informal separations to bigamy, probably escaped the notice of the authorities. The social history of such phenomena is difficult to research because manuscript and archival sources that have been preserved generally do not document the commonplace realities of daily life. Instead, they provide documentation of deviations from standard normative practices. This study is based on material related to separation contained in the Spanish Judicial Records of Louisiana located in the Louisiana Historical Center at the Louisiana State Museum in New Orleans, the Ecclesiastical Notary records of that province in the Civil District Courts Records of Orleans Parish located in the District Courts Building of New Orleans, and the Archivo de Béxar located at the University of Texas at Austin. The latter is widely available in a microform reproduction; the citations in this essay are to the microform edition. For a general discussion of these records, see Henry Putney Beers, *French and Spanish Records of Louisiana: A Bibliographical Guide to Archive and Manuscript Sources* (Baton Rouge: Louisiana State University, 1989), 30–31, 34–35, 150–80; and Adán Benavides Jr., comp. and ed., *The Béxar Archives (1717–1836): A Name Guide* (Austin: University of Texas Press, 1989), xi–xxii.

2. The period concerned here is the mid-1760s to the mid-1830s. During these decades, Texas was a Spanish province until 1821, then part of independent Mexico. In terms of civil, judicial, religious, and military jurisdiction, it was never linked with Louisiana, which existed as a Spanish province from 1766 to 1803. Moreover, Spanish Louisiana—although an imperial province of strategic importance to the Indies during the late eighteenth century—had a much greater geographical extent and a more diverse ethnic population than did relatively more homogeneous Texas. The territory of colonial Louisiana included most of the western Mississippi valley and, during the 1780s and 1790s, extended across the northern Gulf coast to encompass parts of the modern states of Mississippi, Alabama, and Florida. This latter area was known as West Florida, first having been a British colony from 1763 to 1783, then Spanish from 1793 until 1819. Louisiana's large Gallic population, coupled with an increasing Anglo-American migration, gave the province a greater cultural and demographic variety than that found in Texas during that period. For recent historical literature on these provinces, see Light T. Cummins, "Texas under Spain and Mexico," in *A Guide to the History of Texas*, ed. Light T. Cummins and Alvin R. Bailey Jr. (New York: Greenwood, 1988), 3–16; Cummins, "Spanish Louisiana," in *A Guide to the History of Louisiana*, ed. Light T. Cummins and Glen Jeansonne (Westport, CT: Greenwood, 1982), 17–25; and Cummins, "Colonial Louisiana," in *Louisiana: A History*, ed. Bennett H. Wall et al., 2nd ed. (Arlington Heights, IL: Harlan-Davidson, 1990), 52–67.

3. The institutionalization of Hispanic-frontier scholars into two schools, those of the southeast and the southwest, is historiographical reality, heightened by the fact that the manuscript records for Louisiana and Texas are generally maintained as parts of different archival collections. Such separation is an appropriate historiographical distinction, but only as long as historical analysis focuses on the institutional aspects of the Spanish imperium in the Indies: studies of government and colonial administration, international rivalry and Native American relations, methods of frontier organization and expansion, and commercial development. In these aspects of political and economic institutions, Hispanic Texas and Louisiana probably show more historical disparities than similarities. For a fuller discussion, see David J. Weber, "Turner, the Boltonians, and the Borderlands," *American Historical Review* 91 (1986): 66–81; and Michael C. Scardaville, "Approaches to the Study of the Southeastern Borderlands," *Alabama and the Borderlands: From Prehistory to Statehood*, ed. R. Reid Badger and Lawrence C. Clayton (Tuscaloosa: University of Alabama Press, 1985), 184–96.

4. Silvia M. Arrom, *The Women of Mexico City, 1790–1857* (Stanford, CA: Stanford University Press, 1985), 206–7.

5. Richard Boyer, "Women, *La Mala Vida*, and the Politics of Marriage," in *Sexuality and Marriage in Colonial Latin America*, ed. Asunción Lavrín (Lincoln: University of Nebraska Press, 1989), 258–59.

6. Roderick Phillips, *Putting Asunder: A History of Divorce in Western Society* (Cambridge: University of Cambridge Press, 1988), 3; "Información de Pedro Josef Boydant para hacer constant el primer matrimonio subsistente de su mujer," July

1784, Acts of S. de Quiñones, vol. 3, Orleans Parish Notarial Archives, Civil District Court Building, New Orleans; "Memoria de Don Antonio Marmillon," Acts of S. de Quiñones, vol. 1, ibid.

7. Phillips, *Putting Asunder*, 12–13; Arrom, *Women of Mexico City*, 208.

8. Arrom, *Women of Mexico City*, 208.

9. Phillips, *Putting Asunder*, 13.

10. Vaughn Baker Simpson et al., "Le Mari Est Seigner: Marital Laws Governing Women in French Louisiana," in *Louisiana's Legal Heritage*, ed. Robert R. Macdonald and Edward Haas (New Orleans, 1983), 12–13.

11. Arrom, *Women of Mexico City*, 209–10.

12. Ibid., 209.

13. "Royal Decree on Divorce Case of Josefa Castañeda," Archivo de Béxar, roll 18, ff. 92–94.

14. For a full discussion of marriage contracts, see Hans W. Baade, "Marriage Contracts in French and Spanish Louisiana: A Study in Notarial Jurisprudence," *Tulane Law Review* 53 (1979): 1–93. See also Joseph W. McKnight, "Spanish Law for the Protection of Surviving Spouses in North America," *Anuario de historia del derecho español* 57 (1989): 367–406.

15. For representative examples of this literature, see Nancy Cott, "Eighteenth Century Family and Social Life Revealed in Massachusetts Divorce Records," *Journal of Social History* 10 (1976): 20–43; Sheldon S. Cohen, "'To Parts of the World Unknown': The Circumstances of Divorce in Connecticut, 1750–1797," *Canadian Review of American Studies* 11 (1980): 275–93; and María Beatriz Nizza da Silva, "Divorce in Colonial Brazil: The Case of Sao Paulo," in Lavrín, *Sexuality and Marriage in Colonial Latin America*, 313–40.

16. This finding is consistent with Silvia M. Arrom's study of early nineteenth-century Mexico City. She notes that "physical abuse was the primary reason women gave for seeking divorce." Arrom, *Women of Mexico City*, 232.

17. "María Antonia Rodríquez contra Josef Molina, su marido, sobre divorcio," Acts of S. de Quiñones, vol. 1, Orleans Parish Notary Archives, Civil District Courts Building, New Orleans.

18. "Información producida por Margarita Prudome de los malos tratos que Pedro Duranton, alias Lecouture, su marido le da," Acts of S. de Quiñones, vol. 3, March 29, 1784, Orleans Parish Notary Records.

19. "Doña Catalina Toupar contra Don Luis Lorsel, su marido, sobre separación," Acts of S. de Quiñones, vol. 5, Orleans Parish Notary Archives.

20. Action of Bernardo Castillo and José María Jiménez, Archivo de Béxar, February 19, 1829, roll 169, f. 689.

21. The court granted the separation. See Jack D. L. Holmes, "'Do It, Don't Do It': Spanish Laws on Sex and Marriage," in Macdonald and Haas, *Louisiana's Legal Heritage*, 32.

22. "Phillipe Flotte v. Marie Theresa Leiveille, his wife, to prevent her from giving away her property," May 25, 1773, in "Index to Spanish Judicial Records of Louisiana," trans. Laura Porteous, *Louisiana Historical Quarterly* 9 (1926): 543–44.

23. Ibid., 544.

24. "Margarita Mellieur v. Claudio La Coste, her husband, to demand from him her dowry and community property," February 10, 1784, in "Index to Spanish Judicial Records of Louisiana," trans. Laura Porteous, *Louisiana Historical Quarterly* 20 (1937): 529.

25. "Elizabeth de Villiers v. Francisco de Volsay, her husband," January 27, 1780, in "Index to Spanish Judicial Records of Louisiana," trans. Laura Porteous, *Louisiana Historical Quarterly* 15 (1932): 548–49.

26. "Feliciana Fourganger v. Josef Duget, her husband," October 28, 1787, in "Index to Spanish Judicial Records of Louisiana," trans. Laura Porteous, *Louisiana Historical Quarterly* 25 (January 1942): 284–85.

27. Holmes, "'Do It, Don't Do It,'" 19–20.

28. Arrom, *Women of Mexico City*, 240–41.

29. Case for Separation, María Casimira Benítez and Juan José Flores, March 5, 1808, Archivo de Béxar, roll 37, f. 809.

30. "Suit for Separation of Daniel Callaghan," Acts of S. de Quiñones, 17 May 1785, vol. 4, f. 81, Orleans Parish Notary Archives.

31. This verdict was acceptable to Allon, who apparently wanted his wife back. "Benito Allon contra su Mujer," Acts of Quiñones, October 1796, vol. 8, f. 515, Orleans Parish Notary Archives.

32. "Isabel Alexandre contra Luis Forneret," May 1793, Acts of Quiñones, vol. 6, f. 134, Orleans Parish Notary Archives.

33. "Francisco López to Juana Antonia Ocona," July 23, 1812, Archivo de Béxar, roll 51, ff. 962–64.

34. "Joseph Molina contra su mujer," May 9, 1793, Acts of S. de Quiñones, vol. 6, f. 130, Orleans Parish Notary Archives.

35. "Memorial of Severo Ruiz," July 4, 1829, Archivo de Béxar, roll 123, ff. 986–87.

36. "Genova Goder contra Joseph Lubiere sobre renunciar al matrimonio," Acts of S. Quiñones, May 1788–July 1793, f. 117, Orleans Parish Notary Archives.

37. "Testimonio de diligencias sobre deunar de Don Fernando Rodríquez, residente en esta, con su mujer Antonia Aguilar, residente en Islas Canarias," January 19, 1786, Acts of S. de Quiñones, 4:573.

38. In his 1990 Presidential Address to the American Historical Association, the late David Herlihy made an impassioned plea for the study of the family as an important object of historical analysis. As he explained his purpose: "I want to examine the emergence of the family in the West as a moral unit and a moral universe: a unit in the sense that it is sharply differentiated from the larger associations of kin and community, and a universe in the sense that human relations within it are very different from human relations outside its limits." Herlihy, "Family," *American Historical Review* 96, no. 1 (1991): 1. For a general overview of the family in western culture, see Tamara K. Hareven, "The History of the Family and the Complexity of Social Change," *American Historical Review* 96, no. 1 (1991): 95–124.

CHAPTER 11

Across the Sabine

The Stephen F. Austin Family in Spanish and Antebellum Louisiana

In 1921, Mattie Austin Hatcher, an archivist at the University of Texas, published an essay in the *Southwestern Historical Quarterly* entitled "The Louisiana Background to the Colonization of Texas, 1763–1803." She surveyed Spanish policies, especially those of Esteban Miró, which first opened Louisiana to English-speaking migrants. Her analysis stopped with the Louisiana Purchase. In 1927, this historical essay became the basis of a more comprehensive monograph entitled *The Opening of Texas to Foreign Settlement, 1801–1821*, which examined the origins of the Anglo-American movement from Louisiana into Texas. Hatcher's work has not had the influence on subsequent scholarship to the extent it deserves, much of that historical analysis instead being atomized by a state-based approach. In addition, since her work crossed the defined historiographical divide between the "southeastern" and the "southwestern" Spanish Borderlands, few scholars over the years have linked Texas and Louisiana together into integrated research projects.

That atomization has certainly been true in the scholarly literature dealing with the Anglo-American settlement of Texas. Moses Austin and the other empresarios of the 1820s sometimes spring to life in the general historical literature with little emphasis on the historical antecedents that made their activities possible. They are examined as Anglo-

Americans who first appear on the historical stage when they organized settlement ventures in Texas without discussion of earlier endeavors that motivated their arrival. Such is not accurate. The activities of Moses Austin in settling the lead-mining districts south of St. Louis, however, had a definite influence on his Texas venture. Even earlier, he had owned lead mines in Virginia in the 1790s before traveling to upper Louisiana, later Missouri, to profit from the mining and smelting carried on there. At that time, he brought with him Anglo-American families, founding the towns of Potosi and Herculaneum. Although he lived under Spanish rule there for only a few years before the 1803 Louisiana Purchase, Austin learned how to deal with Spain's administrators and gained an understanding of land law as it related to the settlement of people from the United States. The Ozark Plateau settlements he established became a proving ground for his plans to bring English speakers into Texas. The essay below analyzes the relationship between Louisiana and Texas during and after the time English speakers moved west of the Sabine River, concentrating on the members of the Austin family, who played a public and prominent role in that demographic movement. What is said about them, however, was true as well for many other Anglo-Americans who settled in Texas during the 1820s and 1830s. Anglo-American Texas at that time constituted a hinterland of New Orleans. It should be noted that this essay does not distinguish between Texas as first a Spanish province and thereafter part of Mexico because the land policies that began under Spain continued under Mexican sovereignty, especially as they touched on the empresario system. My biography of Stephen F. Austin's sister, *Emily Austin of Texas, 1795–1850*, develops in more detail the points made below regarding the strong ties between Anglo-American Texas and New Orleans.

Light Townsend Cummins, "Across the Sabine: The Stephen F. Austin Family in Spanish and Antebellum Louisiana," *Louisiana History* 55 (Spring 2014): 389–408.

SOMETIME IN early 1796, Moses Austin, a lead-mine owner in the New River valley of Virginia, read a letter published in a local newspaper. The Marquis Pierre Charles DeHault DeLassus, the Spanish commandant at the settlement of Nuevo Bourbon south of St. Louis, had written this letter, which had been translated into English and reprinted in a number of gazettes throughout the United States. DeLassus hoped to encourage immigration of English speakers into Spanish Louisiana from their homes along the Eastern Seaboard. He provided much favorable description of conditions in the Mississippi valley. He wrote in part: "There is in this country a great quantity of iron, lead and copper ores." This statement caught the attention of Moses Austin, whose Virginia lead mines were beginning to play out. That December, armed with letters of recommendation to several Spanish officials in the region, Austin left his wife and young family in Virginia to visit the lead-mining district of upper Spanish Louisiana. After weeks of exhausting travel in the worst of winter weather, including a dangerous time when he got lost in the snow, Austin arrived at St. Louis on January 15, 1797. He met personally with DeLassus, who gave him letters of introduction to Commandant Francois Valle at Ste. Genevieve in the heart of the lead-mining district.[1]

Moses Austin liked what he found. Within the year, he had moved his mining operations to Spanish Louisiana. This presaged the Austin family's successful settlement of Anglo-Americans in Texas by exactly twenty-five years and began their three-generation-long relationship with Louisiana. The Austin family's connection with Louisiana has been obscured in the historical literature dealing with their contributions to American history. Such is the case because many scholars who have researched and written on the history of Louisiana as a territory and a state look to the north and to the east. They focus on the impact New Orleans and the lower Mississippi valley has had on the economic and demographic growth of the American South and the Atlantic-coast ports cities without giving much attention to Texas. Many historians conceptualize the lower Mississippi watershed before the Civil War as "southern" instead of "western." This, of course, is not an incorrect vantage point. Such a historical viewpoint, however, does not give full justice to considering the history of Texas and its relationship to Louisiana before the 1860s. From the second decade of the nineteenth century down to the period of Reconstruction, Anglo-American areas of Texas existed as a financial and commercial hinterland of Louisiana, especially New Orleans. Cultural ties between the two also moved along these lines of contact. Such proved the case until the late 1860s, when long-distance steamship service from Galveston to the East Coast, along with the expansion of the national railroad network into Texas, broke the Lone Star State's dependency on Louisiana.[2]

The historiographical conceptualization of Texas being a hinterland of Louisiana is founded in the perspective of looking at both places as neighboring parts of what had once been the Spanish Borderlands. As such, they were concurrent provinces of the Spanish colonial imperium. Historians writing from borderlands perspectives have long understood that Texas had a strong geographical connection to Louisiana. The Sieur de la Salle set in motion the Spanish settlement of Texas when he established an abortive French settlement on Lavaca Bay after having earlier floated down the Mississippi River from Canada. A generation later, the journey of Louis Juchereau de St. Denis from Natchitoches to San Juan Bautista on the Rio Grande prompted a renewed effort on the part of Spain to establish viable settlements in Texas. Thereafter, the opening of the Camino Real, with its eastern terminus at Los Adaes near Natchitoches, created regular contact and much illegal trade between Texas and Louisiana. The Mallet Brothers and others routinely journeyed into Spanish Texas from Louisiana to trade, while individuals such as Athanase de Mèziéres effectively ignored imperial boundaries in dealing with Native American peoples of the region.[3]

The American Revolution had a profound impact on linking Texas and Louisiana. By that time, Louisiana had become a Spanish possession. The colonial revolt in British North America constituted a welcome opportunity for Spain to weaken her centuries-old international rival Great Britain by supporting the rebellion that began at Lexington and Concord. In particular, Spain's influential Gálvez family saw an important role for the Gulf coast and lower Mississippi valley in the conflict. Jose de Gálvez served as Spanish colonial minister, his brother Matias as the viceroy of New Spain, and Matias's son Bernardo as governor of Louisiana. In particular, Bernardo de Gálvez turned to Spanish Texas for the purpose of provisioning his military forces and, in turn, those of the American rebels. In that regard, Governor Gálvez sent an agent from New Orleans to Texas for the purpose of procuring a steady supply of Texas beef to feed his army. The American Revolution thus witnessed the first Texas cattle drives as Spanish ranchers moved their herds from the San Antonio and Guadalupe river valleys eastward across the Sabine River to provision the armies of Bernardo de Gálvez. Modern estimates hold that between 1779 and 1782, over 15,000 head of Texas cattle went to Louisiana during the course of this supply effort. Some of this beef found its way from the Mississippi valley to the rebel armies. The jerky and salt meat consumed by the Continental Army at Saratoga came from Texas by way of Natchitoches and New Orleans. Thereafter, a regular cattle trade between Texas and Spanish Louisiana motivated a profitable commerce between the two, taking place well into the nineteenth century. These efforts also expanded to include a lively trade in horses since purchasers in Louisiana greatly desired Spanish mustangs. By the 1790s, Barr and Davenport, an English-speaking merchant house at Natchitoches, had received Spanish approval to engage in trade between Texas and Louisiana.[4]

By the time Moses Austin became a legal resident of Spanish Louisiana, the province and its capital at New Orleans had begun attracting much attention in the United States. New Orleans existed as a burgeoning port city with an expanding economic hinterland that afforded many possibilities for trade and commerce with the Gulf coast, the Caribbean, the United States, and the entire Atlantic commercial world.[5]

The Austin family, especially Moses and his son Stephen, constitute a valid case study that highlights the fact that Texas existed as a cultural and economic hinterland of Louisiana during the period of English-speaking settlement during the empresario era.[6] The experience of three generations from this Texas family proved very typical in this regard. For over fifty years—from the 1820s to the 1870s—the Austins lived with close, strong, and regular economic ties to Louisiana, especially New Orleans. They existed prior to the Civil War as the "first family" of Texas, and to this day, descendants play significant economic roles in Texas as bankers, oil executives, business leaders, and other individuals who have financial and social standing throughout the state. Importantly, because of the Austin family's prominence, there exists today a large and relatively complete collection of historical papers that covers generations of their personal, public, and commercial activities from the 1780s until the early twentieth century.[7]

The Austin family saga on the frontier begins in Spanish Louisiana, and it is more appropriately a part of the history of that larger region than it is purely a Texas story. Moses Austin came to Spanish territory on the west bank of the Mississippi as part of a determined Anglo-American frontier advance that had begun during the American Revolution. Fort Jefferson, located at the juncture of the Mississippi and Ohio Rivers in the 1780s, proved to be the vanguard of this movement in the mid-Mississippi valley. Spanish immigration policies after the American Revolution encouraged English-speaking entrepreneurs to settle people from the infant United States all along the river, including at places such as New Madrid, Nuevo Bourbon, and eventually the Felicianas of modern Louisiana. Moses Austin became one of these entrepreneurs. By 1799, he had brought over a hundred people from the United States to settle Potosi, a town he founded in the lead-mining district south of Spanish St. Louis near Ste. Genevieve. He also established a settlement at Herculaneum, the location of a large lead smelter he constructed. That smelter, greatly expanded and modernized, is still in operation today. Moses Austin became very familiar with Spanish land laws. He also became adept at working with Spanish governmental officials. His two sons, Stephen and Browne, grew to adulthood at Potosi, as did his daughter, Emily.[8]

The Austin children knew firsthand the business and commercial activities in which their father engaged, eventually becoming personally involved in them as they came of age.[9] Almost all of these economic activities demanded regular contact with New Orleans by means of river transport on the Mississippi, especially after the Louisiana Purchase of 1803, when the region began to experience marked demographic and commercial expansion. Moses Austin built a grand, palatial home at Potosi he named Durham Hall after the town of his birth in Connecticut. All of the fittings, furniture, and embellishments for this grand residence came from New Orleans. His wife, Maria Austin, who considered herself the social arbiter of the English-speaking community south of St. Louis, looked to New Orleans for fashion, cultural news of interest, and examples of up-to-date social conventions. The Austin lead mines relied exclusively on New Orleans merchants, both for the financing of its operations and the sale of its smelted ingots.[10]

By his late teenage years, Moses's son Stephen F. Austin superintended the family's lead shipments from Herculaneum to New Orleans.[11] In one memorable year, Stephen's journey took him through the extensive damage wrought by the New Madrid earthquake, destruction he vividly recounted in his letters home. On a later trip, his barge sank in the Mississippi south of Baton Rouge. He spent several weeks supervising the successful salvage of its lead and other cargo. The Austin lead business gave both Moses and Stephen great familiarity with New Orleans and its business community. Both men made Louisiana contacts that would be crucial in the later Anglo-American settlement of Texas.[12]

One of these connections would have a profound impact on Austin's later efforts. In May 1801, Moses Austin traveled for business reasons to New Orleans, where he negotiated legal documents with the notary Pedro Pedesclaux and thereafter lodged at a local hostelry. A frontier entrepreneur named Phillip Neri, better known as the Baron de Bastrop (a fictitious title he had invented for himself), was also notarizing documents with Pedesclaux and staying at the same lodgings. Austin and Bastrop met at that time. Like Austin, Bastrop had been a land agent during the Spanish period, in his case associated with Louisiana's Matson Rouge grant. Bastrop would later work closely in partnership with the Austins in settling Anglo-Americans west of the Sabine. Today both Texas and Louisiana have towns named for him.[13]

The economic depression that occurred on the Mississippi River frontier after the War of 1812 brought financial ruin to many of the businesses and economic enterprises in the region. The Austins lost their lead mines, and all of their other investments evaporated. Moses, along with son Stephen, soon hatched a plan to regain the family's wealth. They would involve themselves in settling areas to the southwest of Missouri, starting with Arkansas and then Texas. Along with James Bryan, who had married Stephen's sister, Emily, they heavily invested in

New Madrid land claims.[14] Stephen F. Austin and James Bryan founded Little Rock, later establishing the town of Fulton north of present-day Shreveport on the Red River. Stephen made his residence at a plantation on that river in what is today the heart of the Ark-La-Tex region, moving there in 1820 as migrants journeyed down the Old Southwest Trail to places such as Arkadelphia (a town founded by James Bryan) and Old Washington. Stephen served a term as a district judge in Miller County, Arkansas, while his brother-in-law Bryan encouraged the arrival of more settlers. A worsening economic crisis, now known as the Panic of 1819, dashed the profitability of these ventures, followed by the subsequent death of James Bryan from a lingering fever. Stephen gave up his Arkansas plans and moved to New Orleans, where he secured a position for himself in the law office of attorney Joseph H. Hawkins. Stephen had years earlier been a schoolmate of Hawkins's brother. It was young Austin's intention to make the Crescent City his permanent home.[15]

While Stephen and James Bryan attempted to settle Arkansas, Moses Austin undertook efforts to bring English speakers into Spanish Texas. He hoped to become a land agent for the second time in his career, empowered by the Spanish colonial government to sponsor a colonization scheme west of the Sabine. Moses traveled to San Antonio in 1820 and met with Texas governor Antonio Martinez. Austin received a contract to bring three hundred families from the United States into the province. During that visit, Moses renewed his friendship with the Baron de Bastrop, who was then also in San Antonio de Bexár. The two formed a partnership for this settlement enterprise, an agreement cut short by Moses Austin's death in 1821, just as the venture was starting. On hearing of his father's passing, Stephen agreed to replace Moses in this project. The Anglo-American settlement of Texas thus continued under the auspices of Stephen F. Austin. New Orleans merchants and businessmen underwrote most of Stephen's financial expenses in this massive venture. Joseph H. Hawkins signed a contract with Stephen that gave him part ownership in the Austin land grants, and by the time of his passing several years later, the New Orleans attorney had provided over thirty thousand dollars to underwrite Austin's expenditures, a tremendous amount of money for the time. New Orleans investors chartered the sailing ship *Lively*, which brought the initial settlers from New Orleans to Velasco at the mouth of the Brazos. They also made loans to prospective colonists who desired the funds necessary to move into the Austin colony.[16]

New Orleans resident Samuel May Williams became one of Austin's chief associates in the venture. In 1819 Williams worked for the mercantile house of Morgan, Dorsey, and Company, located at the corner of Magazine and Gravier Streets in New Orleans, where he first met Stephen F. Austin. As his biographer Margaret Sweatt Henson has noted: "Williams understood commerce and banking and had valuable mercantile contacts."[17] The young New Orleans merchant followed Austin to Texas, where he became the main business manager of the colonial venture, a position he retained for the remainder of the colonization period. Williams often turned for interim financing in Texas to his brother-in-law Samuel St. John, who served as New Orleans business agent for the eastern investment-banking firm of Joseph D. Beers and Company. Such fundraising accelerated during the Texas Revolution, when both Austin and Williams raised monies for the Texas cause, not only at New Orleans but also in cities and towns all along the Mississippi and Ohio Rivers northward into Kentucky.[18]

It was, however, the plantation economy of Anglo-American Texas that created the most profound link with New Orleans and Louisiana. No better evidence of this can be found than in the development of the Austin family plantation Peach Point, founded in 1832 by Moses Austin's daughter, Emily. Since Stephen never married, he made his home there with his sister and her family until his death in 1836. Peach Point became one of the most prosperous plantations in Texas, and it still exists today in the hands of a descendant. Like most of the other cotton plantations along the lower Brazos River, then the heart of such agriculture for the region, Peach Point had close contact with New Orleans and its business community. Its correspondence, records, and business ledgers are replete with the regular mention of Louisiana people, mercantile firms, and cultural events. Members of the family regularly traveled to New Orleans for both business and pleasure. The Austin family was not alone in this. By the late 1830s, regular packet ships plied the sea lanes between the

Crescent City and Texas ports, including Galveston, San Luis, Velasco, and Indianola, carrying passengers and hauling freight.[19]

Most of the cotton, and later sugar, grown by Texas plantations went to market at New Orleans. This proved such a lucrative commerce that, in the late 1820s, Stephen's younger brother Browne organized with their cousin John Austin a maritime shipping venture specializing in the route between the Brazos River and New Orleans. They purchased the schooner *Eclipse,* which was one of the first vessels in this trade. During an August 1829 trip to New Orleans, Browne contracted yellow fever and died in the home of business associate John Collier. Browne Austin lies today in an unmarked grave in one of the Crescent City's cemeteries. As the cotton trade accelerated, several New Orleans banking and mercantile firms developed strong relationships with Texas planters. Beverly Chew of the New Orleans Canal and Banking Company underwrote loans to Texans. On occasion, these loans kept the plantations afloat when bad weather spoiled the annual crop. New Orleans merchant George Hammekin also proved to be an important business contact for the Texas plantation belt, especially for the Austin family at Peach Point. He had known Moses Austin and maintained contact with the family for two generations thereafter. Hammekin handled many of the Austin family's business arrangements in New Orleans, especially the purchase of agricultural equipment, planting supplies, and staples needed to operate the plantation. This sometimes involved shipping high fashion to the women of the family, along with an array of housewares and personal items. One of these, a silver tea service, became a treasured heirloom. In the late 1840s, the family shipped to New Orleans the small silver service that had belonged to Moses Austin. There, the firm of Hyde and Goodrich melted it down, added more sterling silver, and crafted a large, elegant service more suited to the needs of a prosperous plantation. That silver tea set made in New Orleans is today on display at Houston's Bayou Bend Museum.[20]

As did other Texans, the Peach Point family regularly ordered medical supplies from New Orleans. They also traveled to New Orleans for medical treatment when they needed something more sophisticated than what was available in Texas, especially before the founding of the hospital at Galveston. This included slaves from Peach Point as well. In one case, a female slave developed breast cancer. After treatments in Texas proved of no avail, one of Moses Austin's grandsons accompanied her to New Orleans, where doctors at the Medical College of Louisiana, now the Tulane University Medical School, operated on her. She remained thereafter at a boarding house on Coliseum Square for several weeks in the company of a family member before returning to Peach Point for additional recuperation. The historical record does not record the ultimate success of her treatment.[21]

The Texas Revolution of 1836 had a profound impact on the Austin family, along with everyone else living west of the Sabine. Not surprisingly, Louisiana played a role in this conflict. United States secretary of war Lewis Cass dispatched troops commanded by General Edmund P. Gaines to Fort Jessup in Louisiana for the purpose of keeping armed volunteers from entering into Texas. As well, Gaines attempted to maintain peace among the Indians of the region while he stood guard to keep armed conflict from spilling over from Texas into Louisiana. The presence of these military forces east of the Sabine also contributed to a mass exodus from the Anglo-American parts of Texas. Known as the "Runaway Scrape," this constituted a movement of several thousand civilians eastward in an attempt to escape the advancing Mexican army commanded by Antonio López de Santa Anna. Roads running to Louisiana teemed with masses of people, some with carts and wagons hauling their possessions, all of them bound toward safety in the American state. Emily Austin Perry and her family participated in this flight. Her son Guy Bryan recalled: "We joined the throng of fleeing people. As far as the eye could see, extended backward and forward, was an indiscriminate mass of human beings, walking, riding, and every kind of vehicle." The road was clogged with "men, women, and children, walking, riding on horseback, in carts, sleds, wagon, and every kind of transportation known to Texas." One participant who made it all the way to Louisiana remembered: "The road from Nacogdoches to the Sabine is one unbroken line of women and children, on foot, with nothing but their clothes on their back." Emily and her family were still passing through East Texas when Houston's victory at the Battle of San Jacinto ended their exodus, but many of their neighbors did cross the Sabine. Some of those Texans who made it to Louisiana remained for over a year, planting corn crops to raise funds to underwrite their return home.[22]

Many residents of New Orleans supported the revolutionary cause in Texas. In October 1835, just as the conflict was beginning, a group of pro-Texas partisans held a public meeting in Bank's Arcade in the Crescent City. The owner of this building, Thomas Banks, had long been a supporter of Anglo-American settlement in Texas. He was joined that evening by Adolphus Sterne, a merchant who had befriended Sam Houston before the latter moved to Texas. Sterne, who would eventually become a Texan, seized the opportunity presented by the meeting to assist in raising two companies of volunteer Louisiana soldiers to fight in the Texas Revolution. Over one hundred men joined the units created that night, taking as their name the New Orleans Greys. Two field companies of these men left for Texas. Some of them joined the defenders of the Alamo, where they lost their lives with the rest of that ill-fated garrison. Others of the New Orleans Greys fought with the Texan forces commanded at Goliad by James Fannin and were massacred with his men. The remainder of these Louisiana soldiers joined Sam Houston's forces at San Jacinto. All of the New Orleans Greys fought with distinction, serving as evidence of the support Louisiana had for the Texas Revolution.[23]

Even before the Texas Revolution, Mary Austin Holley, first cousin to Stephen F. Austin and his sister, Emily, played a significant role in forging strong bonds between Anglo-American Texas and Louisiana. This is especially the case because Mary made her residence at New Orleans starting in 1829, where she lived off and on until her passing in 1846. Born at New Haven, she was the daughter of Moses Austin's older brother. She grew up in Connecticut, married the Reverend Horace Holley, and had two children, a son and a daughter. Reverend Holley served as president of Transylvania College in Kentucky prior to his death in 1827. Thereafter searching for a means of livelihood, Mary took a position two years later as governess to the children of the LaBranche family at New Orleans. This family constructed the eleven structures along Royal Street in New Orleans that today constitute a tourist attraction known as the LaBranche Buildings. Mary witnessed the construction of these buildings and lived in one of them. She routinely traveled between New Orleans and Texas. In addition to her Austin cousins at Peach Point, her brother Henry resided in Texas at his plantation, Bolivar. Like her brother, Mary also owned land in Texas and, on more than one occasion, attempted to develop it unsuccessfully.[24]

Mary Austin Holley became a well-known personality at New Orleans and did much to popularize an interest about Texas among residents of Louisiana. For example, her letters record the experiences she had during one trip from the Crescent City to Galveston in 1838. Holley's departure by ship from New Orleans proved to be a very public event. "It was thought that 3,000 people were collected on the levee and steamboats to see us depart," Holley wrote her daughter. "I assure you that Texas makes a sensation in New Orleans."[25] Mary's cousin Stephen F. Austin also visited in New Orleans at various times, one of which was on his 1835 return from Mexico City en route back to Texas. On arrival in the Crescent City, he told Mary, "I am once more in the land of my birth, and of freedom—a word I can well appreciate." Stephen did avail himself of some urban opportunities in New Orleans during that stay, for example visiting the Hotchkiss bookstore located on Chartres Street. There he purchased the published letters of Robert Walpole, a volume by Sir Walter Scott, Washington Irving's book on the conquest of Granada, and Dr. Johnson's dictionary.[26]

Mary Austin Holley's greatest contribution to the development of Texas came through the several bestselling books she wrote that praised the economic possibilities available for those who moved there. She wrote some of these from her base in New Orleans. In 1833, she published *Texas: Observations, Historical and Geographical.* This volume, part travelogue and part history, presented the reader with glowing possibilities about the agricultural and commercial benefits to be found in Texas by those who moved there. This book proved a material force in motivating immigration west of the Sabine, a portion of which came from Louisiana. Three years later, Holley published *Texas: A History,* which also trumpeted the opportunities available in the province. In the mid-1840s, she visited Texas for the purpose of writing a biography of her cousin, Stephen F. Austin, a project cut short by her death from yellow fever in 1846. Mary Austin Holley was buried in the Saint Louis Cemetery at New Orleans.[27]

The Austin family also played an important role in establishing the Episcopal Church in Texas because their family had long been members of that denomination. Although Emily's second husband, James Perry, was a Presbyterian, her Bryan children remained Episcopalians, and she worked to bring that denomination to Texas. This involved recruiting Episcopal priests from Louisiana. In 1838, the Reverend Caleb Ives established Christ Church at Matagorda, opening a school affiliated with it. Emily's sons Stephen and Henry enrolled in the school, and she often attended Sunday worship services there. Emily's daughter Eliza wrote to her brother, then studying in Ohio: "The Reverend Mr. Ives of Matagorda came to us for a visit about a week ago, he preached on the Sabbath and all of the neighbors attended." Emily invited Bishop Leonidas Polk of the Episcopal Diocese of Louisiana to visit Texas, which he did. Bishop Polk held services at Peach Point Plantation, along with others held at nearby places, including Columbia, Brazoria, Velasco, Quintana, and Matagorda. Emily made a large donation to the Episcopal Diocese of Louisiana and urged the bishop at New Orleans to help organize a church governing structure for Texas. In February 1844, Episcopal bishop George Washington Freeman visited Peach Point for the purpose of seeking Emily's support in organizing a missionary diocese in Texas. Emily's sons Guy and Austin Bryan also met with Bishop Freeman on this visit to Texas. Assisted by three priests, the bishop held a Eucharist at the Peach Point chapel attended by "a congregation of thirteen gentlemen, six ladies, and five children," including Emily. Within a few months, Texas had become part of the missionary district governed by the Episcopal bishop at New Orleans.[28]

The Austin family at Peach Point forged an even closer relationship to Louisiana after the annexation of Texas. By 1846, the cotton-planting lands of the Brazoria plantation belt had begun to play out and increasingly failed to produce profitable harvests. Emily's husband, James F. Perry, led in the effort to convert agricultural production in the region from cotton to sugar cane. Louisiana, of course, became the model for this. Perry visited the lower Mississippi, hiring overseers and sugar refiners for the expansion of this crop into Texas.[29] By 1851—the year of Emily's death as the last surviving member of her generation of Austins—Peach Point had been fully converted to sugar production, including the existence of a large refining mill on the property. Stephen Perry, the son of Emily and James, inherited the plantation and continued the sugar operations until his passing in the 1870s. Additional close ties to Louisiana occurred in the 1840s, when another Austin grandson, Moses Bryan from Emily's first marriage, married a woman from Rapides Parish, Adeline LeMothe. He had met her on one of his trips to Louisiana from Peach Point. They took up residence at a nearby plantation, Reterio, and maintained close contact with relatives and friends in Louisiana. It was Moses Austin Bryan's generation of family members who fought in the Civil War. This conflict had a tremendous impact on them and everyone else in Texas.

This was in part because the Civil War marked the end of the era in which Texas existed as a hinterland of New Orleans and Louisiana. Three major economic changes in the late 1860s broke the commercial and cultural ties antebellum Texas had enjoyed with the Pelican State. First, replacement of coastal packet vessels by long-distance steamships bound for large port cities on the East Coast fractured the reliance Texas had on New Orleans as the center of its maritime commerce. Transportation and marine shipping from west of the Sabine had relied, during the antebellum years, on a coastal trade plied by ships mainly going back and forth between New Orleans and Galveston, the latter of which had emerged as the major export location for Texas cotton. Steam-packet service between Galveston and New Orleans had begun in 1837, when the Morgan Line vessel *Columbia* started regular service to and from the Crescent City for Texas.[30] In the ten years after Texas statehood in 1845, the number of ships leaving Galveston grew to almost six hundred a year, with many of these vessels bound for New Orleans. These early steamships, however, were all side-wheelers suited only to coastal trade. After the Civil War, the arrival of long-distance, ocean-going steamships quickly fractured the longstanding ties Texas had heretofore maintained with New Orleans through the port of Galveston. In 1866,

C. L. Mallory and Company, an East Coast shipping firm, began regular steam-packet service between New York City and Galveston, thereby completely bypassing New Orleans. Ocean-worthy steamships operated by the Mallory Line made almost two dozen trips between Galveston and New York City during their first year of operation in Texas. Each year thereafter witnessed a growth in the number of such roundtrips, thus tying Texas directly to the major port cities of the Eastern Seaboard. By 1870, other shipping lines were also offering direct passenger and cargo service between Texas and Atlantic-coast port cities.[31] This new commerce bypassed New Orleans.

Second, the rise of the cattle industry after the Civil War transformed the Texas economy, in the process weakening commercial and economic ties with Louisiana. During the late 1850s, several Texas cattlemen had begun shipping Texas beef to New Orleans by coastal trading ships after it had been slaughtered at Texas Gulf-coast ports. One of them built an ice plant at Copano Bay to facilitate this commerce. The war, however, made the maritime and overland shipping of cattle to Louisiana difficult, with the result that the number of Texas beeves grew tremendously throughout the rangelands of the state. The rise of the beef-canning industry in the Midwest, first seen during the Civil War, created a new demand for larger numbers of Texas cattle at places such as St. Louis and Chicago once the conflict had ended. Starting in the late 1860s, Texas cattle went north to markets located in the Midwest instead of those at New Orleans or elsewhere in Louisiana.

The widespread conversion to cattle went hand in hand with the third major change that ended the status of Texas as a Louisiana hinterland; namely, railroad expansion in the years after the Civil War. The arrival of transcontinental railroads in the Lone Star State during the late 1860s and early 1870s considerably weakened ties with Louisiana. This was especially the case because Galveston lagged behind the rest of Texas in railroad development.[32] This trend began as early as 1865, when Texas cattlemen undertook the famous trail drives to the railheads of Missouri and Kansas. This eventually brought trackage linked to the national railway network directly into Texas as part of the cattle-shipping economy. The most significant of these rail lines proved to be the Missouri,

Kansas, and Texas Railroad, which crossed the Red River north of Dallas, heading south into Texas during 1872. The Katy Railroad, as it was popularly known, eventually reached Central Texas, thus hauling cattle by rail directly to rendering plants in Kansas, Missouri, and Illinois.[33] Railroad passenger and cargo service quickly reoriented Texas to direct contact with St. Louis, Chicago, and other points to the north and east. Louisiana ceased to be a destination for Texans and their commerce, instead becoming a place to be passed through by means of the national rail network, if at all.

These post–Civil War changes notwithstanding, the Anglo-American settlement and development of Texas from the 1820s until the late 1860s would not have been possible except for the fact that it existed as a dependency of Louisiana. The Stephen F. Austin family of Texas was explicitly involved in this close, regular, and significant relationship with the lower Mississippi valley, Louisiana, and New Orleans. Numerous historical sources confirm that they were not unique in that regard. All of the English-speaking families of Texas who lived outside of the Hispanic zones of San Antonio and South Texas also functioned as part of an economic hinterland of Louisiana for several decades after the empresario era of the 1820s. Gazettes and newspapers throughout Texas during the antebellum era routinely featured articles reprinted from Louisiana newspapers, along with advertisements for every manner of products, goods, and services imported from Louisiana. Letters, diaries, and other primary sources across Texas during those decades are replete with regular references to Louisiana. Most English-speaking Texans considered themselves as part of the commercial and cultural appendages of New Orleans prior to the 1860s. Nonetheless, by the 1870s, the strong economic, commercial, social, and cultural ties that Texas had enjoyed as a hinterland of Louisiana were clearly passing into history. The state was entering a new era that would increasingly move its economy, culture, and society away from the South and from the southern identifications exemplified by the Stephen F. Austin family.[34]

Notes

1. John F. McDermott, ed., "The Diary of Charles de Hault de Lassos," *Louisiana Historical Quarterly* 30 (Fall 1989): 359–438; Carl J. Ekberg, *French Roots in the Illinois Country: The Mississippi Frontier in Colonial Times* (Urbana: University of Illinois Press, 2000); George P. Garrison, "A Memorandum of M. Austin's Journey from the Lead Mines in the County of Wythe in the State of Virginia to the Lend Mines in the Province of Louisiana West of the Mississippi, 1796–1797," *American Historical Review* 5 (1900): 518–23.

2. Mattie Austin Hatcher, *The Opening of Texas to Foreign Settlement, 1801–1821* (Austin: University of Texas Press, 1927). This perspective was subsequently carried forward in two additional pre–World War II studies, Julia K. Garrett, *Green Flag over Texas: A Story of the Last Years of Spain in Texas* (New York: Cordova, 1939); and Harris G. Warren, *The Sword Was Their Passport: A History of American Filibustering in the Mexican Revolution* (Baton Rouge: Louisiana State University Press, 1943).

3. See the three studies by Robert S. Weddle that developed this history: *Changing Tides: Twilight and Dawn in the Spanish Sea, 1763–1803* (College Station: Texas A&M University Press, 1995); *The French Thorn: Rival Explorers in the Spanish Sea, 1682–1762* (College Station: Texas A&M University Press, 1991); and *Wilderness Manhunt: The Spanish Search for LaSalle* (Austin: University of Texas Press, 1973). See also Donald E. Chipman, *Spanish Texas, 1519–1821*, rev. ed. (Austin: University of Texas Press, 2010).

4. Light Townsend Cummins, *Spanish Observers and the American Revolution, 1775–1783* (Baton Rouge: Louisiana State University Press, 1991); Robert H. Thonhoff, *The Texas Connection with the American Revolution* (Austin, TX: Eakin, 1992); J. Villasana Haggard, "The House of Barr and Davenport," *Southwestern Historical Quarterly* 49 (1945): 66–88.

5. See the following studies for a history of the development of New Orleans as a significant port city with a hinterland centered in the lower Mississippi valley and Old Southwest: John G. Clark, *New Orleans, 1718–1812: An Economic History* (Baton Rouge: Louisiana State University, 1970): Daniel H. Usner, *Indians, Settlers, and Slaves in a Frontier Exchange Economy: The Lower Mississippi Valley before 1783* (Chapel Hill: University of North Carolina Press, 1992); and Lawrence N. Powell, *The Accidental City: Improvising New Orleans* (Cambridge, MA: Harvard University Press, 2012).

6. The definitive biography of Moses Austin is David B. Gracy II, *Moses Austin: His Life* (San Antonio: Trinity University Press 1987). Two additional historical studies make seminal contributions to assessing Moses Austin and his family, especially his son Stephen F. Austin. Eugene C. Barker, *The Life of Stephen F Austin, Founder of Texas, 1793–1838: A Chapter in the Westward Movement of the Anglo-American People* (Nashville, TN: Cokesbury, 1925; rev. ed., 1968); and Gregg Cantrell, *Stephen F. Austin: Empresario of Texas* (New Haven, CT: Yale University Press, 1999). For a biography of Moses Austin that examines him and his family

during the years they lived in Missouri, see James A. Gardner, *Lead King: Moses Austin* (St. Louis: Sunrise, 1980). The only book-length study dealing with Emily Austin is Light Townsend Cummins, *Emily Austin of Texas, 1795–1851* (Fort Worth: Texas Christian University Press, 2009). For the birth of Emily at Austin Ville, see ibid., 52. See also Marie Beth Jones, *Peach Point Plantation: The First 150 Years* (Waco, TX: State House, 1982).

7. There are two collections of family papers, the Moses and Stephen F. Austin Papers and the James F. and Stephen S. Perry Papers, both located at the Dolph Briscoe Center for American History, University of Texas at Austin. The Moses and Stephen F. Austin Papers have been transcribed, edited, and published. See Eugene C. Barker, ed., *The Austin Papers*, 3 vols. (Washington, DC: American Historical Association, 1924–28). The James F. and Stephen S. Perry Papers are available in a microfilm edition, Kenneth M. Stampp,, ed., *Records of Antebellum Southern Plantations from the Revolution through the Civil War Series G, Selections from the Center for American History, University of Texas at Austin, Part One* (Frederick, MD: University Publications of America, 1987).

8. Gertrude R. Rath. "The Life and Times of Moses Austin in Missouri" (M.A. thesis, Hollins College, 1924), 6; "Genealogical Notes," in Barker, *Austin Papers*, 1:6; "Elias Bates," Perry Family Vertical File, Brazoria County Historical Museum, Angleton, TX (hereafter cited as Perry File).

9. Walter A Schroeder, *Opening the Ozarks: A Historical Geography of Missouri's Ste. Genevieve District, 1760–1830* (Columbia: University of Missouri Press, 2000), 290. For the development of this region, see also Carl J. Ekberg, *Colonial Ste. Genevieve* (Tucson: Patrice, 1996), 153.

10. Gracy, *Moses Austin*, 178.

11. Between 1809 and 1815, 65 percent of the firm's shipments to New Orleans consisted of smelted lead. John L. Trevebaugh, "Merchant on the Western Frontier: William Morrison of Kaskaskia, 1790–1837" (Ph.D. diss., University of Illinois, 1962), 196–99; Ruby J. Swartzlow, "The Early History of Lead Mining in Missouri," pt. 5, *Missouri Historical Quarterly* 29 (1935): 195–205. For an early inventory from the store, see "Store at Mines for Mr. Bryan," James Bryan Papers, box 2N248, Briscoe Center.

12. Gracy, *Moses Austin*, 183; "Stephen F. Austin Diary," in Barker, *Austin Papers*, 1:204–9.

13. Jennie Melly Mitchell and Robert D. Calhoun, "The Marquis de Maison Rouge, the Baron de Bastrop, and Colonel Abraham Morehouse: Three Ouachita Valley Soldiers of Fortune," *Louisiana Historical Quarterly* 20 (1937): 291–462; Charles A. Bacarisse, "Baron de Bastrop," *Southwestern Historical Quarterly* 58 (1955): 319–30.

14. Stephen Aron, *American Confluence: The Missouri Frontier from Borderland to Border State* (Bloomington: University of Indiana Press, 2006), 166.

15. James Cummins to James Bryan, July 15, 1819, Barker, *Austin Papers*, 1:45–46; Stephen F. Austin to James Bryan, December 31, 1818, ibid., 335; Stephen F. Austin to James Bryan, November 2, 1818, ibid., 333–34; James Cummins to James Bryan, July 15. 1819, ibid., 345–46. All of the following citations are from the Southwest

Arkansas Regional Archives, Washington, AR: Receipt of James Bryan, SMF 489; James Cummins to James Bryan, July 15, 1819, SMF 489; and Stephen F. Austin to James Bryan, January 8, 1818, SMF 489.

16. The career of Hawkins, whose descendants later moved to Texas, is surveyed in Margaret L. Furse, *The Hawkins Ranch in Texas: From Plantation Tunes to the Present* (College Station: Texas A&M University Press, 2014), 206–7. See also Cantrell, *Stephen F. Austin*, 81–90.

17. Margaret S. Henson, *Samuel May Williams: Early Texas Entrepreneur* (College Station: Texas A&M University Press, 1976), 10.

18. Earl W. Forneli, *The Galveston Era: The Texas Crescent on the Eve of Secession* (Austin: University of Texas Press, 1961), 44; Cantrell, *Stephen F. Austin*, 151; Ruth G. Nichols, "Samuel May Williams," *Southwestern Historical Quarterly* 56 (1952): 189–210.

19. David G. McComb, *Galveston: A History* (Austin: University of Texas Press, 1986), 47; Richard V. Francaviglia, *From Sail to Steam: Four Centuries of Texas Maritime History* (Austin: University of Texas Press1981), 125–27; Gary Cartwright, *Galveston: A History of the Island* (New York: Anteneum, 1991), 77.

20. Hallie Bryan Perry, "Family Notes by Request," typescript, Texas State Library, Austin; Receipt of Hyde and Goodrich (in the amount of $647), March 20, 1849, Perry File, A-15; Jones, *Peach Point Plantation*, 115; George L. Hammeken to Emily Perry, September 22, 1848, Perry File, A-11; George L. Hammeken to Emily Perry, December 18. 1849, S. S. Perry Papers, Austin College Archives, Sherman, TX.

21. Joel Bryan to James F. Perry, October 7, 1840, Perry File, A-10. This situation continued until the Civil War, when transportation routes through Louisiana became disrupted. Even so, during the early years of that conflict, the Confederacy developed a supply line that ran from Louisiana through Texas to the Rio Grande valley. F. James Perry to Stephen F. Perry, February 29, 1844, ibid.

22. Light Townsend Cummins, "Up Buck, Up Ball! Do Your Duty! Women and the Runaway Scrape," in *Women and the Texas Revolution*, ed. Mary L. Scheer (Denton: University of North Texas Press, 2012), 153–78; Carolyn Callaway, 'The Runaway Scrape: An Episode of the Texas Revolution" (M.A. thesis, University of Texas, 1942). When the Perry family finally did arrive back at Peach Point, they found hundreds of chickens had roosted in their house. This had the unanticipated benefit of providing them with eggs to eat for several weeks.

23. The battle flag of the New Orleans Greys was captured by General Santa Anna. It remains in Mexico City to this day. At various times in recent years, Texas officials have attempted unsuccessfully to have this historic standard returned to the state. Edward L. Miller and Peter Stines, "New Orleans Greys at San Antonio de Bexár, 1835," *Military Collector and Historian* 48 (1996): 40–41. For the full story of the Greys, see Edward L. Miller, *New Orleans and the Texas Revolution* (College Station: Texas A&M University Press, 2004).

24. Rebecca S. Lee, *Mary Austin Holley: A Biography* (Austin: University of Texas Press, 1962); Mettle A. Hatcher, *Letters from an Early American Traveler:*

Mary Austin Holley, Her Life and Her Works, 1784–1846 (Dallas, TX: Southwest, 1933).

25. Hatcher, *Letters from an Early American Traveler*, 68: Lee, *Mary Austin Holley*, 280.

26. Stephen F. Austin to James F. Perry, July 13, 1835, in Barker, *Austin Papers*, 3:90–91; Cantrell, *Stephen F. Austin*, 297–98, 305; Austin to Mary Austin Holley, August 21, 1835, in Barker, *Austin Papers*, 3:101; "Bought of Hotchkiss and Company," ibid., 101.

27. Lee, *Mary Austin Holley*, 361–62.

28. Lawrence L. Brown, *The Episcopal Church in Texas, 1838–1874: From Its Foundation to the Division of the Diocese* (Austin, TX: Eakin, 1963), 7–11; Eliza Perry to Stephen S. Perry, April 16, 1844, Perry File, A-11; DuBose Murphy, "Early Days of the Protestant Episcopal Church in Texas," *Southwestern Historical Quarterly* 34 (1931): 293–316.

29. Jones, *Peach Point Plantation*, 99, 123.

30. Francaviglia, *From Sail to Steam*, 128–29.

31. James P. Baughman, *The Mallorys of Mystic: Six Generations in American Maritime Enterprise* (Middletown, CT: Wesleyan University Press, 1972); Harold M. Hyman, *Oleander Odyssey: The Kempners of Galveston, Texas, 1854–1980* (College Station: Texas A&M University Press, 1990); S. G. Reed, *A History of the Texas Railroads* (1941; repr., New York: St. Clair, 1981).

32. John M. Carroll, *Galveston and the Gulf: Colorado and Santa Fe Railroad* (Galveston, TX: Center for Transportation and Commerce, 1985), 89. By the end of the 1880s, Texas had 8,486 miles of railway track in the state, 6,046 of which had been built since 1879. Earle B. Young, *Tracks to the Sea: Galveston and Western Railroad Development, 1886–1900* (College Station: Texas A&M University Press, 1999), 159.

33. V. V. Masterson, *The Katy Railroad and the Last Frontier* (Norman: University of Oklahoma Press, 1962), 219. The main line from New Orleans into Texas, the Southern Pacific, suffered from slow construction. It did not link New Orleans to Houston until 1881. Donovan L. Hafsommer, *The Southern Pacific, 1901–1985* (College Station: Texas A&M University Press, 1986), 210.

34. These changes are discussed further in Light Townsend Cummins, "History, Memory, and Rebranding Texas as Western for the 1936 Centennial," in *This Corner of Canaan: Essays on Texas in Honor of Randolph B. Campbell*, ed. Richard B. McCaslin et al. (Denton: University of North Texas Press, 2013), 37–60.

Bibliographic Essay

THE DISCUSSION of secondary sources that follows contains citations to more recent publications that update the footnotes in the various chapters. Because many newer works cut across the coverage of several chapters, it seemed fruitful to note them by means of a selected general bibliography instead of employing updated annotations on a chapter-by-chapter basis. The sources noted in the citations of the forgoing essays are not, for the most part, included here. Neither are published primary works and the articles, which can be accessed through the respective bibliographies of the noted book-length studies. The discussion below does not constitute a complete survey of all important works of scholarship dealing in comprehensive fashion with the geographical and time periods represented by the parameters of essays in this book. Instead, that large literature has been culled to denote only those studies that make explicit commentary on the phenomenon of English-speaking migration. Even those that focus on tangentially related topics have been excluded, mainly for reasons of limited space.

There exists today a considerable number of published bibliographies and historiographical guides to which those interested can turn in order to put themselves in touch with the myriad of studies across the generations of scholarship dealing with this frontier expansion. Today, in an era of postmodern scholarly orientation, academic historians approach the expansion of Anglo-Americans into the Mississippi valley and Gulf coast from a number of diverse perspectives, many of which are atomized because little effort has been made to craft a unified or all-encompassing historiographical synthesis. Historians of the Spanish Borderlands, the

Hispanic frontier of North America, the American South, and the US colonial era have been attracted to the topic, along with scholars who study Native Americans, African Americans, and other racial minorities. Anthropologists, archeologists, ethnographers, and sociologists have also written on the topic. Finally, there is a vibrant literature with a state-based orientation focused on Texas and Louisiana history that considers Anglo-American demography from a restricted conceptualization that seldom goes beyond the boundaries of those modern states. Unfortunately, there is no single historiographical reference work that contains a unified bibliography to scholarship over the last four decades dealing in summary fashion with the Anglo migration into Spanish Louisiana and Mexican Texas. I have participated in editing several state-based references that contain bibliographic information on this topic, namely, *A Guide to the History of Louisiana, A Guide to Texas History,* and *Discovering Texas History*. The various chapters in these volumes note recent studies on the topic, as do the books *Texas through Time* and *Texas beyond Time* edited by Walter L. Buenger and others.[1] There are several academic history journals that routinely publish essays touching on Anglo-American migration and customarily review books dealing with the topic.[2]

Recent decades have witnessed the publication of a substantial number of books and articles by academic historians dealing with the migration of English-speaking settlers across the Mississippi valley and into Mexican Texas. In part, this results from an increased awareness regarding the diversity of the American frontier experience in the years between the American Revolution and the American Civil War. Historians have become concerned with the interaction between various groups that played a role in the territorial expansion of the United States from the time of the Revolution to the Anglo-American settlement of Texas. For that reason, studies over recent decades have embraced this topic from several distinct viewpoints, depending on the historiographical orientation held by the historian studying the phenomenon. There are three major analytical perspectives manifested in this literature: first, historians of the United States who study the westward-moving frontier as a national-level occurrence; second, historians of the Spanish Borderlands who have adopted a Hispanic frame of reference that considers the expansion from the reverse side of the historical experience; and third, historians who write from a state-based perspective, mostly from that of Louisiana or Texas, in considering how the Anglo-American migration into their areas influenced regional development, a perspective that rests almost exclusively on considering the historical movement of Anglo-Americans into each future state without attempting to link this into a larger, national perspective.

The colonial viewpoint, as the first of these orientations, is embodied in the mainline national history of the United States. Its practitioners have produced a great deal of scholarship over the last three to four decades regarding the Anglo-American territorial expansion into Spanish Louisiana and Texas. Most all of this literature is written from the standpoint of US history, with the framework of colonial, Revolutionary, and early national-period scholarship as its fundamental orientation. As well, it is often based on research conducted in sources that speak to US history. One strain has adopted a viewpoint known as Atlantic World history, based on viewing the lower Mississippi valley and Gulf coast as a particular part of an expanding trade zone of hemispheric scope. This had its beginning in the world-systems approach first broached by scholars such as Immanuel Wallerstein.[3] This interpretive orientation is transnational, viewing each locality (such as Louisiana or Texas) as a part of an integrated system, comprising both Europe and North America, based on economics as the major motivation for historical change, including Anglo-American expansion. Those who study Atlantic World history recognize no center or periphery when it comes to a frame of reference. They consider in holistic fashion all geographical areas as part of a balanced system of interlocking parts, each of which enjoys its own historical significance in a symbiotic relationship. Such analyses view historical events in any specific locality as part of a globalized, capitalistic world economy.

In a few very general respects, Atlantic World history can be considered as an interpretive extension of the "imperial school," developed by historians such as Charles M. Andrews during the 1920s and 1930s, but with broader parameters. Atlantic World history has its roots in intellectual developments that began in the 1990s. Harvard historian Bernard Bailyn sponsored in that decade an international seminar on the history of the Atlantic World, providing a foundation for this new historiographical approach. A scholarly journal, *Atlantic Studies*, began publication in 2004. Historian David Armitage has defined three different strains of Atlantic World history: circumatlantic, which takes a systemic approach encompassing the entire frame of reference; transatlantic, which employs a comparative approach between several of its components; and cisatlantic, which provides a focus only on one part of the wider system while explicitly conceptualizing its place inside the larger scheme.[4]

The Atlantic World framework gives much attention to the movement of people in a demographic sense, thus providing a context in which to consider westward-moving Anglo-American migrations of the late eighteenth and early nineteenth centuries. For historians writing in this viewpoint, the larger context of that movement is just as important as the particular historical events associated with it. As an emerging field over the last several decades, Atlantic World studies have been proliferating. The Oxford University Press maintains an online bibliography that provides an updated assessment of new studies across the entire spectrum of this historiographical orientation.[5] Two books provide succinct introductions to the viewpoints embodied in this approach. Karen Ordahl Kupperman's *The Atlantic in World History* (New York: Oxford University Press, 2012) is a solid overview of the subject. Bernard Bailyn's *Atlantic History: Concept and Contours* (Cambridge, MA: Harvard University Press, 2005) offers the reader a full explanation of the analytical assumptions upon which the Atlantic World orientation is based.

Noted British historian J. E. Elliott provides a cogent analysis of this same phenomenon, examined on a larger scale for the English- and Spanish-speaking components of the Atlantic World approach. His *Empires of the Atlantic World: Britain and Spain in America, 1492 to 1830* (New Haven, CT: Yale University Press, 2006) views Anglo-American expansion in North America as a meaningful part of this historical context. Elliott summarizes this process as one continuous process from its beginnings to the end of the era. He makes the succinct observation that "as each new generation of settlers outnumbered the generation that proceeded it and immigrants swarmed into the mainland colonies of British North America, the frontiers of settlement were constantly begin pushed forward in the search for new land."[6] What started on the Atlantic Seaboard eventually passed through Spanish Louisiana, entered Spanish and Mexican Texas, and finally moved beyond to the shores of the Pacific Ocean. Louisiana and Texas thus constitute the middle chapters of a longer story told within the context of the Atlantic World and its expansion. A summary of these population movements can be found in a college-level textbook on Louisiana history, especially the chapters written by me in the section entitled "The Anglo-American Influx," which traces this demographic movement from its beginnings with the establishment of British West Florida in the early 1760s.[7]

Historians attracted to the Atlantic World approach have published in recent decades a number of studies that specifically consider Anglo-American migration into the Mississippi valley and Texas within this context. Bernard Bailyn's study *The Peopling of British North America: An Introduction* (New York: Knopf, 1986) broke new ground by undertaking a sophisticated demographic analysis of population movements in North America prior to the American Revolution. The volume was one of several Bailyn undertook to analyze population movements in North America from the 1550s to the mid-nineteenth century. *The Peopling of British North America* pays special attention to the English-speaking settlement of the lower Mississippi valley and Gulf coast in British-controlled areas contiguous to Spanish Louisiana. This same orientation can be seen in Alan Taylor's *American Colonies: The Settling of North America,* which includes a focus on the Anglo-American demographic movement into Spanish and French territories, although it ends its analysis in the mid-eighteenth century.[8] Ira Berlin brings a similar orientation to his study of the lower Mississippi valley in the late eighteenth and early nineteenth centuries, with special emphasis on slavery and the role it played in the English-speaking expansion into the Mississippi valley and Gulf coast. His *Many Thousands Gone: The First Two Centuries of Slavery in North America* (Cambridge, MA: Harvard University Press, 1998) analyzes how slavery motivated the westward expansion of

Anglo-American settlement. In so doing, Berlin pays special attention to the development of slavery in Louisiana and the lower Mississippi, both before and after the Louisiana Purchase (1803). The strong links he establishes between the expansion of slavery and the Anglo-American demographic movement has informed almost all subsequent studies.

Recent decades have witnessed for Louisiana new historiographical approaches with marked Atlantic World frames of reference. For example, Bradly Bond's essay collection *French Colonial Louisiana and the Atlantic World* (Baton Rouge: Louisiana State University Press, 2005) carries forward this approach by looking at the founding and early growth of the colony from a world-systems perspective within an inherently larger context. As Bond notes, "because Louisiana remains outside the dominant national story of English-speaking settlement and westward expansion into that heartland, the heirs of American exceptionalism and the assigns of patrician historians consider French colonial Louisiana, if not a phantom place, then a peculiar place that is tangential to the stories they tell."[9] Historian Cécile Vidal has led the way in advocating a broad-based reorientation of the history of colonial Louisiana based on the Atlantic World approach. She sponsored an international conference based on applying Atlantic World history to Louisiana that met in two sessions, one at Tulane University in New Orleans and the other in Paris at the École des Hautes Études en Siences Sociales. The historians participating in these two seminars examined various aspects of Louisiana history from a variety of perspectives within the Atlantic context. This resulted in the publication of a book of essays entitled *Louisiana: Crossroads of the Atlantic World.*[10] Containing a historiographical introduction by Vidal, eight topical chapters, and a concluding assessment by historian Sylvia Frey, this collection provides solid examples of how race and slavery, trade, gender relationships, and matters of trade economy can be applied to Louisiana within this larger system.

In addition to the Atlantic World scholars, historians of the Spanish Borderlands have also studied the Anglo-American influx into Louisiana and Texas from the era of the American Revolution to the 1830s. This historical school of analysis flowed in large part from the work of Herbert Eugene Bolton at the University of California, Berkeley, during the first half of the twentieth century. Bolton examined the colonial history of those Spanish colonies that eventually became part of the United States, from Florida in the East to California in the West. Several generations of Borderlands scholars have focused on the role that Spain played as a governmental entity in those regions, with much emphasis on Native peoples. These scholars interpret the Borderlands as a zone of imperial conflict between English- and Spanish-speaking colonies in North America. They have produced a vast literature, much of which speaks to the Anglo-American movement into Louisiana and Texas. One of Bolton's graduate students, Abraham Nasatir, provided a summary examination of this scholarship in his *Borderland in Retreat,* which chronicles the advancing English frontier from the viewpoint of the Spanish colonies it encroached from the 1760s until the 1840s.[11] The decades since the publication of Nasatir's analysis have seen a significant change in the viewpoint of Borderlands scholars, some of which is reflected in the analyses they have made of the Anglo movement into the lower Mississippi valley and Gulf coast.

Historian David Weber emerged by the 1980s as the prime motivator of these historiographical changes, initiated by his landmark volume *The Mexican Frontier.*[12] This study examines the complex relationships between Native Americans, Spaniards, and English speakers in an integrated fashion, thus departing from the emphasis on the Hispanocentric orientation embraced earlier by Bolton and his students. Weber's book provides a broad synthesis that examines the entire Southwest as one region, thereby permitting him to categorize Anglo expansion as one continuous movement affecting both Native Americans and Spanish settlers. His assumptions have become mine as well, reflected in the interpretive underpinnings of my *To the Vast and Beautiful Land.* Weber considers a wide variety of religious, ethnic, cultural, economic, and political aspects involved in this demographic movement. A later work by Weber, the *Spanish Frontier in North America,* embraces this approach on a larger scale, providing a full synthesis of Borderlands scholarship over the generation prior to its publication.[13] The concept of a moving frontier between Spain and English-speaking areas on the continent became the primary organizing concept, with added emphasis on the historical participation of the region's Native Americans. A third book by Weber greatly expanded the analysis of Native peoples in this tripartite frontier. Entitled *Barbaros,* this volume essentially reversed the longstanding viewpoint of Borderlands scholarship by conceptualizing the frontier experience from a non-European perspective.[14]

Although *Barbaros* is not focused on Louisiana or Texas, its orientation has helped many historians reconceptualize their interpretations of those two areas, including the manner in which the Anglo-American influx is treated in the current literature. Juliana Barr, for example, in her study *Peace Came in the Form of Women,* has examined the role women played in the complex iterations between various Native American tribes, the Spanish, and Anglo-American migrants into Louisiana and Texas. Tribes relied on female interaction and trade to bolster relations between them in diplomatic and military matters, which eventually included taking Anglo-American women as captives, a process not understood by English speakers. In effect, Barr's book adopts a Native American frame of reference in considering the migrations of Euromericans into the region.[15] This orientation presaged publication of *The Comanche Empire,* by Pekka Hämäläinen, a comprehensive study that views the Comanche as an imperial force, coequal in standing to the Spanish and Anglo-American entities on the southwestern frontier during the eighteenth and nineteenth centuries.[16] This volume conceptualizes the migration of both Spaniards and Anglo-Americans from the Native American viewpoint. Gary Clayton Anderson employs this same frame of reference to reinterpret the Anglo-American colonization of Texas during the early 1800s, presenting well-known interactions between English speakers and Native Americans as counterpoints to the perspectives in the traditional literature. Anderson contends, in basic summary, that this migration constituted the foundation for a calculated genocide of Native Americans in the region.[17]

The Sabine River watershed constituted, in effect, a transition zone between Southwestern and Southern Native American groups that interacted with Anglo-Americans as they migrated westward. A historiographical essay by Matthew Babcock is a useful place to encounter the burgeoning historical literature dealing with Texas Indians, especially for the era of Anglo-American migration into the state.[18] Anthropologist Charles M. Hudson pioneered modern studies of Native peoples in the American South with his 1976 book, *The Southeastern Indians.* In recent decades, historical perspectives have changed in the wake of Hudson's work to consider Native Americans on their own terms, especially regarding their relationships and rivalries with English speakers on the westward-moving frontier. This orientation is the interpretive basis for a conceptual reexamination provided by James Axtell in his 1996 Walter Lynnwood Fleming lectures at Louisiana State University.[19] Daniel K. Richter's *Facing East from Indian Country,* although its chronological focus ends before Anglo-American movement into Louisiana and Texas, solidified this viewpoint. Richter considers European–Native American contacts in the colonial period from the perspective of the latter group, thus providing a paradigm shift away from the traditional Anglo-centric assumptions.[20] Studies of Louisiana Native American groups have constituted another important area of scholarship for almost a generation. Daniel H. Usner's groundbreaking study *Indians, Settlers, and Slaves* laid the scholarly foundation for the Atlantic World frame of reference in this field. His book provides a cogent analysis of the westward movement of English speakers into the Mississippi valley within the context of Native American relations while examining the role slavery played in the process. In particular, he provides a focused analysis of cultural and economic relations between the three groups in Louisiana.[21]

An analysis of French Louisiana by Sophie White considers cultural relations between colonists and Native Americans within a framework of material-culture interactions. Her book, *Wild Frenchmen and Frenchified Indians,* establishes that the two groups influenced each other in a symbiotic relationship that changed each of them in significant ways.[22] The foundations of French–Native American relations form the basis of George Milne's *Natchez Country.*[23] Although this study does not address the later era of Anglo-American migration into the lower Mississippi, it does provide an interpretive context in which to consider that occurrence. Two studies bring these perspectives to the current scholarship with a focus much later than colonial Louisiana, although their conclusions are applicable to the lower Mississippi valley. In *An Infinity of Nations,* Michael Witgen examines how Indian groups changed and adapted to the encroachment of European civilization, creating new historical spaces for themselves. Jace Weaver carries forward this perspective by examining the entire chronology of European bearing on Indian civilizations from the Native American perspective. In particular, his book *The Red Atlantic* concentrates on the role indigenous groups played in the development of the Atlantic World economy.[24]

The Native American history of Louisiana prior to European contact is the subject of a volume of essays, *The Archaeology of Louisiana,* that sets intro perspective the tribes first encountered by European settlers.[25] Daniel H. Usner's *American Indians in the Lower Mississippi Valley* provides a solid overview of Louisiana Native Americans.[26] This study is significant because it covers the period of Anglo-American migration into the region with special emphasis on the role cotton planting played. The Choctaws, who lived to the east of Louisiana along the Gulf coast, are the subject of Greg O'Brien's *Choctaws in a Revolutionary Age,* a study that provides commentary about the relations of this group to Anglo-American settlers in that region.[27] Morris Arnold has chronicled the history of the Quapaw, who lived in the regions between St. Louis and New Orleans, with special reference to this tribe's interaction with Europeans.[28] The Caddo people were the most significant of the Native American groups who interacted with Anglo-American immigrants in Louisiana and Texas during the late eighteenth and early nineteenth centuries because their homelands straddled the Sabine River, giving them an historical presence in both provinces. Additionally, the geopolitical power of the Caddo remained a constant well into the antebellum period. Cecile Elkins Carter, herself a Caddo, provides a solid introduction to this group from an ethnographic perspective. Her study offers a comprehensive summary of that Native group's social and culture traditions from colonial times to the present day.[29] In addition to ethnohistorians, archeologists have been particularly interested in the Caddo during recent decades because of their importance at the crossroads of French, Spanish, and Anglo-American expansion, coupled to the fact that they resisted European domination longer than any other tribal group in the

Texas-Louisiana region. Timothy Perttula, one of the most active of these archeologists, edited a volume in 2009 containing facsimile reproductions of important articles about the Caddo appearing between 1934 and 1953 in the *Bulletin of the Texas Archeological and Paleontological Society*. He also has written or edited several other volumes that have greatly advanced archeological knowledge of these Native Americans. His most recent volume (coauthored), *Caddo Landscapes in East Texas Forests*, uses archeological and anthropological approaches to analyze cultural and social developments from prehistoric times to the mid-nineteenth century, when the tribe finally succumbed to Anglo-American domination.[30]

In addition to archeologists and ethnographers, academic historians have also paid a great deal of attention to the Caddo. F. Todd Smith, a scholar with established expertise on that tribe, has written several books that focus on the Caddo, along with the Wichita, and their relations with Europeans moving into the region. His *Caddo Indians: Tribes at the Convergence of Empires* provides a detailed and comprehensive analysis regarding how they interacted with French, Spanish, English migration to their region from the time of Cabeza de Vaca to the decade prior to the American Civil War. Written from the historical perspective of the Caddo, it surveys each of the tribe's three branches as they interacted with the encroachments of Europeans into their domains. Smith's book *From Dominance to Disappearance* expands his historical analysis to comprehend all of the Native American tribes of the Louisiana-Texas region from the late eighteenth century to the start of the Civil War, a story significant to understanding the Anglo-American migrations into the region. Viewing these events from a Native American perspective instead of a European one, Smith finds similarities between the way the Caddo and other tribes experienced European migration, thus causing him to apply his historical commentaries to other tribes of the region as well. In that regard, Smith's *The Wichita Indians* assesses the role that tribe played in the crucial era of European territorial advance into the areas of Spanish Louisiana and Texas, especially analyzing the important role they played in trade and commerce with settlers along with other tribes. Smith completes this story, dealing entirely with the Anglo-American period, in *The Caddos, the Wichitas, and the United States*, which surveys the relations between those tribes and Anglo-American civilization from the antebellum period to the start of the twentieth century.[31]

Historian David La Vere has written several books about Native Americans that provide a backdrop for understanding the Anglo-American migration into Louisiana and Texas. Importantly, he has written a summary overview of the tribes in Texas, thereby providing a clear exposition across time from European contact to the present day. In so doing, he combines historical research with ethnography, anthropology, and archeology. La Vere's study of Caddo leadership and the organization of their geopolitical polity provides a cogent understanding necessary to appreciating the difficulties Anglo-Americans faced in establishing dominance over these Native Americans. He also has edited the Works Progress Administration interviews conducted during the 1930s. Held in manuscript form at the Oklahoma Historical Society in Oklahoma City, these interviews contain much ethnographic information about the Caddos of Texas. Although the main focus is not on Texas, where federal Indian policy never took root, La Vere's analysis of the removal efforts of the nineteenth century in his book *Contrary Neighbors: Southern Plains Indians and Removed Indians in Indian Territory* (Norman: University of Oklahoma Press, 2000) does provide additional context.

Texas tribes have also attracted the attention of scholars in recent decades. The Comanche, of course, constitute the most significant group other than the Caddo in terms of interacting with Anglo-American immigrants in Texas. A number of studies (in addition to Hämäläinen's landmark volume noted above) have appeared in recent decades about this tribe and its influence on the region. Building on Stanley Noyes's influential *Los Comanches: The Horse People, 1751–1845* (Albuquerque: University of New Mexico Press, 1993), several works have carried forward the historical examination of this important Native American group. Thomas W. Kavanagh's *Comanche Political History* provides useful information about their geopolitical organization, while Gerald Betty comments on the final days of their dominance in *Comanche Society*.[32] Robert A. Ricklis has surveyed the Karankawas from their origins to their extinction at the hands of Europeans, while Kelly F. Himmel presents a sociological examination in *The Conquest of the Karankawas and the Tonkawas*.[33] The latter volume concentrates on the era of Anglo-American migration into Texas, thereby providing a useful exposition on how these two tribes fell victim to this influx of settlers. Jacki Thompson Rand's *Kiowa Humanity and the Invasion of the State* provides a useful examination of that tribe, while *The Texas Cherokees* by Diana Everett remains an important study of that group.[34] The Apache have also attracted much scholarly attention, although the focus of many modern studies goes well beyond the boundaries of Texas. Sherry Robinson's *I Fought a Good Fight* provides the most up-to-date analysis. Two additional studies provide important focus of the Lipan Apache: Nancy McGown Minor's *The Light Gray People* and Thomas A. Britten's *The Lipan Apaches*.[35] Thomas B. Hook has analyzed the Alabama-Coushatta in a timely volume that sets them in historical perspective.[36]

Although the French and the Spanish naturally had first contact with the Native Americans of Louisiana and Texas, the historic arrival of Anglo-Americans took place in the 1760s, with the British settlement of West Florida and the coming of the American Revolution. That conflict motivated an English-speaking commercial interest in the Mississippi valley and Gulf coast that paved the way for migration.[37] Eric Beerman's study, available only in Spanish, provides a comprehensive overview of Spain's participation in that struggle. The best English-language study remains Thomas E. Chavez, *Spain and the Independence of the United States*.[38] The role the Spanish played diplomatically, with special focus of Louisiana, is developed in Light Townsend Cummins's *Spanish Observers in the American Revolution*. William R. Nester's biography of George Rogers Clark, with emphasis on his role in the American Revolution, places his campaigns into larger perspective while presenting a full assessment of Clark's complex personality. Two books provide an assessment of the role Texas manifested in the American colonial revolt: Robert H. Thonhoff, *The Texas Connection with the American Revolution*, and *Drama and Conflict*, by Thonhoff and Robert S. Weddle.[39] A recent study by Larrie D. Ferreiro, *Brothers at Arms*, examines the role played by France and Spain as allies of the rebels during the American Revolution, with emphasis on military and commercial support considered within an international context. Kathleen DuVal's *Independence Lost* contains interesting and informative biographies of significant English speakers who were involved in the Gulf coast during the Revolution, including Oliver Pollock. The role of Louisiana governor Bernardo de Gálvez is the subject of Carmen de Reparaz's *I Alone,* a translation from the original Spanish version.[40] Gonzalo M. Quintéro Saravia wrote a 2015 doctoral dissertation at the Universidad Complutense in Madrid that provides a detailed biography of Gálvez. It has been translated into English and forms the basis for a biography of this Spanish general recently published in the United States.[41]

The important role West Florida played as a fulcrum and jumping-off point for the Anglo-American movement into the lower Mississippi valley and Gulf coast is detailed in a book edited by Samuel A. Hyde, *A Fierce and Fractious Frontier.*[42] Andrew McMichael's comprehensive study, *Atlantic Loyalties,* concentrates on the relationship between the Spanish government and the English-speaking settlers who came to the province in the several decades after the American Revolution.[43] McMichael embraces a thorough Atlantic World frame of reference as he links most of the developments in the colony to the wider world of hemispheric development. In so doing, he provides a comprehensive analysis of Anglo-American migration into the Baton Rouge District, thereby laying the motivational background for the West Florida Revolt of 1810. Richmond Brown's edited volume, *Coastal Encounters,* contains an eclectic series of essays that examine Native American–European relations during the eighteenth century along the Gulf coast while also focusing on West Florida in the American Revolution and the rise of ranching in Texas.[44] A volume of essays edited by Gene A. Smith and Sylvia Hilton examines the effects of Anglo-American migration into Spanish Louisiana and the Gulf coast during the late eighteenth century. It contains biographies of significant English speakers who came to the region, along with an analysis of the motivations that produced this migration.[45]

David E. Narrett's *Adventurism and Empire* constitutes a wide-ranging analysis of Anglo migration into the Gulf coast and lower Mississippi valley prior to the Louisiana Purchase. This volume carries back into the late eighteenth century the topics examined for the nineteenth century in the now-classic study *The Old Southwest,* by Thomas D. Clark and John D. W. Guice.[46] Narrett cogently traces the rivalry between Spain and the expanding Untied States from the end of the Seven Years' War in 1763 to the Purchase of 1803. He highlights the activities of noted frontiersmen and filibusters, outlines the various intrigues that took place as Anglo-Americans moved into the region, and focuses these discussions within the larger context of Atlantic World history. Several state-based historical studies also survey the period of Anglo-American movement into the lower Mississippi valley and Gulf coast from the perspectives of the modern states of Louisiana, Arkansas, and Missouri, all once part of the Spanish province governed from New Orleans. F. Todd Smith's sweeping overview *Louisiana and the Gulf South Frontier* constitutes a narrative recounting of the development of the colony as both a French and Spanish province. He surveys settlement activities by colonists from those nations before providing close attention to what he styles the "Anglo Protestant Influx" as it created a new hegemony for Louisiana by the early nineteenth century.[47]

The Louisiana Purchase of 1803 marks an absolute historical tipping point in the Anglo-Americanization of the lower Mississippi valley and Texas. The bicentennial of the Purchase in 2003 motivated a number of scholars to revisit the events surrounding it, a topic that had already acquired a large and detailed bibliography. Paul Hoffman edited a volume of essays presented at a conference sponsored by the Historical New Orleans Collection in 2003 that brought together many historians whose works deal with the Purchase, including aspects of Anglo-American migration.[48] Peter J. Kastor has provided a modern synthesis of the purchase in *The Nation's Crucible,* with special attention given to the manner in which it shaped the American identity. Along with Francois Weil, Kastor has also edited a series of essays dealing with the international aspects of the purchase from the viewpoint of Atlantic World history.[49] John Kulka, like Kastor, has written an overview of the Purchase that concentrates on the role Jefferson and his party played in achieving it, with additional analysis of population movements into its territories.[50] The influences of slavery as a southern institution as related to the Purchase is explored in *Mr. Jefferson's Lost Cause,* by Roger G. Kennedy.[51]

It was the movement of the cotton economy into the lower Mississippi valley after the Louisiana Purchase that greatly accelerated the Anglo-American influx. There existed profound reasons why the "cottonocracy" expanded with such speed and vigor in Louisiana and the cis-Mississippi starting in the 1790s. The perfection of the cotton gin proved a significant impetus to this expansion since it simplified cotton processing and made more profitable the shipping and sale of each year's crop. In *Inventing the Cotton Gin,* Angela Lakwete places its appearance within the context of the Atlantic World economy, substantiating the explosive expansion of planting that the machine's perfection motivated.[52] Karen Gerhardt Britton Fort has provided a cultural history of cotton ginning that explains in clear terms the tremendous influence this invention had on the southern way of life.[53] A second factor further motivated the Anglo American influx into Louisiana and Texas: soil exhaustion. The growing of cotton proved particularly injurious to southern land because it leached vital nutrients from the soil. This presented planters with two choices: either fertilize and restore the nutriments where they were, or move to new areas of planting. Although fertilization constituted a process most agrarians understood during that era, moving to new land proved to be the cheapest, most efficient, and most easily accomplished strategy. In *Southern United States,* Donald E. Davis and his coauthors substantiate that the major areas of cotton production shifted from the Atlantic coast early in the nineteenth century to Texas in the decade before the American Civil War.[54] Although Christopher Morris's *The Big Muddy* considers the environmental history of the river to the present day, the eighteenth and nineteenth centuries receive due attention.[55]

This expansion of English speakers into the Mississippi valley is succinctly surveyed in *South by Southwest,* by James David Miller.[56] This study traces the demographic expansion of the cotton-planting South from the end of the War of 1812 to the start of the Civil War. Miller ties together the need for geographical expansion of the crop across time to the creation of a planter mentality. This duality gave rise, he contends, to a conservative worldview of the economic order held by the planter class in which the acquisition of slaves became more important than owning land in a particular place. Slavery became more important in their minds than place, a factor that can explain the rapidity with which both the lower Mississippi valley and Texas were settled in the decades after the Louisiana Purchase. English speakers moving into the eastern part of the Gulf coast and southern Atlantic coast of Florida during the early years of the nineteenth century are detailed in John Cusick's *The Other War of 1812*.[57] This study analyzes the policies of the Madison administration in its successful efforts to bring Florida into the national domain, in the process making commentary on Anglo-American migration along the entire Gulf coast. Analogous population movements into West Florida during the same period emphasized Anglo-American expansion into the areas bordering Louisiana and Texas. Frank L. Owsley Jr. and Gene A. Smith's *Filibusters and Expansionists* constitutes a detailed study that greatly expands our historical understanding of the English-speaking influx in the Mississippi valley and central Gulf coast.[58] Two case studies of specific areas in the region provide a further understanding of the effects of Anglo-American advances into the region: Sophie Burton and Todd Smith, in a more broad-based study of Natchitoches, Louisiana, substantiate the racial diversity of that settlement, which eventually became a significant center linking Texas and Louisiana in the late eighteenth and early nineteenth centuries.[59] Robert V. Haines considers the Anglo-American influx into what would become the state of Mississippi, starting in the late eighteenth century and continuing until after the War of 1812. He analyzes racial diversity, especially between Native Americans and Anglos, to show how English-speaking hegemony occurred in that area of the lower Mississippi valley.[60]

The institution of slavery is historiographically inseparable from any consideration of the Anglo-American migration into Louisiana and Texas. Randolph B. Campbell's *An Empire for Slavery* provides a careful analysis and comprehensive discussion of slavery in Anglo-American Texas.[61] Gwendolyn Midlo Hall's *Africans in Colonial Louisiana*, examines the places of origin in Africa for Louisiana's slave populations and relates those to the social and cultural construct of the region's symbiotic Afro-Creole culture. A larger context for the development of slavery in the region is found in the previously mentioned volume by Ira Berlin, *Many Thousands Gone*. Berlin provides a sweeping narrative that traces slavery from the Atlantic coast in the colonial era to the Mississippi valley during the era of Anglo-American migration. In so doing, he captures the episodic nature of slavery's expansion to the lower Mississippi as part of a two-century-long process, providing a platform for the eventual expansion of the institution from there into Texas.[62] Thomas N. Ingersoll's *Mammon and Manon in Early New Orleans* provides a comprehensive overview of that institution in Louisiana, with special reference to New Orleans as the colonial center. Jennifer M. Spear's study of the relationships between the sexes in New Orleans shows that patriarchal domination, to the point of sometimes becoming abusive, formed a constant in the daily life of the colony, with a focused influence on the nature of Louisiana slavery.[63] Gilbert C. Din, one of the most distinguished historians of Spanish colonial Louisiana, has written an institutional history of slavery in the province during the period of Spanish domination.[64]

Considering slavery from the viewpoint of the slaves themselves, with attention given to the forging of identity, Caryn Cosse Bell traces the formation of black leadership. Her *Revolution, Romanticism, and the Afro-Creole Protest Tradition in Louisiana* relates to the Anglo-American power structure of the antebellum era as she examines available eighteenth-century evidence for clues on how the colony's black population later reacted to the American Civil War.[65] Although it presents a comprehensive urban history across the entire history of New Orleans, from its establishment to the present day, *The Accidental City*, by Lawrence N. Powell, has much to say about slavery in is larger assessment of the city and its history.[66] A study by Rashauna Johnson concentrates of slave labor as employed at New Orleans during the late eighteenth and early nineteenth centuries. Her *Slavery's Metropolis* postulates that the urban growth of the city during the early period of American domination took place because of the rapid growth of slavery. The migration of slaves to Louisiana because of the Haitian Revolution of 1796 took place in tandem with the massive arrival of Anglo-Americans. This produced a period of economic boom in which New Orleans prospered, though with slave labor as its significant commodity to such an extent that, by the mid-1820s, enslaved persons constituted one-third of the population.[67]

Two studies dealing with blacks in late eighteenth- and early nineteenth-century Louisiana offer windows into relations between that group and the Anglo-Americans establishing hegemony in the region. Kimberly S. Hanger wrote a detailed study assessing free African Americans in Louisiana during the Spanish period. Her book, *Bounded Lives, Bounded Places,* has much to say about how Spain conceptualized slavery and the manner in which arriving immigrants from the United States had different views of the institution. In effect, this study notes how the free-black population accommodated itself to changing conditions, including references to somewhat seamy practices, such as the keeping of octoroon women by Europeans men. No person of mixed heritage in New Orleans was better known than Myra Clark Gaines, whose life constitutes one of the most historically fascinating stories of that era regarding a woman of color. The daughter of an Anglo-American father, who had migrated to Louisiana, and an African mother, Gaines eventually was named heir to a financial fortune and spent most of her adult life involved in litigation seeking to legitimize her claim. Elizabeth Urban Alexander's *Notorious Woman* recounts this personal history in detail, a saga directly related to the Anglo-American migration into Louisiana.[68]

This English-speaking influx also changed the law and the administration of justice in both Louisiana and Texas. The arrival of Anglo-American legal practices to lower Mississippi after the Purchase of 1803 radically altered the administration of justice, especially with property rights. These developments are elegantly developed in a volume of legal history by Mark Fernandez that cogently illustrates the influence the Common Law worked on the lower Mississippi valley and Gulf coast. *From Chaos to Continuity* provides a sweeping survey detailing the complex interplay between the French, Spanish, and Anglo legal systems.[69] Judith Kelleher Schafer, in a more focused study, has examined how laws regarding slavery transitioned from the French and Spanish systems into an English one, resulting in a hybrid system. She examined over one thousand legal cases regarding slavery in antebellum Louisiana, in the process showing how the law over time increasingly became more "Americanized."[70] A volume edited by Warren M. Billings and Mark Fernandez contains nine essays that consider various aspects of Louisiana law during the antebellum era, with special reference to the influence of English law on Louisiana practices that previously flowed from the Code Napoleon and the Siete Partidas.[71] The evolution of the law in Arkansas as an area once part of Spanish Louisiana is the subject of Morris Arnold's *Unequal Laws unto a Savage Race*.[72]

The legal system in Texas also experienced change because of the Anglo-American influx, like Louisiana becoming a mixture of two different European systems. Charles R. Cutter's *The Legal Culture of Northern New Spain* provides a baseline by examining in detail the administration of justice that characterized legal practices in Spanish Texas. He shows clearly that legal systems in that province had already experienced a distinctness because of the area's remoteness from central Mexico and the seat of authority.[73] Jean Stuntz, in *Hers, His, and Theirs,* provides much information about how Spanish law treated women in Texas prior to the arrival of the Common Law, practices that eventually modified the way the Anglo-American legal system dealt with them differently there than east of the Sabine.[74] The early chapters, dealing with the settlement period, of a larger, chronologically comprehensive study by Michael Ariens contains a useful analysis of the legal ramifications the arrival of Anglo-Americans had on Texas law.[75] A volume edited by Randolph B. Campbell, *The Laws of Slavery in Texas,* contains historical essays and documents that illustrate how the arrival of the Common Law in Texas combined with Spanish practices to create a legal system of slavery.[76] John Martin Davis has published an extensive documentary compendium of land grants in Texas that establishes the relationship between Hispanic and Anglo-American legal systems in that state.[77]

A state-based perspective, the third area of scholarly orientation, has also provided the motivation for a number of important historical studies. Arkansas existed as colonial territory of French and Spanish Louisiana. Morris Arnold has examined the colonial history of this area, with attention given to the beginnings of Anglo-American migration in two separate studies. His *Colonial Arkansas* offers a history of the province from its first settlement to the Louisiana Purchase, while his narrative analysis of the Arkansas Post assesses the historical importance of that frontier establishment as a center for European advancement into the lower Mississippi region from the time of Henri de Tonti to Stephen F. Austin.[78] Missouri played an important role in the Anglo-American influx, especially in the early nineteenth century as the frontier home of the Austin family. Carl Ekberg has published several studies that examine the colonial history of Ste. Genevieve, most notably a biography of Francois Valle, the administrator who granted Moses Austin his first Spanish colonization contract south of St. Louis in the late 1790s.[79] William E. Foley's *The Genesis of Missouri: From Wilderness Outpost to Statehood* (Columbia: University of Missouri Press, 1989) traces the history of that state from European settlement to its admission as a state in 1821. Historical geographer Walter A. Schroeder's *Opening the Ozarks: A Historical Geography of Missouri's Ste. Genevieve District, 1760–1830* (Columbia: University of Missouri Press, 2002) contains much useful information about the Anglo-American settlers who migrated into southeastern Missouri starting in the late eighteenth century, when it was still part of Spanish Louisiana. They eventually became, by the American period, the demographic majority southeast of St. Louis. In particular, a number of the settlers noted in this volume eventually traveled the Old Southwest Trail to settle in Texas in the 1820, including the Austins and their associates.

The Anglo-American influx into Texas has been a significant topic in historical writing for over a century. The era of the filibusters, the arrival of the Austins, and the establishment of the empresario era have attracted the attention of historians since the early twentieth century. Scholarship over recent decades has sometimes provided reinterpretations, while it has also brought to light new parts of the story previously unknown. By way of example, Andres Recendez significantly recast understandings of the relationships between those Texans of Hispanic and Anglo descent starting in the early nineteenth century. In *Changing National Identities at the Frontier*, Recendez concludes that these two groups occupied different spaces that permitted them to form distinct identities, thereby bringing a cultural plurality to the region. Despite efforts by the Mexican government to control these provinces, the pull of the US economy proved too strong and resulted in Anglo hegemony.[80] Roger G. Kennedy, a public historian who served as director of the National Park Service, has written a summary overview of the Anglo-American migration into Texas, with special emphasis on the role cotton played as a prime motivating factor. Drawn mostly from secondary academic sources, his *Cotton and Conquest* provides a broad-based narrative that ties together the history of cotton planting in the South, its movement into western regions, and its entry into Texas, thereby covering in sweeping narrative fashion much of the detail contained in more focused monographic studies.[81]

Several studies have shed new light on the empresario era in Texas, especially the settlements set in motion by Moses Austin and completed by his son, Stephen F. Austin. David B. Gracy II wrote a through biography of Moses Austin that places this seminal figure in the full context of his era, with equal emphasis on his career in both Virginia and Missouri as important for Anglo-American frontier development from the 1780s until his death in 1821. Gregg Cantrell's *Stephen F. Austin* expands Eugene C. Barker's 1927 biography into a full and completely contextualized analysis that assesses Austin in light of modern scholarship. The Stephen Austin of this study emerges as a more complex figure than previously understood, while it also provides a full understanding of the various motivations for the Anglo-American influx into Texas.[82] My biography, *Emily Austin of Texas,* completes the story of the Moses Austin family in the settlement of Texas by considering the role Stephen's sister played in helping solidify the Anglo-American presence in the state. After her brother's death in 1836, she became, by inheritance, one of the wealthiest individuals in Texas and perhaps its largest landowner. She was, along with her husband and sons, an entrepreneurial force in the development of the state in addition to being one of the social leaders of its Anglo-American community.[83] The history of the Austin family in Texas can be seen in larger context by considering other empresarios who brought settlers to the state, including Martin de Leon, who enjoyed this distinction by sponsoring Hispanic colonization in the 1820s. Ana Caroline Castillo Crimm details this empresarios project in her family history *De Leon*. Two books by Jesús F. de la Teja dealing with San Antonio also provide important context for understanding the Anglo-American influx.[84]

Andrew J. Torget's *Seeds of Empire* has subjected questions relating to slavery, cotton, and the Anglo-American entry into Mexican Texas to a full-scale reevaluation. This volume, based on extensive research in both English-language sources in the United States and in Mexican materials, presents a picture of Anglo-Mexican interactions seemingly more complex than historians have previously understood. Mexican views about the institution of slavery were not monolithic. Tejano residents, Torget notes, proved ready to join in common cause with Anglo-American settlers pushing cotton and slavery westward across the Sabine River. In that regard, residents of Mexican heritage in Texas opposed abolitionist policies coming from Mexico City in favor of alliances with English-speaking slaveholders. Together, they forged common cause against the Mexican national leadership that, when the Texas Revolution took place, permitted the Anglo-Americans to emerge victorious and, in the process, establish one of the most viable slave societies in the Atlantic World.[85]

The vibrancy and fresh approach to the topic seen in Torget's study substantiates the reality that much still needs to be done in researching and writing about the Anglo-American influx into the region. And, as these studies are undertaken, they must be based on the historical reality that the Anglo-American migration into Spanish Louisiana and Mexican Texas should be viewed as a single, continuous process that carried English speakers from the lower Mississippi valley and the Gulf coast directly across the Sabine River into Texas—and eventually beyond to California.

Notes

1. Light Townsend Cummins and Glen Jeansonne, eds., *A Guide to the History of Louisiana* (New York: Greenwood, 1982); Cummins and Alvin R. Bailey Jr., eds., *A Guide to the History of Texas* (New York: Greenwood, 1988); Bruce Glasrud, Light Townsend Cummins, and Cary D. Wintz, eds., *Discovering Texas History* (Norman: University of Oklahoma Press, 2015); Walter L. Buenger and Robert

A. Calvert, eds., *Texas through Time: Evolving Interpretations* (College Station: Texas A&M University Press, 1991); and Walter L. Buenger and Arnoldo de Leon, *Beyond Texas through Time: Breaking Away from Past Interpretations* (College Station: Texas A&M University Press, 2011).

2. These include the *East Texas Historical Journal*, the *Journal of the Early Republic*, the *Journal of Southern History*, *Louisiana History*, the *Southwestern Historical Quarterly*, and the *William and Mary Quarterly*. Hypertext bibliographic searching in specialized databases such as JSOTR and Project Muse increasingly provide quick and efficient avenues into this literature to the point that bibliographies and historiographical guides published in paper format may eventually become obsolete.

3. Immanuel Wallerstein, *World Systems Analysis: An Introduction* (Durham, NC: Duke University Press, 2004).

4. David Armitage, "Three Concepts of Atlantic History," in *The British Atlantic World, 1500–1800*, ed. Armitage and Michael J. Braddick (New York: Palgrave Macmillan, 2002), 11–27.

5. Trevor Burnard, ed., "Oxford Bibliography in Atlantic History," *Oxford Bibliographies*, http://www.oxfordbibliographies.com/obo/page/atlantic-history (accessed June 7, 2017).

6. Elliott, *Empires of the Atlantic World*, 265.

7. Light Townsend Cummins, "The Anglo-American Influx," in *Louisiana: A History*, ed. Bennett H. Wall et al., 9th ed., ed. John Rodrique, Light Townsend Cummins, et al. (New York: Wiley Blackwell, 2016).

8. Bernard Bailyn, *Voyagers to the West: The Peopling of America on the Eve of Revolution* (New York: Knopf, 1986); Alan Taylor, *American Colonies: The Settling of North America* (New York: Penguin Books, 2002).

9. Bond, *French Colonial Louisiana and the Atlantic World*, xii.

10. Cécile Vidal, ed., *Louisiana: Crossroads of the Atlantic World* (Philadelphia: University of Pennsylvania Press, 2014).

11. Abraham P. Nasatir, *Borderland in Retreat: From Spanish Louisiana to the Far Southwest* (Albuquerque: University of New Mexico Press, 1976). Specific additional titles from this perspective are noted in "Spanish Louisiana," in Cummins and Jeansonne, *Guide to the History of Louisiana*, 17–34; and "Spanish and Mexican Texas," in Cummins and Bailey, *Guide to the History of Texas*, 3–16.

12. David Weber, *The Mexican Frontier, 1821–1846: The American Southwest under Mexico* (Albuquerque: University of New Mexico Press, 1983).

13. David Weber, *The Spanish Frontier in North America* (New Haven, CT: Yale University Press, 1994).

14. David Weber, *Barbaros: Spaniards and Their Savages in the Age of Enlightenment* (New Haven, CT: Yale University Press, 2006). The changes in Borderlands scholarship as represented in Weber's works are fully assessed in a timely historiographical volume: Samuel Truett and Elliott Young, eds., *Remapping US–Mexico Borderlands* (Durham, NC: Duke University Press, 2004).

15. Juliana Barr, *Peace Came in the Form of a Woman: Indians and Spaniards in the Texas Borderlands* (Chapel Hill: University of North Carolina Press, 2009).

16. Pekka Hämäläinen, *The Comanche Empire* (New Haven, CT: Yale University Press, 2009).

17. Gary Clayton Anderson, *The Conquest of Texas: Ethnic Cleansing in the Promised Land, 1820–1875* (Norman: University of Oklahoma Press, 2005). An earlier book by Anderson, *The Indian Southwest, 1580–1830: Ethnogenesis and Reinvention* (Norman: University of Oklahoma Press, 2009), employed a similar viewpoint to examine how trade and interaction between Native groups created tribal polities that affected interaction between Indians and European civilizations in the region.

18. Matthew M. Babcock, "Native Americans," in Glasrud, Cummins, and Wintz *Discovering Texas History*, 15–30.

19. Charles M. Hudson, *The Southeastern Indians* (1976; repr., Knoxville: University of Tennessee Press, 1989); James Axtell, *The Indians' New South: Cultural Change in the Colonial Southeast* (Baton Rouge: Louisiana State University Press, 1997). See also Theda Purdue and Michael D. Green, *The Columbia Guide to American Indians of the Southeast* (New York: Columbia University Press, 2001).

20. Daniel K. Richter, *Facing East from Indian Country: A Native History of Early America*, rev. ed. (Cambridge, MA: Harvard University Press, 2009).

21. Daniel H. Usner Jr., *Indians, Settlers, and Slaves in a Frontier Exchange Economy: The Lower Mississippi Valley before 1783* (Chapel Hill: University of North Carolina, Press, 1992). The classic overview of tribal organization in the lower Mississippi valley is provided in Fred B. Kniffen et al., *The Historic Indian Tribes of Louisiana: From 1542 to the Present* (1987; repr., Baton Rouge: Louisiana State University Press, 1992).

22. Sophie White, *Wild Frenchmen and Frenchified Indians: Material Culture and Race in Colonial Louisiana* (Philadelphia: University of Pennsylvania Press, 2012).

23. George Milne, *Natchez Country: Colonists and the Landscape of Race in French Louisiana* (Athens: University of Georgia Press, 2015).

24. Michael Witgen, *An Infinity of Nations: How the Native New World Shaped Early North America* (Philadelphia: University of Pennsylvania Press, 2013); Jace Weaver, *The Red Atlantic: American Indigenes and the Making of the Modern World, 1000–1927* (Chapel Hill: University of North Carolina Press, 2014).

25. Mark A. Rees, ed. *The Archeology of Louisiana* (Baton Rouge: Louisiana State University Press, 2010).

26. Daniel H. Usner Jr., *American Indians in the Lower Mississippi Valley: Social and Economic Histories* (Lincoln: University of Nebraska Press, 2003).

27. Greg O'Brien, *Choctaws in a Revolutionary Age, 1750–1830* (Lincoln: University of Nebraska Press, 2002).

28. Morris Arnold, *Rumble of a Distant Drum: The Quapaws and Old World Newcomers, 1673–1804* (Fayetteville: University of Arkansas Press, 2007).

29. Cecile Elkins Carter, *Caddo Indians: Where We Come From* (Norman: University of Oklahoma Press, 1995).

30. Timothy Perttula, ed., *Caddo Archeology* (Davenport, IA: Gustav's Library, 2009). Other important volumes include Jeffrey S. Girard, Timothy Perttula, and Mary Beth Trubitt, *Caddo Connections: Cultural Interactions within and beyond the*

Caddo World (New York: Rowan and Littlefield, 2014); Perttula, *The Prehistory of Texas* (College Station: Texas A&M University Press, 2012); Perttula and Charles Walker, eds., *The Archeology of the Caddo* (Lincoln: University of Nebraska Press, 2010); Perttula, *The Caddo Nation: Archaeological and Ethnohistoric Perspectives* (Austin: University of Texas Press, 2010); and Perttula, Robert Cast, and Ross C. Fields, *Caddo Landscapes in East Texas Forests* (Philadelphia: Oxbow Books, 2017).

31. F. Todd Smith, *Caddo Indians: Tribes at the Convergence of Empires, 1542–1854* (College Station: Texas A&M University Press, 1995); Smith, *From Dominance to Disappearance: The Indians of Texas and the Near Southwest, 1786–1859* (Lincoln: University of Nebraska Press, 2006); Smith, *The Wichita Indians: Traders of Texas and the Southern Plains, 1540–1845* (College Station: Texas A&M University Press, 2000); Smith, *The Caddos, the Wichitas, and the United States, 1846–1901* (College Station: Texas A&M University Press, 1996).

32. Thomas W. Kavanagh, *Comanche Political History: An Ethnohistorical Perspective, 1706–1875* (Lincoln: University of Nebraska Press, 1996); Gerald Betty, *Comanche Society: Before the Reservation* (College Station: Texas A&M University Press, 2002).

33. Robert A. Ricklis, *The Karankawa Indians of Texas* (Austin: University of Texas Press, 1996); Kelly F. Himmel, *The Conquest of the Karankawas and the Tonkawas, 1821–1859* (College Station: Texas A&M University Press, 1999).

34. Jacki Thompson Rand, *Kiowa Humanity and the Invasion of the State* (Lincoln: University of Nebraska Press, 2008); Diana Everett, *The Texas Cherokee: A People between Two Fires, 1819–1840* (Norman: University of Oklahoma Press, 1990).

35. Sherry Robinson's *I Fought a Good Fight: A History of the Lipan Apaches* (Denton: University of North Texas Press, 2013); Nancy McGown Minor, *The Light Gray People: A Ethno-History of the Lipan Apaches of Texas and Northern Mexico* (Lanham, MD: University Press of America, 2009); and Thomas A. Britten, *The Lipan Apaches: A People of Wind and Lightening* (Albuquerque: University of New Mexico Press, 2009).

36. Thomas B. Hook, *The Alabama-Coushatta Indians* (College Station: Texas A&M University Press, 1997).

37. One recent study, Shannon Lee Dowdy, *Building the Devil's Empire: French Colonial New Orleans* (Chicago: University of Chicago Press, 2009), provides a summary of historical development in Louisiana during the French era. For a solid overview of Spain's colonial experience in Texas, see Donald Chipman, *Spanish Texas, 1519–1821* (Austin: University of Texas Press, 1992).

38. Eric Beerman, *Espana y la independencia de los Estados Unidos* (Madrid: Editorial Mapfre, 1992); Thomas E. Chavez, *Spain and the Independence of the United States: An Intrinsic Gift* (Albuquerque: University of New Mexico Press, 2002).

39. Light Townsend Cummins, *Spanish Observers and the American Revolution* (Baton Rouge: Louisiana State University Press, 1992); William R. Nester, *George Rogers Clark: I Glory in War* (Norman: University of Oklahoma Press, 2012); Robert H. Thonhoff, *The Texas Connection with the American Revolution* (Austin,

TX: Eakin, 1981); Thonhoff and Robert S. Weddle, *Drama and Conflict: The Texas Saga of 1776* (Austin, TX: Madrona, 1976). Clark's efforts to found Fort Jefferson are detailed in Kenneth C. Carstens, *George Rogers Clark's Fort Jefferson, 1780–1781: Kentucky's Outpost on the Western Frontier* (Berwyn Heights, MD: Heritage Books, 2005).

40. Larrie D. Ferreiro, *Brothers at Arms: American Independence and the Men of France and Spain who Saved It* (New York: Knopf, 2016); Kathleen DuVal, *Independence Lost: Lives on the Edge of the American Revolution* (New York: Random House, 2015); Carmen de Reperaz, *I Alone: Bernardo de Gálvez and the Taking of Pensacola in 1781, a Spanish Contribution to the Independence of the United States* (Madrid: Ediciones de Cultura Hispánica, 1993).

41. Gonzalo M. Quintéro Saravia, "Bernardo de Gálvez y América a finales del siglo XVIII" (Ph.D. diss., Universidad Complutense de Madrid, 2015); Quntéro Saravia, *Bernardo de Gálvez: Spanish Hero of the American Revolution* (Chapel Hill: University of North Carolina Press, 2018).

42. Samuel A. Hyde, ed., *A Fierce and Fractious Frontier: The Curious Development of Louisiana's Florida Parishes, 1699–2000* (Baton Rouge: Louisiana State University Press, 2004).

43. Andrew McMichael, *Atlantic Loyalties: Americans in Spanish West Florida, 1785–1810* (Athens: University of George Press, 2008).

44. Richmond Brown, *Coastal Encounters: The Transformation of the Gulf South in the Eighteenth Century* (Lincoln: University of Nebraska Press, 2007).

45. Gene A. Smith and Sylvia Hilton, eds. *Nexus of Empire: Negotiating Loyalty and Identity in the Revolutionary Borderlands, 1760s–1820* (Gainesville: University Press of Florida, 2010).

46. David E. Narrett, *Adventurism and Empire: The Struggle for Mastery in the Louisiana-Florida Borderlands, 1762–1893* (Chapel Hill: University of North Carolina Press, 2015); Thomas D. Clark and John D. W. Guice, *The Old Southwest, 1795–1830: Frontiers in Conflict* (Norman: University of Oklahoma Press, 1996).

47. F. Todd Smith, *Louisiana and the Gulf South Frontier, 1500–1821* (Baton Rouge: Louisiana State University Press, 2014).

48. Paul E. Hoffman, ed., *The Louisiana Purchase and Its Peoples: Perspectives from the New Orleans Conference* (Lafayette: University of Louisiana at Lafayette Press, 2004).

49. Peter J. Kastor, *The Nation's Crucible: The Louisiana Purchase and the Creation of America* (New Haven, CT: Yale University Press, 2004); Kastor and Francois Weil, eds., *Empires of Imagination: Transatlantic Histories of the Louisiana Purchase* (Charlottesville: University of Virginia Press, 2003).

50. John Kulka, *A Wilderness So Immense: The Louisiana Purchase and the Destiny of America* (New York: Knopf, 2003).

51. Roger G. Kennedy, *Mr. Jefferson's Lost Cause: Land, Farmers, Slavery, and the Louisiana Purchase* (New York: Oxford University Press, 2003).

52. Angela Lakwete, *Inventing the Cotton Gin: Machine and Myth in Antebellum America* (Baltimore: Johns Hopkins University Press, 2005).

53. Karen Gerhardt Britton Fort, *Bales o' Cotton: The Mechanical Art of Cotton Ginning* (College Station: Texas A&M University Press, 2015).

54. Donald E. Davis et al., *Southern United States: An Environmental History* (Santa Barbara, CA: ABC-Clio, 2006). See also Eugene V. Genovese, *The Political Economy of Slavery: Studies in the Economy and Society of the Slave South*, 2nd ed. (Middleton, CT: Wesleyan University Press, 1989).

55. Christopher Morris, *The Big Muddy: An Environmental History of the Mississippi and Its Peoples from Hernando de Soto to Hurricane Katrina* (New York: Oxford University Press, 2012).

56. James David Miller, *South by Southwest: Planter Emigration and Identity in the Slave South* (Charlottesville: University of Virginia Press, 2002).

57. John Cusick, *The Other War of 1812: The Patriot War and the American Invasion of Spanish East Florida* (Gainesville: University Press of Florida, 2003).

58. Frank L. Owsley Jr. and Gene A. Smith, *Filibusters and Expansionists: Jeffersonian Manifest Destiny, 1800–1821* (Tuscaloosa: University of Alabama Press, 1997).

59. Sophie Burton and Todd Smith, *Colonial Natchitoches: A Creole Community on the Louisiana-Texas Frontier* (College Station: Texas A&M University Press, 2008). For a study that notes the Anglo-American influx, see Christopher Morris, *Becoming Southern: The Evolution of a Way of Life, Warren County and Vicksburg, Mississippi, 1770–1860* (New York: Oxford University Press, 1995).

60. Robert V. Haines, *The Mississippi Territory and the Southwest Frontier, 1795–1817* (Lexington: University of Kentucky Press, 2010).

61. Randolph B. Campbell, *An Empire for Slavery: The Peculiar Institution in Texas, 1821–1865* (Baton Rouge: Louisiana State University Press, 1991).

62. Gwendolyn Midlo Hall, *Africans in Colonial Louisiana: The Development of Afro-Creole Culture in the Eighteenth Century* (Baton Rouge: Louisiana State University Press, 1992); Ira Berlin, *Many Thousands Gone: The First Two Centuries of Slavery in North America* (Cambridge, MA: Harvard University Press, 1998).

63. Thomas N. Ingersoll, *Mammon and Manon in Early New Orleans: The First Slave Society in the Deep South, 1719–1829* (Knoxville: University of Tennessee Press, 1999); Jennifer M. Spear, *Race, Sex, and Social Order in Early New Orleans* (Baltimore: Johns Hopkins University Press, 2009).

64. Gilbert C. Din, *Spaniards, Planters, and Slaves: The Spanish Regulation of Slavery in Louisiana, 1763–1803* (College Station: Texas A&M University Press, 1999).

65. Caryn Cosse Bell, *Revolution, Romanticism, and the Afro-Creole Protest Tradition in Louisiana, 1718–1868* (Baton Rouge: Louisiana State University Press, 1997).

66. Lawrence N. Powell, *The Accidental City: Improvising New Orleans* (Cambridge, MA: Harvard University Press, 2013).

67. Rashauna Johnson, *Slavery's Metropolis: Unfree Labor in New Orleans during the Age of Revolutions* (Cambridge: Cambridge University Press, 2016).

68. Kimberly S. Hanger, *Bounded Lives, Bounded Places: Free Black Society in Colonial New Orleans, 1769–1803* (Durham, NC: Duke University Press, 1997); Elizabeth Urban Alexander, *Notorious Woman: The Celebrated Case of Myra Clark Gaines* (Baton Rouge: Louisiana State University Press, 2001).

69. Mark Fernandez, *From Chaos to Continuity: The Evolution of Louisiana's Judicial System, 1712–1862* (Baton Rouge: Louisiana State University Press, 2001).

70. Judith Kelleher Schafer, *Slavery, the Civil Law, and the Supreme Court of Louisiana* (Baton Rouge: Louisiana State University Press, 1997). Schafer wrote a second book, which carries the evolution of Louisiana law from the mid-antebellum era to the Civil War, especially in the areas of manumission and the laws of slavery: *Becoming Free, Remaining Free: Manumission and Enslavement in New Orleans, 1846–1862* (Baton Rouge: Louisiana State University Press, 2003).

71. Warren M. Billings and Mark Fernandez, eds. *A Law unto Itself?: Essays in the New Louisiana Legal History* (Baton Rouge: Louisiana State University Press, 2001).

72. Morris Arnold, *Unequal Laws unto a Savage Race: European Legal Traditions in Arkansas, 1686–1836* (Fayetteville: University of Arkansas Press, 1985).

73. Charles R. Cutter, *The Legal Culture of Northern New Spain* (Albuquerque: University of New Mexico Press, 2001).

74. Jean Stuntz, *His, Hers, and Theirs: Community and Property Law in Spain and Early Texas* (Lubbock: Texas Tech University Press, 2005).

75. Michael Ariens, *Lone Star Law: A Legal History of Texas* (Lubbock: Texas Tech University Press, 2011).

76. Randolph B. Campbell, ed., *The Laws of Slavery in Texas: Historical Documents and Essays* (Austin: University of Texas Press, 2010).

77. John Martin Davis Jr., *Texas Land Grants, 1750–1900: A Documentary History* (Jefferson, NC: McFarland, 2016).

78. Morris Arnold, *Colonial Arkansas, 1686–1804: A Social and Cultural History* (Fayetteville: University of Arkansas Press, 1993); Arnold, *The Arkansas Post of Louisiana* (Fayetteville: University of Arkansas Press, 2017). See also Charles Bolton, *Territorial Ambition: Land and Society in Arkansas, 1800–1849* (Fayetteville: University of Arkansas Press, 1993); and Bolton, *Remote and Restless: Arkansas, 1800–1860* (Fayetteville: University of Arkansas Press, 1998).

79. Carl Ekberg, *François Valle and His World: Upper Louisiana before Lewis and Clark* (Columbia: University of Missouri Press, 2017). See also Eckberg, *French Roots in the Illinois Country: The Mississippi Frontier in Colonial Times* (Urbana: University of Illinois Press, 2000).

80. Andres Recendez, *Changing National Identities at the Frontier, Texas and New Mexico, 1800–1850* (Cambridge: Cambridge University Press, 2004).

81. Roger G. Kennedy, *Cotton and Conquest: How the Plantation System Acquired Texas* (Norman: University of Oklahoma Press, 2015).

82. Gregg Cantrell, *Stephen F. Austin: Empresario of Texas* (New Haven, CT: Yale University Press, 1999).

83. Light Townsend Cummins, *Emily Austin of Texas, 1705–1851* (Fort Worth: Texas Christian University Press, 2009).

84. Ana Carolina Castillo Crimm. *De Leon: A Tejano Family History* (Austin: University of Texas Press, 2004); Jesús de la Teja, *San Antonio de Béxar: A Community on New Spain's Northern Frontier* (Albuquerque: University of New Mexico

Press, 1996); de la Teja, *Faces of Bexár: Early San Antonio and Texas* (College Station: Texas A&M University Press, 2016).

85. Andrew J. Torget, *Seeds of Empire: Cotton, Slavery, and the Transformation of the Texas Borderlands, 1800–1850* (Chapel Hill: University of North Carolina Press, 2015).

Index

Other Books in the Elma Dill Russell Spencer Series in the West and Southwest

Aspects of the American West: Three Essays
Joe B. Frantz and W. E. Hollon

Trader on the American Frontier: Myth's Victim
Howard R. Lamar and Kristin E. Parsons

America's Frontier Culture: Three Essays
Ray A. Billington and W. T. Jackson

How Did Davy Die?
Dan Kilgore

Grave of John W. Hardin: Three Essays on Grassroots History
C. L. Sonnichsen

Juan Davis Bradburn: A Reappraisal of the Mexican Commander of Anahuac
Margaret S. Henson

Civil War Recollections of James Lemuel Clark
L. D. Clark

Texas Longhorn: Relic of the Past, Asset for the Future
Donald E. Worcester

Red Hole in Time
Muriel Marshall

Travels in Mexico and California
A. B. Clarke

Mexican War Journal and Letters of Ralph K. Kirkham
Robert R. Miller

Regional Studies: The Interplay of Land and People
Glen E. Lich
Immigrant Soldier in the Mexican War
Frederick Zeh and William J. Orr

Where Rivers Meet: Lore from the Colorado Frontier
Muriel Marshall

Massacre on the Lordsburg Road: A Tragedy of the Apache Wars
Marc Simmons

Geronimo's Kids: A Teacher's Lessons on the Apache Reservation
Robert S. Ove and H. Henrietta Stockel

Defiant Peacemaker: Nicholas Trist in the Mexican War
Wallace L. Ohrt

Life among the Texas Indians: The WPA Narratives
David La Vere

Plains Indians
Paul H. Carlson

Conquest of the Karankawas and the Tonkawas, 1821-1859
Kelly F. Himmel

Chiricahua Apache Women and Children: Safekeepers of the Heritage
H. H. Stockel

Hispanics in the Mormon Zion, 1912-1999
Jorge Iber

Comanche Society: Before the Reservation
Gerald Betty

True Women and Westward Expansion
Adrienne Caughfield

Robertsons, the Sutherlands, and the Making of Texas
Anne H. Sutherland

Life Along the Border: A Landmark Tejana Thesis
Jovita González and Maria E. Cotera

Lone Star Pasts: Memory and History in Texas
Gregg Cantrell and Elizabeth H. Turner

Secret War for Texas
Stuart Reid

Colonial Natchitoches: A Creole Community on the Louisiana-Texas Frontier
H. S. Burton and F. Todd Smith

Yeomen, Sharecroppers, and Socialists: Plain Folk Protest in Texas, 1870-1914
Kyle G. Wilkison

More Zeal Than Discretion: The Westward Adventures of Walter P. Lane
Jimmy L. Bryan

On the Move: A Black Family's Western Saga
S. R. Martin

Texas That Might Have Been: Sam Houston's Foes Write to Albert Sidney Johnston
Margaret S. Henson

Tejano Leadership in Mexican and Revolutionary Texas
Jesús F. De la Teja

Texas Left: The Radical Roots of Lone Star Liberalism
David O. Cullen

How Did Davy Die? And Why Do We Care So Much?
James E. Crisp and Dan Kilgore

Drumbeats from Mescalero: Conversations with Apache Elders, Warriors, and Horseholders
H. H. Stockel

Turmoil on the Rio Grande: History of the Mesilla Valley, 1846-1865
William S. Kiser

Texas Right: The Radical Roots of Lone Star Conservatism
David O' Donald Cullen and Kyle G. Wilkison

We Never Retreat: Filibustering Expeditions into Spanish Texas, 1812–1822
Ed Bradley

General Alonso de León's Expeditions into Texas, 1686–1690
Lola Orellana Norris

Comanches and Germans on the Texas Frontier: The Ethnology of Heinrich Berghaus
Daniel J. Gelo and Christopher J. Wickham, with contributions by Heide Castañeda

Murder and Intrigue on the Mexican Border: Governor Colquitt, President Wilson, and the Vergara Affair
John A. Adams

Woolly West: Colorado's Hidden History of Sheepscapes
Andrew Gulliford

Preserving German Texan Identity: Reminiscences of William A. Trenckmann, 1859–1935
Walter L. Buenger

Civil War on the Rio Grande, 1846–1876
Roseann Bacha-Garza, Christopher L. Miller, and Russell K. Skowronek

www.ingramcontent.com/pod-product-compliance
Lightning Source LLC
Chambersburg PA
CBHW071344011025
33062CB00072B/35